DONNE AND THE POLITICS
OF CONSCIENCE
IN EARLY MODERN ENGLAND

STUDIES IN THE HISTORY
OF
CHRISTIAN THOUGHT

EDITED BY

HEIKO A. OBERMAN, Tucson, Arizona

IN COOPERATION WITH
HENRY CHADWICK, Cambridge
JAROSLAV PELIKAN, New Haven, Connecticut
BRIAN TIERNEY, Ithaka, New York
ARJO VANDERJAGT, Groningen

VOLUME LXI

MEG LOTA BROWN

DONNE AND THE POLITICS
OF CONSCIENCE
IN EARLY MODERN ENGLAND

DONNE AND THE POLITICS
OF CONSCIENCE
IN EARLY MODERN ENGLAND

BY

MEG LOTA BROWN

E.J. BRILL
LEIDEN · NEW YORK · KÖLN
1995

The paper in this book meets the guidelines for permanence and durability of the Committee on Production Guidelines for Book Longevity of the Council on Library Resources.

Library of Congress Cataloging-in-Publication Data

Brown, Meg Lota.
    Donne and the politics of conscience in early modern England / Meg Lota Brown.
       p.   cm. — (Studies in the history of Christian thought, ISSN 0081-8607 ; v. 61)
    Includes bibliographical references (p.) and indexes.
    ISBN 9004101578 (cloth)
    1. Donne, John, 1572–1631—Political and social views.
2. Politics and literature—England—History—16th century.
3. Christianity and politics—History—16th century.   4. Conscience—
–Religious aspects—Christianity.   5. Donne, John, 1572–1631–
–Religion.   6. Donne, John, 1572–1631—Ethics.   7. Conscience in literature.   I. Title.   II. Series.
PR2248.B76   1995
821'.3—dc20
                                       94–42409
                                           CIP

Die Deutsche Bibliothek - CIP-Einheitsaufnahme

Brown, Meg Lota:
Donne and the politics of conscience in early modern England / by Meg Lota Brown. – Leiden ; New York ; Köln : Brill, 1995
   (Studies in the history of Christian thought ; Vol. 61)
   ISBN 90–04–10157–8
NE: GT

ISSN   0081-8607
ISBN   90 04 10157 8

PRINTED IN THE NETHERLANDS

For Rick

A mathematical certitude, which is manifest by Demonstration, and impossible to be false, is in vain to be expected in morals, by reason of the infinite variety of Circumstances, and the uncertainty of Humane affairs...

-- Robert Sanderson, Bishop of Lincoln
<u>Lectures on Conscience and Human Law</u>

Except Demonstrations, (and perchance there are very few of them) I find nothing without perplexities. I am grown more sensible of it by busying myself a little in the search of the eastern tongues, where a perpetual perplexity in the words cannot choose but cast a perplexity upon the things.

-- John Donne, Letter

CONTENTS

ACKNOWLEDGMENTS

Support for the research and writing of this book was provided by the University of California at Berkeley, the University of Arizona, the Steinfeld Grant, and the National Endowment for the Humanities. Portions of the work have been published elsewhere, and I owe thanks to the publishers for permission to reprint. Part of chapter four appeared as "'In that the world's contracted thus': Casuistical Politics in Donne's 'Sunne Rising.'" In *"The Muses Common-Weale": Poetry and Politics in the Seventeenth Century*. Eds. Claude Summers and Ted-Larry Pebworth. Columbia: University of Missouri Press, 1988, pp.23-33. Part of chapter two was published in *Renaissance and Reformation*, and portions of chapter three appeared in *Seventeenth-Century Texts and Studies* and *The John Donne Journal*.

For their helpful responses to drafts of the manuscript, I thank Joel Altman, Donald Friedman, Fred Kiefer, Peter Medine, Heiko Oberman, Michael Schoenfeldt, and Barbara Shapiro.

For their example, wisdom, and generosity, I will always be grateful to Heather Laycock Wilson, Rick Teagarden, Nancy Simpkins, Susan Derwin, and Laura Berry.

Rick, Aaron, and Mallory Brown have my deepest gratitude and love.

CHAPTER ONE

INTRODUCTION: "NOTHING WITHOUT PERPLEXITIES"

This book examines the responses of Donne and his culture to post-Reformation debate about authority and interpretation. My governing assertion is that the legal and epistemological principles, as well as the narrative practices, of casuistry provided an important resource for those caught in the welter of conflicting laws and religions. While my focus is on Donne's poetic and prose works, I am also looking at the culture encoded in those works—at the historical, theological, and political discourses in which Donne's view of authority and interpretation took shape. My sources include continental and English polemics about the deficiencies of language, law, and reason, as well as cases of conscience and treatises on moral theology from Italy, Spain, Germany, England, France, and the Netherlands. The organizing principle is that casuistry affords a theoretical and historical framework for examining the prevailing responses in early modern Europe to the epistemological and ethical crises that post-Reformation polemics engendered; specifically, those crises forced questions about whose interpretation of truth is legitimate and who is entitled to authorize action.

Recent approaches to Renaissance studies have demonstrated the "interinanimation" of legal, theological, political, and literary discourses. My own comparative analysis proposes that casuistry affords a nexus for the interpretive strategies of these discourses in early modern England. Drawing on the hermeneutics of casuistry in both Protestant and Catholic polemics, this study locates Donne in contemporaneous debate about the limits of knowledge and the cultural construction of authority. My contextualization of Donne enables a previously unexplored approach not only to his work, but also to the political culture it shaped and was shaped by. Recent work on Donne himself lacks any extended consideration of both his prose and his poetry within the context of post-Reformation debate about authority and interpretation; indeed, most scholars focus on either the prose or the poetry, thereby confining their treatment of the sites of conflict and play shared by both modes. Placing Donne in the context of early modern casuistry, I argue that his works occupy a philosophical and historical position that has not before been investigated.

Also called practical theology or case divinity, casuistry is a method of adjudicating the conflicting claims of self and law. Its purposes are to address the tensions that arise from legal or ethical antinomies, and to respond to those who are uncertain about "acceptable conduct." Indeed, casuistry is necessary because there is no easy definition of acceptable conduct. Practical theology is a system of directives to reason and conscience that defines, interprets, and applies general laws according to the circumstances of a specific case. My study argues that casuistry acknowledges the pressure of epistemological anxiety and the indeterminacy of language—that it recognizes, as does Donne throughout his works, that language and law are ambiguous, moot, unstable. At the same time, casuistry enables one, however precariously, to impose form on uncertainty, to justify action on the basis of probability and circumstantiality, to reason towards practical responses to the conflicting claims of absolutist authorities.

Case divinity constitutes a significant body of Renaissance literature, one that literary critics and historians have not substantially mined. It is significant in the sheer volume of its production and significant because intellectually crucial to a great many writers of the period. From the mid-sixteenth to the mid-seventeenth centuries, tens of thousands of cases of conscience were published in England and on the continent. Attention to practical theology was more widespread during Donne's lifetime and the fifty years that followed than at any other time. This was largely because the issues of conscience and conduct that are the staple of casuistry were extraordinarily charged during the period; they informed in material and urgent ways the lives not only of individuals but of entire nations. Indeed, as Keith Thomas remarks, "The seventeenth century can justly be called the Age of Conscience. Certainly, there has been no period in English history when men and women were subjected to so many religious and political conflicts of duty and allegiance or responded to them in so intensely scrupulous a fashion." Moreover, as the following chapters demonstrate, casuistical epistemology influenced a great deal of post-Reformation thought. "Recent scholarship has made it abundantly clear that it was casuistry which provided the context for some of the most crucial developments in seventeenth-century political thought. Grotius, Ascham, Filmer, and Locke can all be better understood when fitted into the casuistical tradition." [1] Not surprisingly, such a significant force in the shaping of early modern discourse is manifested in the literature of the period as well as in the political theory. And yet little attention has been given to the influence of case divinity on seventeenth-century literature. Reading Donne through casuistry, my study both examines the effects of epistemological controversy in the

---

[1]   Keith Thomas, "Cases of Conscience in Seventeenth-Century England" in *Public Duty and Private Conscience in Seventeenth-Century England*, eds. John Morrill, Paul Slack, and Daniel Woolf (Oxford: Clarendon Press, 1993), p.29 and pp.44-45.

Reformation, and demonstrates the ways in which Donne invokes the principles and methods of practical theology as he explores valid criteria for judgment. One of my objectives in reading Donne through casuistry is to augment our understanding of the intellectual and emotional conflicts that inform his works, as well as our appreciation of the playfulness, tension, and vitality of his writing.

Throughout, my study is concerned with the political factionalism that increased the need for, and popularity of, early modern casuistry. Treated by contemporaries as "the central, if controversial, instrument for drawing order out of a chaotic landscape of conflicting moral, political, and social hierarchies," practical theology was the resource of moderates, nonconformists, conservatives, Puritans, Anglicans, Catholics, governments, and the disenfranchised.[2] No perplexing detail of private life was too quotidian for casuistical consideration; at the same time, most rulers of early modern Europe invoked the principles and methods of practical theology when weighing policies of national and international significance. For example,

> In 1539 at the request of Emperor Charles V, Francisco Vitoria, Professor of Theology at Salamanca, wrote *Relectio de Indis et de Jure Belli*, a case study on the government of the indigenous people of the newly discovered Americas. In 1613 Francisco Suarez wrote the *Defensio Fidei Catholicae adversus Anglicanae Sectae Errores*, a case study on the obligation of subjects to a heretical ruler, occasioned by the claims of James I over the religious conscience of his Catholic subjects. Casuists became counselors to kings and popes. It was not uncommon for rulers to summon a commission of casuists to render expert advice on a political case . . . Casuists wrote the *Pacis Compositio* (1628), interpreting the obligations arising from the Peace of Augsburg of 1555, and the *Justa Defensio* (1631), which unraveled the complex issue of property rights relative to restitution of monastic properties in formerly Protestant domains. The hundred years beginning around 1550 were made for the casuists, and the casuists made the most of them. [3]

Whether public or private, every act was considered a "moral" act, and therefore within the purview of case divinity. At all levels, casuistry was central to the politics of conscience in early modern Europe.

---

2   Lowell Gallagher, *Medusa's Gaze: Casuistry and Conscience in the Renaissance* (Stanford: UP, 1991), p.2.

3   Albert R. Jonsen and Stephen Toulmin, *The Abuse of Casuistry: A History of Moral Reasoning* (Berkeley: Univ. of California Press, 1988), pp. 144-145.

"Who but a monomaniac...?:"
Reading Donne and Casuistry

A fellow editor of Donne's prose once wrote to Evelyn Simpson, "Who but a monomaniac would read *Pseudo-Martyr* through?" [4] The critic's exasperation was in response to the distinctions, qualifications, and exceptions that saturate Donne's casuistical defense of the Oath of Allegiance. Such a reaction is not uncommon among readers of casuistry, [5] and perhaps explains the dearth of critical attention to the influence of practical theology on Donne's works. But the effect of casuistical procedure on narrative practices and argumentation in Donne's verse and prose merits a great deal more consideration than it has been given. A response to uncertainty about the compass of law, reason, and language, case divinity was an important factor in the theological and epistemological controversies of the period, controversies in which Donne had a profoundly personal stake. In addition, "changing social conditions, such as the growth of business and industry, the development of a national poor law, and the emergence of new habits of personal consumption, made the application of traditional principles seem inappropriate." [6] Casuistry provided a means for adjusting to social, political, and religious changes in Donne's culture, and, as I will demonstrate, it exerted considerable influence on his works.

Donne's knowledge of case divinity was extensive. His many references to casuistry evince a familiarity with specific details in the debate between Protestants and Catholics about the proper methods of moral deliberation. Izaak Walton reports that Donne kept "Copies of divers Letters and cases of Conscience that had concerned his friends, with his observations and solutions of them; all particularly and methodically digested by himself." [7] Several of Donne's letters, in which he mentions "my Cases of conscience," corroborate Walton's statement.[8] Moreover, both *Biathanatos* and *Pseudo-*

---

[4]   Evelyn Simpson, *A Study of the Prose Works of John Donne* (Oxford: Clarendon Press, 1962), p.179.

[5]   Camille Wells Slights, for example, complains that there is in practical theology "a proliferation of exceptions and qualifications that can try the patience of even the most sympathetic reader." *The Casuistical Tradition in Shakespeare, Donne, Herbert and Milton* (Princeton: UP, 1981), p.63.

[6]   Thomas, p.49. See also Perez Zagorin, *Ways of Lying: Dissimulation, Persecution, and Conformity in Early Modern Europe* (Cambridge, MA: Harvard UP, 1990), p. 153.

[7]   Izaak Walton, *Lives*, ed. George Saintsbury (London: Oxford UP, 1973), p.68.

[8]   John Donne, *Letters to Severall Persons of Honour*, ed. Charles Edmund Merrill (New York: Sturgis and Walton, 1910), pp.173 and 196. In his postscript to a letter written in 1621 either to Sir Thomas Lucy or to Sir Henry Goodyer (see I. A. Shapiro, *RES*, VII [1931], pp. 297-299), Donne asks, "Why

Martyr are casuistical treatises, and the sermon on *Esther 4.16* is a beautifully crafted case of conscience.

It is not surprising, then, that Donne's interest in practical theology is also manifested in his verse. But few critics have investigated the poet's attention to casuistry, and only one has examined how the principles of case divinity operate in the *Songs and Sonets*. As I hope to establish, Donne's poems are casuistical insofar as they are concerned with the justification of doubtful actions, with the relation of the individual to general law or convention, and with the conflict between public code and private conduct. I do not mean to claim, however, that each of the *Songs and Sonets* is a formal case of conscience. Rather, I will argue that a number of the poems inscribe methodological and epistemological concerns of casuistry; and I will examine how specific poems dramatize the principles of case divinity that Donne addresses repeatedly in his other works.

As do *Biathanatos* and many of the *Songs and Sonets*, cases of conscience often support unconventional judgments. The practical instrument of moral theology, casuistry is a process of defining, interpreting, and applying ethical principles according to the idiosyncrasies of each case. Moral theology, in addition, is "concerned not simply with the assessment of value in human actions, but with human actions as they have repercussions both in eternity and time." [9] Casuists presuppose the inability of reason and language to formulate precepts comprehensive enough to solve all moral dilemmas. Consequently, they recognize that the literal application of law is not always just. As Joseph Hall insists, "It is not the bare letter of the law that wise men should stand upon, but the drift and intention of the law." [10] In his description of equity, Aristotle outlines the foundation of case divinity; Aquinas, an authority for both Protestant and Catholic casuists, reproduces the following passage from *Nichomachean Ethics* in his *Summa Theologica*:

---

do you say nothing of, my little book of Cases" (p. 173).

[9] H. R. McAdoo, *The Structure of Caroline Moral Theology* (London: Longmans, Green, 1949), p.16. See also Kenneth E. Kirk, *Conscience and Its Problems* (London: Longmans, Green, 1927), p.111. Not only do cases of conscience teach how to respond to moral exigencies, but they serve as homilies for the Christian life. George Herbert remarks in his *Country Parson* that the ideal preacher "greatly esteems also of cases of conscience, wherein he is much versed. And, indeed, herein is the greatest ability of a parson, to lead his people in the ways of truth, so that they neither decline to the right hand nor to the left." (Quoted in Thomas Wood, *English Casuistical Divinity During the Seventeenth Century* [London: Billing and Sons, 1952], p.34).

[10] Joseph Hall, *Resolutions and Decisions of Divers Practical Cases of Conscience*, Vol. XII of *Works*, ed. John Downame (Oxford: D.C. Talboys, 1937), p.311. Subsequent citations to the *Resolutions* appear in the text.

> Every law is expressed in general terms, and there are some matters that
> cannot be dealt with in general terms. . . In such cases the law lays down
> what is right for the majority of cases, without losing sight of the conse-
> quent inaccuracy [in the remainder]. . .When, therefore, a law is laid down
> generally, but manifest ground for exception appears in a particular case, it
> is right that this failure of the legislator (due to his expressing himself in
> general terms) should be made good exactly as he would make it good if he
> were present, or would amend his law if he took the case into account. [11]

In a sermon preached at Temple Church, Donne echoes the above remarks
about the imprecision of law. He observes that we may neglect a law when
our conscience is convinced "That if this present case, which makes us
break this Law, had been known and considered when the Law was made, he
that made the Law would have made provision for this case." [12] Consulting
conscience, Scriptural principles, and reason, casuists examine the relation
of general laws to particular experience. When public code unduly restricts
private conduct, case divinity attempts to provide a system of equitable
sanctions that protects the integrity of the individual.

Casuistical judgments, then, are always contingent upon circumstances.
Hall remarks that "Justice had wont to be painted blindfold, with a pair of
scales in her hand; wherefore else, but to imply that he who would judge
aright must. . . weigh impartially the true state of the cause in all the
grounds thereof, and sentence accordingly?" (p.314). Likewise, Donne
comments in his *Essays in Divinity* that judgment should be "almost syn-
onimous with Discretion; when we consider not so much the thing which
we do, as the whole frame and machine of the businesse, as it is complex-
ioned and circumstanced with time, place, and beholders." [13] One of my
primary assertions is that the efforts of casuists to reconcile general law and
idiosyncratic experience structure many of Donne's works. The *Songs and
Sonets*, for example, frequently explore the relation of convention to the individual's extenuating circumstances. Whether playful or serious, Donne's
speaker argues for exemption from rules that, by virtue of their generality,
do not accommodate his case. In "The Sunne Rising," he remonstrates that
the convention of arising at daybreak does not apply to lovers. Given his
definition of their circumstances as exceptional, he wittily asserts his exempt status. Similarly, in *Biathanatos* Donne discusses numerous situations

---

[11]   The passage, quoted in Kirk, pp.125-126n., is from *Nichomachean
Ethics*, 1137b in *The Basic Works of Aristotle*, ed. Richard McKeon (New York:
Random House, 1941). It is reproduced in *Summa Theologica*, ed. Anton Pegis
(New York: Random House, 1948), II. 2. 120.

[12]   John Donne, *Sermons*, ed. George R. Potter and Evelyn Simpson
(Berkeley: Univ. of California Press, 1953-62), V, 226.

[13]   John Donne, *Essays in Divinity*, ed. Evelyn Simpson (Oxford: Clarendon
Press, 1952), p.90. Subsequent page references to this edition will appear in the
text.

in which laws against suicide may be ignored or evaded. In letters, sermons, poems, and prose tracts, he warns against rigorism, and urges his readers to investigate the attendant circumstances of an act before deciding upon its moral status.

The need to accommodate law to individual experience is not the only assumption of practical theology that Donne shares. The similarity of his epistemology to that of case divinity is striking. Paradoxically, casuistry exists because imperfect reason can neither formulate absolute principles that apply to every situation, nor easily judge doubtful and perplexing cases; yet casuistry depends on the exercise of reason and on one's ability to achieve "practical knowledge." Throughout this study, I argue that Donne shares casuists' concern with the ambiguous relation between law and its application, between words and their interpretation, and between truth and its imperfect formulations. The first two chapters examine the epistemological and historical contexts of Donne's casuistry, particularly the Renaissance controversy about valid criteria for judgment. Locating Donne in early modern debate about the limits of reason and the relativity of law and ethics, I assert the importance of casuistry for Donne and his contemporaries as a method of treating uncertainty and justifying action. In addition, I examine specific controversies, political and religious, that precipitated the pressing need for, and the enormous popularity of, practical theology.

The third chapter focuses on Donne's prose. I discuss problems of moral decision and action, problems of knowledge and definition in the secular context of the *Paradoxes and Problems* and the theological context of the *Essays in Divinity*. The major portion of the chapter considers how Donne addresses these problems in three casuistical texts: *Biathanatos*, *Pseudo-Martyr*, and the sermon on *Esther 4.16*. Because of the varying context of each of the three works, each poses startlingly different responses to the same legal and moral precepts. If my reading proves fruitful, studying the ways in which Donne both adopts and adapts casuistical methods not only facilitates fuller understanding of the reasoning of his works, but it also enables one to address more encompassing questions about the effects of epistemological controversy on post-Reformation England.

The fourth chapter explores ways in which the *Songs and Sonets* assimilate and wittily subvert practical theology's response to epistemological and linguistic uncertainty. I examine the casuistical dilemmas that confront Donne's personae in a number of his secular lyrics, and I discuss how the poet playfully burlesques the methods of casuistry when addressing those dilemmas. Although the *Songs and Sonets* antedate most of the prose works that I will study, I consider the verse last. My reasoning is that the non-poetic works enunciate principles of practical theology that the *Songs and Sonets* dramatize less explicitly. Understanding Donne's exposition of these principles in his prose will, I believe, illuminate his verse representations of them. Throughout the book, I argue that casuistry provided an allowance for anomaly—indeed, even sanctioned contention—while still containing the anomalous or contentious individual within the authority of established rules and rulers. Insofar as practical theology privileged conclusions of the individual conscience over institutionally mediated truths, it was potentially disruptive of social norms. Accordingly, chapter four examines how Donne's speaker exploits casuistical latitude and exposes the epistemological and political instabilities of casuistical discourse. And yet, I argue, Donne also invokes case divinity as the resource of conservatism and moderation, as did most contemporary casuists. Enabling integration while promising integrity of conscience, casuistry appealed both to Donne's divided culture and to his own ambivalent politics.

Donne's familiarity with case divinity included both Roman and Reformed cases of conscience. As A. E. Malloch observes, Donne quotes a number of Catholic casuists; among the treatises cited are: Martin Azpilcueta's *Enchiridion sive Manuale Confessariorum* (1566); Juan Azor's *Institutiones morales* (1600-1611); Robert Sayr's *Casus conscientiae* (1601); and Ludovico Carbo's *Summae summarum casuum conscientiae* (1606). [14] Censorship was common in England, and it is unclear how easily obtainable such tracts were under the Anglican government. But given James's warm reception of *Pseudo-Martyr*, a work that makes apparent its author's access to Catholic cases of conscience, possessing the tracts was not necessarily incriminating. It is possible that Jesuit casuistry was smuggled into England from the seminaries at Rheims, Douai, and Rome, where studying cases of conscience was part of the curriculum. John Bossy writes of a highly organized network of communication between Continental and English Catholics; the former, operating on the northwest coast of Europe, "saw to the printing of books, or received them from presses inland, packed them up in bales of merchandise and sent them into England." [15] Many of the books were polemical, and their circulation was punishable by death in Elizabeth's reign. Included in the contraband was literature on casuistical

---

[14] A. E. Malloch, "John Donne and the Casuists," *SEL*, 2 (1962), p.58. Another prominent casuist, whom Donne cites on several occasions in *Biathanatos*, is the Dominican friar, Sotus (1495-1560).

[15] John Bossy, "The Character of Elizabethan Catholicism," *Past and Present*, 21 (1962), p.47. J. C. H. Aveling, "The English Clergy in the 16th and 17th Centuries" in *Rome and the Anglicans*, ed. Wolfgang Haase (New York: Walter de Gruyter, 1982), p.94, remarks that in the late sixteenth century, English universities and loyal Anglicans "were using Catholic books extensively. The devotional and academic literature of the day derived in the main from late medieval origins, constantly recast, pirated across national and denominational boundaries, and thinly disguised with Catholic or Protestant terms and polemic."

subjects.[16] In a letter of 1584, Robert Parsons wrote:

> I am obliged to maintain a modest establishment at Rouen which is the most convenient city on account of its nearness to the sea, so that from there someone can make trips to the coast to arrange for boats to carry [priests] across. . .others take charge of the preparation and introduction into the country of books written in English both on spiritual and devotional subjects and on matters of controversy. [17]

Among the "matters of controversy" addressed were cases of conscience prompted by recusancy laws in England. The seminarians' casuistical manuals advised that attending Anglican services was a sin, but that those who conformed because of fear of death or intolerable persecution were pardonable. [18]

Despite such allowances, many of Donne's family members refused to compromise in the politics of conscience. Descended from the martyred Sir Thomas More, Donne's mother was an unswerving recusant who was "presented" by authorities for refusing to attend church and receive communion.[19] His grandfather went into exile rather than conform to Anglicanism. His mother's uncle, Thomas Heywood, was executed for his Catholicism, and two of his own uncles, Jasper and Ellis Heywood, were Jesuits who died abroad. Donne's stepfather, Richard Rainsford, was imprisoned from 1611-1613 for refusing to take the Oath of Allegiance; his fortune and prospects in ruins, he was again indicted in 1613 for disobeying laws against church attendance. Henry, Donne's brother, was jailed for taking confession, and died of the plague in Newgate Prison at the age of twenty. Given Donne's upbringing in a literate and staunchly Catholic family, and given his strong ties to continental seminaries and Catholic casuistical teaching, he is likely to have had access to proscribed texts and casuistical manuals from abroad.

How Donne became acquainted with the practical theology of Protestants is a matter of conjecture. His claim to have "survayed and digested the whole body of Divinity, controverted betweene ours and the

---

16   Patrick McGrath, *Papists and Puritans Under Elizabeth I* (London: Blandford Press, 1967), p.256. See also Leona Rostenberg, *The Minority Press and the English Crown: A Study in Repression, 1558-1625* (Niewkoop: B. De Graaf, 1971) and Hugh Aveling, *The Handle and the Axe: The Catholic Recusants in England for Reformation to Emancipation* (London: Blond and Briggs, 1976).

17   Quoted in McGrath, p.259.

18   P. J. Holmes, ed. *Elizabethan Casuistry*. (London: Catholic Record Society, 1981), pp. 20-21.

19   For a useful discussion of the legal and religious pressures that Donne's mother and her dependents were subject to, see Marie B. Rowlands, "Recusant Women 1560-1640" in *Women in English Society 1500-1800*, ed. Mary Prior (London: Methuen, 1985), pp. 149-180.

Romane Church" undoubtedly includes knowledge of the debate between
Catholic and Reformed casuists. [20] William Perkins (1558-1602), Joseph
Hall (1574-1656), Frederick Baldwin (1575-1627), and William Ames
(1576-1633) were contemporaries of Donne. But it is uncertain how many
of those casuists he knew personally. Izaak Walton reports that Donne attended Cambridge from 1587 to 1590, a period when Perkins' "reputation as
a teacher [at Cambridge] had gone unrivalled." [21] In the late 1580's, Perkins
delivered at the University a celebrated series of lectures on casuistry, which
later formed part of his *Discourse on Conscience* (pub. 1596). It is possible
that Donne knew Perkins during this period, and probable that he knew of
his works by 1600.

Jeremy Taylor, Robert Sanderson, and Richard Baxter published their
works on practical divinity after Donne's death in 1631; but the procedures
of later seventeenth-century casuists unvaryingly follow Perkins' model—a
model that Donne himself imitated (see chapters two and three below). It
could be argued that to know Perkins is to know all of Protestant casuistry.
Although Puritans and Anglicans differed profoundly on other matters of
theology, there were no specifically denominational differences in their work
on practical theology.

That Donne knew Hall, the leading Anglican casuist of his time, is certain. Although Hall's major treatise on moral theology was published after
1631, both men had an abiding interest in the assumptions of case divinity,
and it seems reasonable to assume that, given their intimacy and shared experiences, they were familiar with each other's study of the subject. Hall,
too, was at Cambridge in 1589, and his career parallels Donne's in many
ways. Both satirized contemporary laws and conventions in the 1590's, and
composed religious polemics in the early 1600's, defending the Anglican
liturgy and church government against Catholic and Puritan detractors. Both
accompanied Lord Doncaster on diplomatic missions to the Continent, and
both benefited from the patronage of Sir Robert Drury. Several years after
Donne became Dean of St. Paul's, Hall was appointed Bishop of Exeter,
and later Bishop of Norwich. He oversaw the publication of Donne's
Anniversaries, and Donne bequeathed him his private seal. Unfortunately,
the only certain conclusion one can draw from such biographical data is that
Donne had ample opportunity to know of Hall's concern with case divinity.
From whom Donne learned the tenets of Protestant casuistry is a matter of

---

[20]   John Donne, *Pseudo-Martyr* (Ann Arbor: Univ. Microfilms, 1967), p.5.

[21]   Thomas Merrill, ed. *A Discourse of Conscience* and *The Whole Treatise of
Cases of Conscience* by William Perkins (Nieuwkoop: B. De Graaf, 1966),
p.xvii. R. C. Bald, *John Donne: A Life* (Oxford: Clarendon Press, 1986), pp.46-
47, supports Walton's assertion that Donne was at Cambridge, possibly from
1588-1589.

conjecture, but that he did learn and support them is evident throughout his letters and prose works.

"An affliction which defeats all Magistracy": Donne's Politics & His Readers

Recent criticism has attempted to rehabilitate Donne, whose flagging status in Renaissance studies is partly due to his representation by new critics and early new historicists as an absolutist, monarchist authoritarian. Annabel Patterson notes that such representations are over-simplified and do not take into account either the highly pressurized context of Donne's actions or the indirection and subtly oppositional stances encoded in his works. Similarly, David Norbrook, Arthur Marotti, and Ted-Larry Pebworth point out the critical and resistant positions Donne takes not only in his prose but in his public poetry. [22] Such studies have yielded a far more complicated and richly rewarding Donne, one whose works bear out Gerald Graff's observation that "Literature is a scene of contradictions that cannot be subsumed under any 'totalizing' system or ideology." [23] Other readers of Donne, however, have been perhaps too zealous to identify his political correctness; they tell us, for example, of "revolutionary" subtexts and "radicalism" in Donne's treatment of his culture's repressive institutions. [24] But Donne was not a champion of democracy or even of the limited liberty that Milton espoused. Rather, he was a political moderate under a coercionary regime. More conservative than insurgent, he was a supporter of monarchy and—when he believed circumstances warranted—an apologist for autocratic governance. [25]

---

[22] Annabel Patterson, "All Donne" in *Soliciting Interpretation: Literary Theory and Seventeenth-Century English Poetry*, eds. Elizabeth D. Harvey and Katharine Eisaman Maus (Chicago: UP, 1990), pp. 37-67; David Norbrook, "The Monarchy of Wit and the Republic of Letters: Donne's Politics" in *Soliciting Interpretation*, pp. 3-36; Arthur Marotti, *John Donne: Coterie Poet* (Madison: Univ. of Wisconsin Press, 1986), pp. 183-95; Ted-Larry Pebworth, "'Let Me Here Use That Freedome': Subversive Representation in John Donne's 'Obsequies to the Lord Harrington," *JEGP*, 91, No. 1 (1992), pp. 17-42.

[23] Gerald Graff, "What Has Literary Theory Wrought?" *The Chronicle of Higher Education*, Feb. 12, 1992, p. A48.

[24] William Zunder, "The Poetry of John Donne: Literature, History and Ideology" in *Jacobean Poetry and Prose: Rhetoric, Representation, and the Popular Imagination*, ed. Clive Bloom (London: Macmillan, 1988), pp. 78-95. On the other hand, for a convincing and historically grounded account of Donne's "individualism," see Richard Strier, "Radical Donne: 'Satyre III'" *ELH* 60 (1993), pp.283-322.

[25] See, for example, Donne's fifth Prebend sermon in *Donne's Prebend Sermons*, ed. Janel Mueller (Cambridge, MA: Harvard UP, 1971), pp. 160-179. For an important discussion of the politics of Donne's "absolutist theology,"

But Donne's political analyses, like his support of monarchy, were never unequivocal. His politics were often inconsistent—at times apparently absolutist and at times apparently subversive—because they were typically casuistical. In (c.) 1615, for example, Donne publicly preached in defense of unlawful religious assembly, and he denied the authority of the monarch to enforce unjust conformity: "In times of persecution, when no exercise of true Religion is admitted, these private Meetings may not be denied to be lawful . . .; so, those souls, which without that, must necessarily starve, may steal their Spiritual food in corners, and private meetings." [26] In a sermon preached approximately a decade later, however, Donne urged unrelenting and severe pressure on religious non-conformists, and he proclaimed the monarch to be master "not of bodies onely, but of soules too." The king, he insists, has divine right, "not onely as we worship one God, but as we are to expresse that worship in the outward acts of Religion in the Church. God hath called himselfe King; and he hath called Kings Gods. . . So it is not the King that commands, but the power of God in the King." [27] Motivating the startling differences between Donne's political positions in these two sermons—his claims about the individual's versus the king's control of the soul—is not his aging conservatism, his careerist corruption, or his fear of reprisals; rather, it is the circumstances of the specific cases under consideration that shape the politics of each sermon. Such casuistical contingency informs Donne's politics throughout his works.

Itself both potentially conservative and oppositional, casuistry was particularly well-suited to Donne's interpretive practices and politics. In early modern Europe, casuistry "became a figure of ambiguity: ostensibly the vehicle through which the voice of conscience performed its stabilizing, normative function, it was also the perceived harbinger of the disintegration of communally recognized signs of what belonged inside and what outside the structure of cultural norms." [28] Resistant to fixed prescriptions and totalizing doctrine, casuistry assumes that the meaning of a text—whether legal, biblical, literary, etc.—is contingent and unstable. At the same time, it guides the uncertain or anomalous conscience according to institutionally approved standards for conduct. Paradoxically,

> It reduced anxieties in its capacity as an instrument of pastoral care or social control only to raise others as the vehicle of an epistemology of opacity and contingency and of an interpretive practice that militated against

---

see Deborah Kuller Shuger, *Habits of Thought in the English Renaissance: Religion, Politics, and the Dominant Cluture* (Berkeley: Univ. of California Press, 1990), pp.159-217.

[26] John Donne, *Sermons*, eds. George R. Potter and Evelyn Simpson (Berkeley: Univ. of California Press, 1953-62), V, 218.

[27] *Donne's Prebend Sermons*, ed. Janel Mueller, p. 165.

[28] Gallagher, *Medusa's Gaze*, p. 2.

the authority of final answers—against, for example, the capacity of an au-
thorial voice to delimit the range of meanings or perceived intentions in
texts designated as the representations of the truth of conscience. [29]

The ways in which Donne's own interpretive practices correspond to those
of casuistry is a subject of the following chapters.

One of my objectives in examining a variety of texts in which Donne
manipulates casuistical principles is to suggest a corrective to criticism that
divorces his early and late works. With some significant exceptions, both
past and recent critics have tended to focus exclusively on either the poetry
or the prose. Thomas Docherty, for example, proposes to "open up" or
"undo" Donne, but he rarely mentions the author's prose. Because of
Donne's dramatic shift of circumstances from university wit and court aspirant to Dean of St. Paul's, most readers have isolated his early poems from
his "mature" writing. As a result, criticism has historically posited two
separate Donnes—the libertine lyricist and the pious preacher—with two
very different philosophies. For instance, one critic describes *Biathanatos* as
"Donne putting off the old life that he may put on the new . . . Thus we
may conclude that *Biathanatos* is crucial in Donne's thought because it il-
luminates the intermediary ground between his earlier scepticism and naturalism and his later scepticism and mysticism."[30] Similarly, Louis Bredvold
asserts that Donne's need for a source of order and law outside himself sup-
planted the destructive relativism of his youth. [31] But as Annabel Patterson
has remarked, arguing for such a "sharp break between 'early' and 'mature'
work was a wishful critical construction" that simplified Donne's politics
and his writing. Emphasizing "the continuity between the Elizabethan

---

[29] Gallagher, *Medusa's Gaze*, p. 4. See also Alan Sinfield's account of ways
in which Protestant practices of the period were both subversive of authority and
conservative: *Faultlines: Cultural Materialism and the Politics of Dissident
Reading* (Berkeley: Univ. of California Press, 1992), pp.164-167.

[30] George Williamson, "The Libertine Donne," *Philological Quarterly*, XIII
(1934), p.291. Admittedly, Donne himself originated the notion of two separate
Donnes. In a letter of 1619, written "at my going into Germany," Donne
entrusts to Sir Robert Kerr his manuscript of *Biathanatos*: "let any that your
discretion admits to the sight of it, know the date of it; and that it is a Book
written by *Jack Donne*, and not by D[r]. *Donne*" (*Letters*, p.19). As the rest of
the letter suggests, however, the distinction has more to do with Donne's concern for his public image than with his repudiation of a youthful philosophy.
Indeed, nowhere in the letter does he disavow the content of *Biathanatos*, and
twice he enjoins Kerr never to destroy the manuscript. Appointed Divinity
Reader to the Benchers of Lincoln's Inn only a few months earlier, Donne no
doubt wanted to avoid the scandal that publication of his "misinterpretable subject" might cause.

[31] Louis I. Bredvold, "The Religious Thought of Donne in Relation to
Medieval and Later Traditions," from *Studies in Shakespeare, Milton and Donne*
(New York: Haskell House, 1964), p.201.

satirist and the Jacobean aspirant for something significant to do," Patterson makes an eloquent call for consideration of the discursive relations, as opposed to "the ideal of coherence," among Donne's works.[32] Other exceptions to criticism that bisects Donne's career are Terry Sherwood's *Fulfilling the Circle* and John Carey's *John Donne: Life, Mind, and Art*. While Carey argues for "imaginative continuity" in Donne's works, I look at practical theology as an aspect of their intellectual continuity. I am not, however, arguing for consistency or homogeneity or even an unequivocal assessment of casuistry in Donne's works. Rather, I am suggesting that to deny Donne's early efforts to come to terms with the individual's relation to law is to overlook an important source of dramatic tension and movement in the *Songs and Sonets*. Moreover, to study Donne's concern with the ambiguities of reason, language, and law is to discover an observance of casuistical methods that persisted throughout his career.

Thus, I propose looking at how the principles of case divinity inform a range of works from Donne's early, middle, and late "periods." Certainly the context within which he employs casuistry changes, but the problem of justifying action in the face of conflicting precepts remains. The young Donne abuses logic and burlesques the methods of case divinity when he argues that the exceptional circumstance of a flea bite creates a dispensation for unmarried sex. But at the heart of his specious appeal to reason and conscience are the same principles that lead the author of *Essays in Divinity* to describe famine as "an affliction which defeats all Magistracy; for in it one may lawfully steal" (p.68).

Given Donne's enduring interest in casuistry, it is peculiar that so little attention has been given to the influence of case divinity on his works. The first suggestion of Donne's affiliation with casuistical "habits of thought" is an article published by A.E. Malloch in 1962. "John Donne and the Casuists" discusses the popularity of cases of conscience in the Renaissance, and gives substantial evidence that Donne shared his century's interest in practical theology. Although the article never mentions Donne's verse, it cites several of the prose works in which he evaluates casuistical methods.

Malloch bases his discussion of case divinity on Catholic procedures. His penetrating analysis of probabilism and of Catholic casuists' reliance on Church authorities points out many of the problems and abuses that motivated Protestants to formulate their own system of practical divinity. However, with the exception of a footnote in which he dismisses Donne's interest in Reformed casuistry, Malloch does not distinguish between the Protestant and Catholic systems. Making such a distinction is crucial when considering Donne's comments about case divinity. If one does not differen-

---

[32] Patterson, "All Donne," p. 47, 60, 42.

tiate between the two methodologies, then the criticism of probabilism in *Pseudo-Martyr*, for example, will appear to be a general "condemnation of the casuists." [33] But Donne's repudiation of probabilist tactics found full support in Reformed casuistry. Although Donne objected to many of the practices endorsed by Catholic casuists, he consistently favored those advanced by Protestants.

Malloch's failure to distinguish between the two systems of case divinity leads him to conclude that Donne's attitude towards casuistry was contradictory:

> Nevertheless, in spite of the firmness of all these [anti-Catholic] statements, Donne was curiously drawn to the work of the casuists. For all his uneasiness and dissatisfaction with their methods, he. . . shared with them many of the habits of thought which produced those methods. [34]

But as I hope to establish, Donne's attraction to practical theology was not at all "curious." Malloch is right to suggest that Donne possessed casuistical "habits of thought"; I am interested in demonstrating specifically how they inform his politics and his epistemology as well as how they affect structure, style, and argument in his works.

Of the few critics who have suggested a connection between Donne and casuistry, Dwight Cathcart is the only one who investigates the influence of practical divinity on the *Songs and Sonets*. He observes in *Doubting Conscience* that many of Donne's poems are confrontations between a speaker who must defend his iconoclastic thesis and an auditor whose objections represent conventional laws of behavior. Cathcart argues persuasively that the point of departure in casuistical deliberation is just such a conflict between the individual and an undifferentiating law whose application to an exceptional case may be unjust. However, Cathcart's understanding of the tensions inherent in practical theology, and the conclusions he draws about the effect of casuistry on Donne's arguments, are problematic.

The source of my divergence from *Doubting Conscience* is that it ignores the problems which arise when Donne's speaker applies secular criteria to the principles of a theocentric methodology. Cathcart does concede that Donne, like casuists, believes reason is unable either to know truth or to construct perfect order out of the apparent contradictions of reality. Yet he insists that Donne is untroubled by epistemological uncertainty because of his faith in "the sublime and peaceful order of the world." [35] Donne's putative belief in an ordered universe beyond his perception, however, does not

---

[33] Malloch, p.75.
[34] Malloch, pp.74-75.
[35] Dwight Cathcart, *Doubting Conscience* (Ann Arbor: University of Michigan Press, 1975), p.12. Subsequent citations to this work will appear in the text.

alter the fact that he is confronted with contradictory laws, the limitations of reason, and the problem that truth appears to be contingent upon circumstances. He is still faced with the dilemma of how to justify action. Donne's speaker may try to support his point of view by championing an alternative law (as in "The Flea") or an uncommon love ("The Canonization"), but he knows that his criteria are fallible insofar as they derive from human valuation. In order to defend the exceptionality of his propositions, he adopts the relativity of casuistry without having recourse to its epistemological assurances.[36] The moral theologian who refers a problem of action to the certain criterion of Scripture anchors his judgment to God's truth; although one's reason is weak and its conclusions may be erroneous, casuistical assurances of God's direction mitigate one's anxiety about the validity of the action. But Donne's secular speaker cannot benefit from the final authorization of case divinity. Given his casuistical premise about the inadequacy of man-made precepts, his arguments are ultimately unresolved because he cannot establish that his position is more probable than that of his audience without measuring both against certain truth.

Unlike recent accounts of Donne's fractured subjectivity and of the anxious decentering of late Elizabethan and Jacobean culture, *Doubting Conscience* maintains that Donne believes "multiplicity" is only perceived and not actual. But, again, such a distinction is irrelevant to the speaker, who must act without an infallible standard for correcting perceptual error. Cathcart makes a similar distinction when discussing the confusion that results from linguistic inaccuracy; he states that the speaker "shows repeatedly throughout the *Songs and Sonets* that it is the contradiction between *words* that perplexes—or delights—and that the reality beyond the word is solid and single" (p.40). Cathcart argues that proof of Donne's faith in the world's order and in the unifying power of truth can be seen in his efforts to conflate opposites and to make one entity of two lovers (p.40). My response to such efforts is different; they may suggest Donne's desire for an ordered universe, but, rather than demonstrate coherence, he does violence to

---

[36] Casuistry offers several assurances for those who fear a moral decision may be incorrect because of reason's fallibility. First, God endows individuals with sufficient knowledge for their salvation. According to Hall, God's "justice will require nothing of the creature, but what he hath enabled him to know and do" (*The Old Religion*, Vol. IX of *Works*, ed. John Downame [Oxford: D. C. Talboys, 1937], p.376). See also Donne's *Sermons*, II, 308. Second, God will accept our intention of goodness as tantamount to right action, even if our judgment is wrong and our act unwittingly sinful. William Perkins writes, "God will accept our imperfect obedience, if it be sincere: yea he accepts the will, desire, and indeavour to obey for obedience itselfe" (*A Discourse of Conscience*, p.45). Despite epistemological uncertainty, casuistry is able to authorize actions both by referring them to God's justice and mercy, and by measuring them against the infallible criterion of Scripture.

logic by conjoining opposites and equating two with one. Donne must express what he believes to be truth in terms of paradox and contradiction. Neither of these modes of expression imitates "the sublime and peaceful order of the world" that *Doubting Conscience* sees reflected in the *Songs and Sonets*.

Nevertheless, Cathcart tends to view the methodology of casuistry as a panacea for problems of uncertainty in the *Songs and Sonets*. His analysis of the epistemology of case divinity is often illuminating, but it is not always consistent with his discussion of casuistry in Donne's poems. For example, he rightly observes that "The epistemology of moral theology abandons the necessity for proving an absolute relationship between truth and its formulation, and the moral theologian accepts a probability of truth in the absence of the certainty of it" (p. 51). Yet Cathcart asserts that, as Donne's speaker tries to integrate his private point of view with public law, he "surmounts the failure of reason to deal with the multiplicity of the visible world, joining himself to clear and final truth" (p. 70). Cathcart's claim that casuistry dispels uncertainty in the *Songs and Sonets* contradicts his admission that moral theologians can only discover "a practical if not an ultimate truth" (p. 56). He argues that resolution of tensions in Donne's poems is achieved because of the speaker's "faith in the existence and the final—if not the immediate—accessibility of truth. In that belief, if in few others, the speaker and his lover rest serenely" (p.152). A basic assertion of my fourth chapter, however, is that there is no evidence of epistemological serenity in the *Songs and Sonets*; casuistry appealed to Donne precisely because it recognizes problems of uncertainty and offers, not a catholicon, but methods of compromise and concession.

Despite his disavowal of epistemological tension in Donne's verse, Cathcart does discuss at length the tension between speaker and auditor. Their conflict, he says, is a legal one in which the speaker is initially at a disadvantage because he argues against conventional laws of behavior. "The speaker's view receives no support from general principles and is ... defenseless except for the cogency of his wit" (p. 37). In *Doubting Conscience*, practical theology is more a vehicle for wit or verbal dexterity than a response to the limits of knowledge. Cathcart depicts casuistry as a rhetorical technique with which the speaker wins his legal debate. Right and wrong are untangled, and the speaker arrives at an unequivocal judgment that places him "within the structure of the world and beyond the conflict of law and the disjunction between the one and the many" (p. 140). Once again, Cathcart asserts that Donne's conclusions are untroubled.

While I agree that the conflict among laws is at issue both in the *Songs and Sonets* and in cases of conscience, I will demonstrate that this conflict is only one facet of the complex problems facing the speaker/casuist. Cathcart's focus on legalism leads him to interpret the speaker's contentiousness at its simplest level: his aim is merely to have his own way, and not to address the epistemological ramifications of the disagreement.[37] I would argue, however, that Donne's persona can assert his anomalous propositions only by addressing reason's inability to discern an absolute standard for action. To defend his position, the speaker argues that his interlocutor's criteria for judgment—convention, law, morality—are relative to circumstances. But to make such a claim is tacitly to admit that one's own judgments can have no more than temporary or contingent authority. Since fallen reason can only perceive truth as relative, one is constantly having to determine the right response to new experience. To calm a present doubt or ratify an equitable law is not to insure against alteration. As the speaker of "Woman's Constancy" points out, what is true for love now may be nullified by later circumstances. At best then, the resolutions of the *Songs and Sonets* are precarious; as I will argue, the speaker's contradiction, paradox, self-conscious sophistry, and almost shrill hyperbole betray an uneasiness about his claims to authority. Cathcart is right to suggest that Donne's persona *wants* to assert an unequivocal judgment, but the speaker's premise about the relativity of right action vitiates unconditional conclusions.

The most recent examination of the casuistical context of Donne's verse is a chapter in Camille Wells Slights's illuminating work, *The Casuistical Tradition in Shakespeare, Donne, Herbert, and Milton*. Although Slights sketches the casuistical theses of *Biathanatos* and *Pseudo-Martyr*, her focus is on the satires. In a brief addendum to her chapter on Donne, she asserts that the procedures of moral theology are inapplicable to the *Songs and Sonets*.

> In a broad sense, the casuistical habit of mind animates the intense self-exploration against a backdrop of the temporal and eternal conditions of men's lives in Donne's lyrics. But the lyrics are not casuistical in any precise, specific way. (p. 182)

To support her position, Slights argues that casuists attempt to enable action, whereas Donne's concern is with definition; her distinction suggests that the two endeavors are mutually exclusive. She claims that the *Songs*

---

[37] Clearly, the speaker's aim is to expedite his proposals, but my interest is in exploring specifically how he manipulates casuistical theories in order to justify his position. Cathcart, however, denies Donne's concern with theory: "Donne is not a philosophical poet. That is, the progress of his thought is not directed toward definition of concept but rather toward direction of his action. His investigations are not theoretic but practical. . ."(pp.28-29). My reading of the *Songs and Sonets* will focus on the methods that Cathcart dismisses; the speaker, I will argue, cannot progress "toward direction of his action" without first casuistically establishing the "definition of concept" that gives his circumstances their exceptional status.

and Sonets do not share the objectives of case divinity because "Donne uses analysis and argument not to solve problems and to resolve doubt but to define and communicate emotion" (p.179).

But Slights's distinction is problematic, especially in poems such as "Song: Sweetest Love" and the valedictions, where defining an emotion— the beloved's unreasonable grief or the speaker's love— is the only way to address the problem of how to respond to separation. In cases of conscience, it is the qualitative definition of one's circumstances that determines whether a law is relevant or an action appropriate. Like any casuist, Donne cannot controvert conventional behavior without first defining the exceptional status of his case. The speaker of "A Valediction: forbidding mourning," for example, tells his interlocutor that their unique love is "Inter-assured of the mind" and not dependent on the senses for verification; consequently, "sublunary" lovers' response to parting is not applicable to them.[38] Only by defining the exceptional qualities of their relationship is he able to assert a new law of response: they should "make no noise,/ No teare-floods, nor sigh-tempests move." The problem of parting itself is redefined since physical separation of two who are metaphysically united is not "A breach, but an expansion." The speaker will leave, but his grieving lover is put in the paradoxical position of responding to a situation that does not exist: she mourns the absence of one from whom she cannot be parted. Slights is right to observe that "Donne uses analysis and argument. . . to define and communicate emotion," but he does so in order to defend casuistically the actions or attitudes that he advances. How he effects his defense is the subject of my chapter on the Songs and Sonets.

Thus I share with Slights, Cathcart, and Malloch the persuasion that Donne's casuistical habits of thought invite closer attention to the role of practical theology in his works. But the aims and conclusions of my study differ significantly from those of other critics. I investigate the epistemological context of Donne's casuistry, and I examine his prose and poetic works that invoke the interpretive practices and narrative procedures of cases of conscience. In addition, I demonstrate that his casuistical response to problems of law and uncertainty recurs throughout the various genres and periods in which he writes. As a result, I hope to provide an added dimension to Donne's concern with the process of moral deliberation, and his exploration of criteria for judgment.

---

[38] John Donne, The Complete Poetry, ed. John T. Shawcross (NY: Doubleday, 1967), pp.87-88. All citations of the poems are to this edition.

"Embassadours of Reconciliation": Motives and Narrative Practices of Casuistry

What follows is an outline of casuistical motives and methods that figure prominently in my account in subsequent chapters of Donne's politics and his works. The differences between Roman and Reformed casuistry mentioned below are developed more fully in chapter two. Particularly germane to Donne's prose and poetry are five tenets of case divinity: the practical application of ethics to experience; the relativity of laws to circumstances; the value of disputation in discovering right action; the inviolacy of conscience; and the responsibility of each person to adjudicate his or her own case of conscience. As will be seen, the last two principles are distinctly Protestant, and are crucial to Donne's endorsement of Reformed casuistry. All of the tenets combine to formulate a system of shaping and interpreting experience. The system serves the same heuristic purpose in reading a number of Donne's works.

Donne remarks in his *Essays*, "Morall Divinity becomes us all; but Naturall Divinity, and Metaphysique Divinity, almost all may spare" (p.88). The distinction between casuistry and abstract branches of theology is an important one. Aptly named, practical theologians are concerned with applied morality rather than doctrinal technicalities. Their audience is not limited to Biblical exegetes; it includes anyone who attempts to translate Christian teaching into action. The propagation of casuistical doctrines is itself a practical enterprise: moral theologians compile cases of conscience in which recommended procedures and principles are enacted; not only do the exempla provide resolutions to specific problems, but they demonstrate how to determine the ethical status of any act. As Jeremy Taylor explains in *Ductor Dubitantium*, "although I have not given answers to every doubt, yet I have told what we are to do when any doubt arises; I have conducted the doubting conscience by such rules, which in all doubts will declare her duty." [39] The emphasis of practical divinity is as much on the process of deliberation as it is on the decision. Cases of conscience illustrate the primary thesis of casuists that moral precepts should not be abstracted from experience.

Amplifying Donne's comment above, Joseph Hall writes in his *Resolutions*, "Of all divinity, that part is most useful which determines cases of conscience . . .as action is of more concernment than speculation" (p.270). The utility that Hall commends is reflected in the topics that cases encompass. Practical theologians are "Embassadors of reconciliation," who

---

[39] Jeremy Taylor, *Ductor Dubitantium*, Vol. 3 of *Works* (London: Henry Bohn, 1844), p.53.

attempt to anchor all legal and ethical principles in the quotidian.[40] "We meddle not," Hall continues, "with those secret (and some of them immodest) curiosities, contenting ourselves only with those which meet us every day in the ordinary practice of men" (p.367). Indeed, casuists treat most areas of "ordinary practice"; their subject matter ranges from problems of business and commerce, to matters of warfare and apparel, to parental authority and the rights of pagans and savages. It is not unusual, then, that Donne employs the methods of casuistry to address such disparate issues as government policy and the behavior of lovers. Practical theologians assume that every action is the product of moral choice. One makes casuistical decisions daily. In a sermon of 1621, Donne maintains that, although our endeavors may "seeme but *Morall*, or *Civill*, or *domestique*, yet they have a deeper tincture, a heavenly nature, a relation *to God*, in them." [41] Given that all acts are morally significant, casuistry seeks to identify in them the "deeper tincture" that general laws may not account for.

Practical theologians frequently liken casuistry to equity. Both processes are conditional, and both claim a greater authority than law in negotiating specific problems. William Ames, remarking on the similar functions of equity and casuistry, adds, "Legall Justice taken strictly, considereth the words just as they are written, but Equity considereth the End, scope and intent of the Law, and so hath more Law in it, then Legall Justice, when taken strictly." [42] In a passage that Donne defends on several occasions, Aquinas asserts that general law cannot accommodate "contingent matters, about which human actions are concerned: and consequently, although there is necessity in the general principles, the more we descend to matters of detail, the more frequently we encounter defects." [43] Case divinity tries to correct such defects by measuring the circumstances of an act against the intention or, in Chancery terms, the "spirit" of the law. Any number of factors— new decrees, custom, the unanticipated or extraordinary— may warrant a

---

40   Thomas Pickering, "Letter of Dedication," in William Perkins' *Whole Treatise of Cases of Conscience*, p.83. In his *Christian Directory* (Ann Arbor: Univ. Microfilms, 1970), sig. A 2, Richard Baxter reiterates that the aim of casuists is "the reduction of Theoretical knowledge into *serious Christian* practice."

41   *Sermons*, III, 366.

42   William Ames, *Conscience With the Power and Cases Thereof* in *Works* (Ann Arbor: Univ. Microfilms, 1962), Bk. V, p. 111. The claim that equity "hath more law in it" is fully developed in Christopher Saint German's *Doctor and Student*; one of the most important analyses of common law in the early modern period, *Doctor and Student* was influenced by contemporary casuistical literature on conscience. Christopher Saint German, *Doctor and Student*, ed. T. F. Plucknett (London: Seldon Society, 1974).

43   Aquinas, *Summa Theologica*, I-II. 94. 4. See Donne's *Biathanatos*, ed. Ernest W. Sullivan II (Newark: Univ. of Delaware Press, 1984), p.46.

dispensation. As Donne contends, "No Law is so primary and simple but it fore-imagins a reason vpon which it was founded: and scarse any reason is so constant, but that Circumstances alter it." [44] Like equity, casuistry enables more qualitative considerations than do precisely legal hearings. The latitude accorded to casuistical decisions was greater than the extenuating allowances that Foucault, for example, observes in his account of legal judgments in the early modern period.[45]

Always grounding their judgments in God's Word, casuists claim that Scripture is their precedent for granting exceptions to the law. Perkins, for instance, reasons that in some cases we may disregard even divine commands without breach of conscience:

> And this stands even by the equitie of Gods word. God made a law, that the priests onely should eat of the shew bread; now David being no priest, did upon urgent occasion eate of it without sinne. If this be true in Gods lawe, then it may also be true in the lawes of men, that they may in some cases be omitted without sinne against God. Neither must this seeme strange. For as there is a keeping of a law, and a breaking of the same; so there is a middle or meane action betweene them both, which is, to doe a thing *beside the lawe*, and that without sinne. [46]

Perkins is careful to distinguish between violating and disregarding the law. Insofar as casuistical dispensations insure justice, they are consonant with the purpose of law, even though temporarily and conditionally they may invalidate an ordinance. As any collection of cases from the sixteenth and seventeenth centuries will confirm, few precepts are so comprehensive that they may not on occasion be disregarded. Both Protestant and Catholic casuists grant exceptions to laws against murder, perjury, theft, incest, assault, etc.

Accordingly, Donne argues in *Biathanatos* that there are numerous instances in which prohibitions against suicide are inapplicable. Summarizing a key assumption of case divinity, he writes: "to me there appeares no other interpretation safe, but this, that there is no externall act naturally Euill, and

---

[44] *Biathanatos*, p.47.

[45] Michel Foucault, *Discipline and Punish: The Birth of the Prison* (NY: Vintage, 1979), pp.17-19.

[46] Perkins, *Discourse*, pp.34-5. The New Testament also afforded justification for casuistical practices. Kirk (p.79) observes that, although Christ preached love of God and neighbor, "he would not violate the conscience of the individual Christian or the Church by laying down a cast-iron code of minutiae. He 'taught in parables' instead. This should warn us only too clearly to be both modest and tentative in declaring that any detailed principle of conduct is an immutable law of God. That there are such immutable principles we do not doubt; but the limitations of the human mind, the imperfections of the human vocabulary, and the needs of different ages conspire to introduce a fluctuating element into their temporal promulgation."

that Circumstances condition them, and giue them theyr Nature." [47] Since
no action has an innate moral status, valuation and interpretation are relative
and unstable. Donne espouses the relativity of laws throughout his works.
In a sermon that discusses sumptuary rules, for example, he insists that no
restriction is universally appropriate. Time, place, and person qualify any
act, whether suicidal or sartorial.

> Certainly the limits of adorning and beautifying the body are not so nar-
> row, so strict, as by some sowre men they are sometimes conceived to be.
> Differences of Ranks, of Ages, of Nations, of Customes, make great differ-
> ences in the enlarging, or contracting of these   limits, in adorning the
> body; and that may come neare sin at some time, and in some places, which
> is not so alwaies, nor everywhere. [48]

As laws and conventions vary according to circumstances, so must our actions. Moral judgments, Donne affirms, should be qualitative, contingent,
casuistical.

The conditional nature of casuistry exerts important claims on the individual, especially in Reformed cases. Since detailed formulae for behavior
are impossible, each person must decide the relation of general laws to specific cases. Casuists require that one debate all sides of an issue before determining its moral status. Our resolutions are subject to the approval of
conscience, which proceeds by reason. A faculty of the mind, conscience is
inoperative without knowledge. Donne explains in *Pseudo-Martyr*: "*an act
by which wee apply our knowledge to some particular thing*, the
Conscience ever presumes *knowledge*: and we may not. . . doe any thing
upon *Conscience*: if we doe it not upon *knowledge*."[49] Therefore, each person is responsible for evaluating the facts of his or her own case, and each
is accountable for the reasons that fortify any conclusion. Not only must ratiocinative effort precede action, but to commit an act without the persuasion of reason is to sin.

> *Whatsoever is not of faith*, that is, whatsoever is not done out of a setled
> perswasion in judgment and conscience out of Gods word, howsoever men
> judge of it, *is sinne*. Againe, God regards not the outward pompe of the ac-
> tion or the doer, but. . .the obedience of the heart: Therefore unlesse the
> conscience well informed first of all approove the thing to be good and
> agreeable to Gods will, it can be nothing els but a sinne. [50]

Casuistical emphasis on reason and conscience calls for the individual's full
participation in appraising experience. The need for such participation is, to
anticipate an argument developed in later chapters, a leitmotif in Donne's

---

[47]   *Biathanatos*, p.120.
[48]   *Sermons*, V, 302.
[49]   *Pseudo-Martyr*, p.237.
[50]   Perkins, *Discourse*, p.41.

prose and a point of departure for his poetic argument.

Although Scripture is the primary reference for casuistical adjudication, the directives of reputable authorities should also be taken into account. But the extent to which one must follow other's determinations varies between Protestants and Catholics. The latter give greater credence to the opinions of Church officials than to the conclusions of a layperson's conscience, while the former maintain that no authority—whether positive law or the Pope— is greater than conscience. The distinction is pivotal for Reformed casuistry, and is grounded in far-reaching objections to Catholic mediation between the individual and God.[51] Donne supports the Protestant argument that automatically deferring to anothers' opinion violates both reason and conscience; indeed, he declares the argument to be a motivating factor in his writing *Pseudo-Martyr* and *Biathanatos*. In effect, the self is disqualified from moral judgment when Church officials are the source of all resolutions. Donne protests that to sacrifice reason to human authority is to become like the "uncleane beasts, [who] swallow, and never chaw the cudde"; similarly, Perkins asserts that those who do not debate their own cases lack the

> right and true direction of conscience out of Gods word, and therefore their best actions are sinnes. . .For they doe these actions either of custome, or example, or necessitie, as beasts doe, and not of faith: because they know not Gods will touching things to be done or left undone. The consideration of this point should make every man most carefull to seek for knowledge of Gods word and daily to increase in it, that he may in all his affaires have Gods lawes to be the men of his counsel.[52]

Protestant casuists do not, however, discourage consulting an objective judge about moral dilemmas. On the contrary, they publish cases and resolutions in order to guide the confused Christian. And they admonish cautious and thorough deliberation before acting against approved authority. Like Reformers, Donne advocated the primacy of conscience, but he also criticized those who "contemne the opinion of other men, *Imprudenter agunt & crudeliter*, They deale weakly, and improvidently for themselves, in that they assist not their consciences with more witnesses." [53] Protestant casu-

---

[51]   The primacy of official resolutions of cases over the individual's own sense of rectitude is consistent with other Catholic traditions of intercession— indulgences, confession, penance, petition to saints, etc. The opposing position of Reformed casuists conforms to Protestant faith in the priesthood of all believers, faith in the unmediated relation of the individual to God. The following chapter discusses at length casuistry's place in Reformation polemics.

[52]   Donne, *Pseudo-Martyr*, p.173; and Perkins, *Discourse*, p.43.

[53]   *Sermons*, VI, 250. Similarly, Hall remarks in his *Resolutions* (p.354):
A man would do well betwixt two extremes: the careless neglect of our spiritual fathers on the one side, and too confident reliance upon their power on the

ists seek a balance between radical individualism and unthinking conformity. But as Ames insists, once reason and conscience are persuaded, "it is
not lawful to go against our own opinion (certain or probable) for respect to
other men's authority."[54] In principle, Ames's statement is meant to insure
the inviolacy of conscience, but the Reformed position is clearly vulnerable
to abuse. Chapter four discusses how Donne's poetic speaker exploits the
latitude that casuistry affords to individual determinations.

Protestant and Catholic differences about the individual's role in moral
judgment are epitomized in their presentation of cases. According to
Catholic casuists, anyone who is uncertain about the proper course of action
should search for analogous problems in published cases and apply the authorized resolutions to his or her own dilemma. Rather than suggest ways
in which to evaluate one's circumstances, Roman cases dictate specific decisions based on precedent and canon law. Reformed casuists object that such
a policy transforms morality into disengaged research, and that the inevitable contradictions among resolutions serve only to increase perplexity.
Donne agrees that the myriad prescriptions of Catholic casuists "are indeede,
Nubes Testium: but not in that sense as the holy Ghost used the
Metaphore. For they are such *clouds* of witnesses, as their testimonie ob-
scures the whole matter." [55] According to Donne and Reformers, the moral
legalism of Catholic cases secures conformity at the expense of understanding.

Moreover, Donne remonstrates in *Pseudo-Martyr* that Roman casuistry
fails to instruct its audience in the process of eradicating uncertainty.

> It is impossible to. . .unentangle our consciences by any of those Rules,
> which their *Casuists* use to give, who to strengthen the possession of the
> *Romane* Church, have bestowed more paines, to teach how strongly a con-
> science is bound to doe according to a *Scruple*, or a *Doubt*, or an *Opinion*,

---

other. Some there are that do so overtrust their own judgment, that they think
they may slight their spiritual guides: there can be no safety for the soul but in a
midway betwixt both these.
   See also Keith Thomas, pp. 35-36.
   54   Ames, *Conscience With the Power and Cases Thereof*, Bk.I,16. Donne
concurs with Protestant casuists about the inviolacy of conscience. In *Sermons*,
V, 243, he remarks, "he that sinnes against his Conscience, and is thereby im-
penitible, cannot be pardoned." And writing to Sir Henry Goodyer (*Letters*,
p.76), he expresses the view of Reformed casuists that one is bound to obey
even the erroneous dictates of conscience: "it is sinne to doe against the conscience, though that erre."
   55   *Pseudo-Martyr*, p.231. As Malloch observes (pp.64-65), the Catholic
emphasis on precedent implies that "personal assimilation of truth is not crucial
to moral action. . .The legality of an action is referred, not principally to the
agent's understanding of what is right, but to the whole body of recorded opinion on the subject."

or an *Errour* which it hath conceived, then how it might depose that
Scruple, or cleare that *Doubt*, or better that *Opinion*, or rectifie that
Errour.[56]

The faults that Donne complains of in Catholic casuistry are redressed in
Protestant cases. The first concern of Reformed casuists is to teach the
layperson how to effect his or her own moral judgments. While agreeing
that their resolutions of cases may prove useful for analogous problems,
Protestants insist that their decisions are advisory, not prescriptive. This
stance is central to Donne's arguments in *Biathanatos*. Since conscience
must formulate its own judgments, he does not presume to make final
choices for his readers; instead, like all Reformed casuists, he offers
methodological paradigms for examining conscience and evaluating circumstances in terms of Scripture. Once versed in the process of eradicating
doubt, the individual can apply the safeguards of casuistry to any decision
that might arise. Jeremy Taylor says of his collection of cases: "I intend
here to offer the world a general instrument of moral theology, by the rules
and measures of which. . .men that are wise may guide themselves in all
their proportions of conscience." [57] The specific "rules and measures" to
which Taylor refers are the final consideration of this chapter.

Cases in Point: Hall and Azpilcueta on Homicide

Given the casuistical (and Donnean) preference for demonstration, it is fit-

---

[56] *Pseudo-Martyr*, pp.226-227. Such objections were, of course, partisan.
For an excellent, more temperate, discussion of Catholic casuistry, see P. J.
Holmes, *Resistance and Compromise* (Cambridge: UP, 1982).

[57] *Ductor Dubitantium*, p.53. In his *Resolutions* (p.271), Hall describes the
role of Protestant casuists as counselors rather than enforcers: "It is far from my
thoughts to obtrude these my resolutions, as peremptory and magisterial, upon
my readers; I only tender them submissly; as probable advices to the simpler
sort of Christian, and as matter of grave censure to the learned." Donne, too,
adopts the advisory role of casuists in his sermons; addressing the congregation
at St. Paul's (*Sermons*, III, 374), he remarks, "I appeall to your own
Consciences. . .(not as a *Judge*, but as an *Assistant* to your Consciences, and
Amicus Curiae)." Despite Reformers' claims that their judgments of cases were
not prescriptive, it is important to note, as does Alan Sinfield, that their counsel
(not just that of Catholic casuists) was nevertheless ideologically intrusive.
"Where the Catholic priest had confessed and absolved people in his parish
through the magical properties of the sacrament, the protestant minister was to
interpret the scriptures to them, intervening specifically in their states of
mind...Though in theory every individual was responsible for his or her own
soul, no minister felt that his flock could be left without expert guidance from
himself. John Brinsley the Younger wrote that ministers were 'agents betwixt
God and his people,' and should preach 'as heralds, in the name, in the authority
of him that sendeth them.'"*Faultlines*, p. 171.

ting to study the methods of practical theology as they are enacted. Any number of cases would be exemplary, since each "attempt[s] to imitate the process by which man can reach right decisions, that is, to embody the mode of thinking it recommends." [58] In order to illustrate some of the differences between Catholic and Protestant casuistry, I have chosen two cases, one from Hall's *Resolutions and Decisions of Divers Practical Cases of Conscience* and another from Martin Azpilcueta's *Enchiridion sive Manuale Confessariorum et Poenitentium*. Both consider the extent to which prohibitions against homicide are binding.

Several factors guided my choice of the two representative texts. As mentioned earlier, Hall and Donne were closely affiliated. Given their personal and philosophical connections, as well as their shared allegiance to Reformed rather than Roman casuistry, a case from Hall's treatise is appropriate to later discussions of Donne's own casuistical argumentation. As for Azpilcueta's *Manuale*, it was one of the best known Catholic works of practical theology in the Renaissance. "Between its first appearance [1553] and 1625, eighty-one editions of the *Enchiridion* were issued, as well as another ninety-two revisions, abridgments, and translations into Spanish, Portuguese, French, and Italian." [59] Donne studied Azpilcueta and quoted him on several occasions. The primary textbook on casuistry at the seminaries of Rheims and Douai, the *Manuale* was first published in Spanish in 1553, and was translated into Latin in 1581.[60] Donne could read both Spanish and Latin, and may have had access to the work through his Jesuit uncles, Jasper and Ellis Heywood.[61]

Entitled "Whether, and in what cases, it may be lawful for a man to take away the life of another," Hall's investigation follows the tripartite structure of many cases of conscience. The work opens with general precepts relevant to the topic, then specifies circumstances that qualify or alter the laws, and ends with a contingent judgment that serves in turn as a general rule for analogous cases. As demonstrated in chapter three below, Donne's sermon on Esther proceeds by the same pattern. Hall treats his sub-

---

[58]   Slights, p.52.

[59]   Zagorin, *Ways of Lying*, p. 165.

[60]   Elliot Rose, *Cases of Conscience: Alternatives Open to Recusants and Puritans Under Elizabeth I and James I* (Cambridge: UP, 1975), p.88. See also Holmes, *Elizabethan Casuistry*, p.1.

[61]   Like all Jesuits, Donne's uncles would have been familiar with numerous casuistical treatises and collections of cases, not just that of Azpilcueta. The Constitutions of the Society of Jesus required thorough training in the methods of practical theology. Weekly, a Professor of Cases of Conscience would grill aspirants, referred to as "casistae" in the Constitutions, on resolutions to difficult cases from various casuistical tracts. *Constitutio Societatis Jesu* IV, 5; *Ratio Studiorum*, "de casibus" (1591); *Institutum Societatis Jesu* II, 586; *Epitome* IV, viii, 372. See Jonsen and Toulmin, *The Abuse of Casuistry*, p.149.

ject as one of perplexity. [62] That is, he acknowledges that the laws governing his case are contradictory. On one hand, human life is sacred, and God is
"the only absolute Lord of it" (p.294). On the other hand, everyone is bound
"to use all just means for his own preservation, although it should be the
necessitated destruction of another" (p.295). Since the occasion determines
which law exerts a greater claim, Hall posits a number of hypothetical situations in order to resolve the perplexity. In each situation, the proper course
of action depends on three factors: the intentions and consequences of the
conflicting laws, the motive or state of mind of those involved in the
dilemma, and the exceptional or extenuating circumstances. According to
casuistry, any one of the three factors may exempt the case from conventional rules; Donne's sermon on *Esther*, for example, cites all three factors
to justify Esther's transgression of both positive and natural laws.

Hall asserts that it is justifiable to destroy another life in self-defense
only if one is mortally assaulted. To this already conditional rule, he adds
further restrictions. "I suppose the assault mortal, when both the weapon is
deadly and the fury of the assailant threatens death. As for some slight and
sudden passages of a switch or a cane, they come not under this consideration" (p.295). The assailant's state of mind and the extenuating circumstances of the attack determine both the degree of danger and the vigor of
one's response. The focus of Hall's argument becomes increasingly specific
as he seeks to clarify in practical terms the relation of law to experience. He
constructs in one sentence a dramatic fiction that illustrates the contingency
of rules for self-defense.

---

[62] Casuists divide cases into categories, the most common of which are
perplexity and doubt. Because each category requires slightly different procedures, it is important to establish the status of the case early in one's deliberation. Perplexity occurs when two or more laws conflict, so that to obey one pre-
cept seems to violate another. The casuistical rule in such dilemmas is to follow
the lesser evil or the greater responsibility. A perplexed conscience should
compare the intention and consequences of each law and determine which is more
appropriate to the circumstances. Donne's *Pseudo-Martyr* and his sermon on
Esther are structured according to the rules of perplexity. *Biathanatos*, on the
other hand, treats suicide as a matter of doubt. This second category involves
cases in which the pertinence of a law is questionable, either because strict application of the law would be unjust, or because of uncertainty about interpreting
the law. Anyone caught in a case of doubt must establish whether the circumstances are extenuating. A dispensation may be warranted if any of the following
can be proven: "a real ambiguity in the formulation of the law, the undoubted
tolerance by authority of its neglect, the definite exception from its
operation..., the emergence of an important factor which obviously never
entered into the calculations of those who formulated the law." (Kirk, p.270)
For Donne's familiarity with the technical distinctions among moral problems, see his *Letters*, p.74 and *Sermons*, IV, 222.

> But even in these assaults, except the violence be so too impetuous that it
> will admit of neither parley nor pause, there ought to be, so much as may
> consist with our necessary safety, a tender regard and endeavour to avoid
> the spilling of blood; but if neither persuasion nor the shifting (what we
> may) our station can abate anything of the rage of the assailer, death must;
> yea, if not my brother only, but my father or my son, should in this
> forcible manner set upon me, howsoever I should hazard the award of some
> blows, and with tears beg a forbearance, yet if there would be no remedy,
> nature must pardon me; no man can be so near me as myself.   (p.295)

Hall's fragmented syntax mirrors the complex and conditional nature of casuistry. His subordinate and independent clauses build to a law ("no man can
be so near me as myself") that the preceding distinctions clarify and delimit.
Since their resolutions are contingent, practical theologians qualify their assertions with examples, analogies, exceptions, and definitions. As a result,
cases of conscience have few simple sentences. Restricting clauses, logical
connectives, and "if-then" constructions distinguish casuistical syntax.
Hall's judgment, like that of many cases, is based on his qualitative redefinition of an act; given the circumstances he outlines, killing another is self-
preservation, and therefore is sanctioned. Indeed, Hall's resolution allows
fratricide, parricide, and filicide.

    Having reasoned towards a conjunction of law and experience, Hall tests
his decision against contrary opinions. Consideration of counterarguments
is essential to right action, since Protestant casuistry holds each person accountable for the fully debated reasons that inform each choice. Disputation
not only insures that one weighs all sides of an issue, but it tries the conviction of conscience and reason. Donne remarks in *Biathanatos* that controversy is the most effective method of discovering rectitude: "as in the Poole
of *Bethsaida*, there was no health till the Water was troubled, so the best
way to finde the truith in this matter was to debate and vexe it." Like
Hall— like all Protestant casuists— he examines conflicting authorities in
order to "bring most doubts into disputation, and *so* into clearnesse" (my
emphasis).[63] The contention that characterizes Donne's works is requisite
in case divinity.

    Hall's first refutation is of Leonardus Lessius, a Catholic casuist who
asserts that clergy should submit to murder rather than kill an attacker.
Nowhere does Scripture order such an exception to the rule of self-preservation, Hall argues; nor does "the common law of nature" support Lessius'
claim. Hall cites three examples of Biblical leaders who justly "enjoined
bloodshed" in self-defense, and he proceeds to refute other objections by referring to the same criteria of Scripture and natural law. His address of specific counterarguments further clarifies the resolution that "no man can be
so near me as myself." He concludes his disputation with the inductive

---

[63]   *Biathanatos*, p.30 and p.64.

movement from particular cases to accommodated principles that distinguishes the end— in both senses of aim and completion— of casuistical deliberation: "Shortly, then, if a man will needs be wicked to my destruction, the evil is his own: let him bear his own guilt; let me look to my own indemnity" (p.296).

Hall adds that the rule of self-preservation extends to defense of property. In light of his earlier determinations, he poses a related problem. "If a man will be offering to rob my house or to take my purse, what may I do in this case?" Hall maintains that neither charity nor justice prevent the use of violence in protecting our property. He even sanctions homicide on such occasions, but with an important provision: our intention must be to seek restitution and not retribution. "Charity forbids that this slaughter should be my first intention; which is primarily bent upon my own safety, and the vindication of my own just property. The blood that follows is but the unwilling attendant of my defence. . ." (p.297). That intention determines the moral status of an act is a fundamental tenet of casuistry. It is impossible to evaluate experience justly without taking into account the agent's state of mind. Jeremy Taylor writes, "He that does a good thing while he believes it to be evil, does choose the evil, and refuse the good." [64] And Donne observes similarly that "the intent and end conditions euery action, and infuses the poyson or the nourishment, which they, which follow, suck from thence." [65] Since the same act committed by two different people may be sinful in one and righteous in another, the judgments of Protestant casuists include close attention to motivation. Reformed casuists object to Catholics' applying preformulated resolutions to a case, because such a practice fails to account for possible differences of intention. Unapprised of anothers' state of mind, practical theologians can only recommend methods for reaching a just decision; they can advise what kinds of questions to ask and the criteria for answering them, but the final authority rests with the agent alone.

The authority that Protestant casuists accord to individual conscience and reason is demonstrated in Hall's final remarks on the defense of property. Once again, Hall poses a series of hypothetical circumstances that tests the extent of his resolution. He concludes that, if conscience and our understanding of divine law support our decision, we may without guilt act in direct opposition to positive law.

---

[64] *Ductor Dubitantium*, p.56. See also Perkins' "A Godly and Learned Exposition of Christ's Sermon on the Mount": God "judgeth not the goodness of the work done by the excellency of the matter whereby it is occupied, but by the heart of the doer." Quoted in George Mosse, *The Holy Pretence: A Study in Christianity and Reason of State From William Perkins to John Winthrop* (Oxford: Basil Blackwell, 1957), p.55.
[65] *Biathanatos*, p.127.

> In such a case, if the sum [of stolen money] be so considerable as that it
> much imports my estate, however our municipal laws may censure it, with
> which, of old, even a killing, *se defendendo*, was no less than felony of
> death: my conscience should not strike me, if I pursue him with all my
> might; and in hot chase so strike him, as that by this means I disable him
> from a further escape, for the recovery of my own: and if hereupon his death
> shall follow, however I should pass with men, God and my own heart would
> acquit me. (p.297)

Evident throughout Hall's case is a hierarchy of authority in which human
laws and conventions are less binding than conscience. Although moral theologians are careful to measure against Scripture the latitude allowed to individual judgment, the Protestant criteria of conscience and inner persuasion
are potentially subversive of outside order: "however our municipal laws
may censure it. . .God and my own heart would acquit me." [66] Catholic casuists were quick to point out that giving greater credence to the layperson's
sense of right and wrong than to tradition and approved authorities was tantamount to ethical anarchy. But Donne and other Protestant advocates argued
that the exercise of reason and conscience is a moral responsibility from
which the laity cannot be excluded.

Azpilcueta, also known as Navarrus, argues according to the authoritarian assumptions of Roman casuistry. Like Hall, Azpilcueta weighs contradictory opinions in order to determine when laws against taking another's
life may be disregarded. But unlike Hall, he rarely substantiates his arguments with Scripture, and he rarely invokes conscience as a guide to action.
His criteria for right conduct are official Church policy and approved authorities. Thus, his *Manuale* allows its readers less participation in moral decisions than does Hall's *Resolutions*, which elevates conscience above human
laws and which leaves final determination to the individual.

The structure of the two treatises reflects their different frames of reference. Hall's work is divided into four "Decades" or topics: "Cases of Profit
and Traffick"; "Life and Liberty"; "Piety and Religion"; "Cases
Matrimonial." Each Decade poses ten moral questions that might arise in
the everyday experience of the reader. As with most Reformed casuists,
Hall's point of departure is the idiosyncratic connection between specific
problems and general rules. Navarrus, on the other hand, organizes his treatise according to laws and prohibitions. The first ten chapters discuss rules
of contrition, confession, and penance. The next ten are devoted to the
Decalogue. And the final seven chapters address Church regulations ("De los
mandamientos de la yglesia"): feast days and fasting; mortal sins; the
Sacraments; Church penalties and excommunication; keeping the Sabbath,

---

66 Christopher Hill discusses the potentially subversive implications of
Protestant "individualism" in his *Century of Revolution* (New York: W. W.
Norton, 1966).

etc. [67] The 800-page *Manuale* is twice the length of Hall's *Resolutions*, and is more concerned with legal technicalities and the opinions of theologians than is its case-oriented counterpart.

Although the following chapter examines more fully the legalistic and authoritarian basis of Catholic casuistry, it is worth noting briefly Azpilcueta's attention to technical terms and academic distinctions. While Hall attempts to simplify moral problems and to present them in lay terms, Navarrus seeks out subtle nuances of wrongdoing and creates complex categories of action. For example, the *Manuale* divides misconduct into several classes, each of which has a different set of rules and penalties. Unintentional misconduct is error; intentional misconduct is either irregularity or sin; sin is either venial or mortal ("obra dañada"). To kill another in self-defense, when conceivably the attacker might have been repulsed with less violence, is intentional misconduct; but unless the victim is a neighbor (in which case, different rules apply), such an act is only an "irregularidad," and not a sin. In addition, Navarrus argues that it is less defensible to kill a thief in the day than it is to kill a thief in the night: "aya gran differencia entre el ladron de dia, y el de noche, por la presumpcion que ay en este (que quiere matar) y cessa en el otro" (p.151). And finally, he asserts that it is a sin to wish for someone's death because of a benefit we may thereby receive, but it is permissible to desire another's death, sickness, or loss of property so that his hardship will convert him to God, or will disable him from doing harm to others, including ourself.

> [For] according to Alexand. and holy Thomas. . .many pious men wish death to the Turk if he will not convert: May God free Christianity from his tyranny. Soto judges that we may even desire the death of Christians who unjustly persecute us, if there is no other remedy for our suffering. (p.153)

Alexander, Aquinas, Soto: Azpilcueta's numerous citations throughout the treatise demonstrate that, to a large extent, in Catholic casuistry an action derives its ethical status from the imprimatur of authority. The pronouncements of Church officials are not simply supportive of reasons for or against an act. They *are* the reason; that is, they are sufficient justification in themselves. Unlike Reformed policy, the layperson does not measure official determinations against his or her own conscience. Rather, one measures one's conscience against official determinations.

---

[67] Martin de (Navarrus) Azpilcueta, *Enchiridion sive Manuale Confessariorum et Poenitentium* (Antwerp, 1566). All citations of the work are to this edition. (Although written in Spanish, the work was published with a Latin title.) Subsequent page references appear in the text. English translations throughout are my own. I am indebted to Beatríz M. Brown for her help in translating the Spanish text.

Despite their different approaches to moral problems, Navarrus and Hall arrive at many of the same judgments about homicide. In his discussion of the Fifth Commandment, Azpilcueta lists a number of authorities both for and against killing to defend property; he concludes by agreeing with St. Thomas that such an act is permissible if the amount of property threatened significantly affects "la sustentacion de su vida, y dela de los suyos" (p.148). He also agrees with Aquinas (again, anchoring his observations to approved authorities) that it is lawful to kill in defense of a neighbor's life or essential property, but he adds St. Augustine's qualification that we may not kill in defense of nonessential possessions. Although theologians differ about what constitutes essential property and about how to determine whether an attack is life-threatening, Navarrus remarks that all Church authorities concur on one fundamental principle: to kill another because of hate or vengeance is invariably to sin. "Y todos estos casos convienen en una cosa. . .que en todos ellos peca el matador, si por odio, o para venganca particular mata" (p.148). Intention is central to moral evaluation. As already seen, Hall reaches the same conclusions; his criteria for judgment, however, are Scripture, natural law, and conscience rather than Azpilcueta's cast of authorities.

Like Hall, Navarrus becomes increasingly specific as he qualifies and defines the terms of his argument. Beginning with a general apology for violence in self-defense, he then distinguishes between legitimate and unwarranted violence. The former, he explains, must be commensurate with the attack:

> It would not be permissible to defend oneself with greater violence than is necessary to resist injury, nor with weapons more lethal than those of the assailant, according to accepted authority: except when the fist of the aggressor is more or less as strong as the sword of the assaulted, according to the same approved authorities.   (p.149)

Hall similarly limits the conditions under which self-defense may include homicide, and he agrees with Azpilcueta's restriction that "if the aggressor is already incapacitated, or has desisted and is fleeing, one cannot without sin kill him, as that would be vengeance, and would exceed the limits of our dispensation, according to Richardo" (p.149). In seeking an equitable compromise between rigorism and laxity, both Hall and Navarrus dwell on the exceptions and contingencies that distinguish casuistical reasoning.

Thus, the two discussions of homicide epitomize central differences as well as shared assumptions of Roman and Reformed casuistry. Both Hall and Azpilcueta maintain that law and ethics are relative to circumstances. Even God's Commandments are conditional. Both casuists agree that rectitude depends on motive and on carefully weighing the arguments for and against an action. But the two men differ as to the standards by which moral arguments should be weighed. Hall gives priority to Scripture and conscience, thereby requiring the individual to take an active role in interpreting law and experience. Navarrus, on the other hand, holds that the collected wisdom of Church authorities is a better guide to right conduct than the unsophisticated reasoning of the layperson. It is significant that Azpilcueta introduces or concludes almost all of his judgments with "segun. . ." or "como lo dice. . . ." Such locutions are symptomatic of a fundamental difference between Catholic and Protestant casuistry, a difference that reaches beyond stylistic and methodological habits. Presenting Church officials as the standard of evaluation, Navarrus demonstrates the authoritarian philosophy that prompted Reformers to develop their own system of case divinity. Throughout his discussion of homicide, Azpilcueta assumes that moral adjudication is the province of the initiated; applying the technical terms and categories of the specialist, he writes for a limited audience. Such treatment of approved authorities as the proprietors and dispensers of truth resulted in charges of moral elitism. Protestants insisted that weighing problems of conscience is not a privilege; it is an obligation—one that extends to all Christians.

Thus, at the heart of the dispute between Roman and Reformed casuists are epistemological questions about proper criteria for judgment. The ramifications of the dispute and their important bearing on Donne's own epistemology are subjects of the next chapter.

CHAPTER TWO

THE POLITICS OF CONSCIENCE:
CONTEXTS AND CONTROVERSIES

Paper Wars and the Diplomacy of Conscience:
Reception of Renaissance Casuistry

The appeal of casuistry to Donne and his contemporaries was considerable.
Douglas Patey observes that "every major divine of the period wrote or
spoke on conscience," and he describes the controversy between Protestant
and Catholic casuists as "one of the greatest paper wars of the age." [1]
Debate among practical theologians about the epistemological ramifications of probabilism, for example, profoundly challenged claims to a normative reading, destabilizing notions of authority and interpretive legitimacy; indeed, one intellectual historian claims,

> There was no aspect of action or belief which was not in one way or an-
> other affected by the crisis over probabilism. . .Copernicus, Galileo,
> Descartes, Pascal, and other founders of modern science and philosophy
> (not excluding Newton) cannot be fully understood except in the light of
> the controversies (philosophical, theological, juridical) among proba-
> bilists and anti-probabilists on the nature of knowledge, opinion, certi-
> tude, ignorance, hypothesis, etc.[2]

Clearly, a full examination of the influence of casuistry is inappropriate to
the scope of this study, but the following pages will suggest some of the
ways in which practical divinity responded to historical debate and cultural
disruption in Donne's period.

The publication history of William Perkins' works provides a measure
of Protestant casuistry's popularity in England. The first to systematize a
Reformed version of practical theology, Perkins (1558-1602) was the main-
stay of English casuists. During Donne's life, as many as eleven editions of
Perkins' collected works, both pirated and authorized, were printed. Further
evidence of Perkins' reception can be deduced from the number of his works

---

[1]   Douglas Lane Patey, *Probability and Literary Form* (Cambridge: UP,
1984), p.56.
[2]   Benjamin Nelson, "Response to Edward Grant," *Daedalus*, 91 (1962),
p.614.

included in anthologies; one collection, *A Garden of Spiritual Flowers*, underwent nine printings from 1609-38.[3] According to a modern editor of Perkins' casuistical treatises, the author was better known to his time than was Hooker. His works were translated into six languages, and "in an age when the literature of piety was exceedingly popular, he was probably read more widely than any other preacher of his day." Indeed, his work "made up nearly a quarter of the 200 items published by the university press at Cambridge between 1590 and 1618." [4] Later writers of cases— Ames, Baxter, and Taylor, for example— acknowledged their enormous debt to Perkins. But his influence was not limited to England; in inventories of colonial American libraries, "one of the commonest entries is the work of William Perkins. . .[His] works are found listed in Virginia inventories almost as frequently as in books of New England." [5]

Perkins' popularity is partly attributable to the accessibility and practicality of his material. Stressing the application of Scripture to quotidian activities, he wrote about marital problems, godly speech, family duties, business transactions, etc. His treatise on how to die well not only discusses preparing one's soul for death, but also offers more immediately practical advice about selecting a physician who might be able to postpone the decorous death. Above all, Perkins translated into simpler terms the technical language and subtleties that characterized Catholic cases. His work, like that of his successors, made a system of addressing moral uncertainty available to all. [6]

Thus one reason for the appeal of Protestant casuistry in England was the wide audience at which it aimed. Unlike Catholic cases of conscience, which were usually written in Latin for the priest's use in confessional, Reformed casuistry was almost always in the vernacular, and was intended for every Christian. Endorsing Luther's declaration of "the priesthood of all believers," Protestants insisted that the answers to dilemmas should be

---

[3]   Louis B. Wright, "William Perkins: Elizabethan Apostle of 'Practical Divinity,'" *Huntington Library Quarterly*, 3, No. 2 (1940), p.193.

[4]   Wright, p.196. Alan Sinfield, *Faultlines: Cultural Materialism and the Politics of Dissident Reading* (Berkeley: Univ. of California Press, 1992), p.150.

[5]   Wright, pp.194-5.

[6]   Most Protestant casuists, whether Anglican or Puritan, tried to imitate Perkins' "simpler," more accessible style. Two exceptions, however, were Jeremy Taylor and Richard Baxter, whose "works were far longer . . . as well as considerably more scholastic in character than those of their Protestant predecessors, and resembled the baroque luxuriance of the *summae* of Catholic casuists in their innumerable citations, their sometimes tortuous reasoning, and the range of cases and contingencies they surveyed." Perez Zagorin, *Ways of Lying: Dissimulation, Persecution, and Conformity in Early Modern Europe* (Cambridge, MA: Harvard UP, 1990), p.248.

sought in Scripture before they are sought in institutions or other individuals. As Marx observes, Luther "shattered the faith in authority by restoring the authority of faith. He transformed the priests into laymen by turning laymen into priests. He liberated man from external religiosity by making religiosoty the innermost essence of man." [7] One effect of Luther's emphasis on individual conscience and judgment was that all Christians were encouraged to be their own casuists. Directly accountable to God for their conduct, the laity was more engaged in its own moral direction than ever before. The audience of Protestant casuistry, then, was all believers, and the subject was all their actions.

But if individuals were to determine their own cases of conscience, what function did the hundreds of published cases serve? And what was the role of moral theologians who preached unmediated consultation of Scripture? As mentioned in chapter one, Protestant casuists perceived themselves as advisors rather than legislators. Cases served as paradigms of deliberation, procedural manuals that readers could consult while adjudicating their own decisions. Because the reader's circumstances often varied from those of published cases, moral theologians pointed out that their resolutions were only provisional. Protestant casuists wrote not as absolute judges, but as "reasonable investigators" into all sides of a problem. Jeremy Taylor explains in *Ductor Dubitantium*: "Where I had not certainty in a case, or that the parts of a question were too violently contended for, without sufficient evidence on either side, I have not been very forward to give my final sentence, but my opinion and reason." [8]

Opinion and reason were the province of Reformed casuists. Their role consisted of quieting or aggravating conscience, of setting forth alternatives and consequences, of providing models for weighing moral responsibilities. The judgments of their Catholic counterparts, however, were less tentative. The Roman Church allowed its casuists jurisdiction over conscience. As early as the third century, the *Didascalia* proclaimed that priests "are in the place of God and have received power to bind and loose. This power applies to all sins." [9] The priest's jurisdiction combined with mandatory confession to strengthen the authoritarianism of Catholic casuistry. Reformers objected to such control over conscience; Perkins, for example, criticizes the Roman

---

7   Karl Marx, *Early Writings*, ed. and trans. T. B. Bottomore (NY: McGraw Hill, 1964), p.53.

8   Jeremy Taylor, *Ductor Dubitantium*, Vol. 3 of *The Whole Works*, 3 vols. (London: Henry Bohn, 1844), p.52.

9   John T. McNeill and Helena M. Gamer, eds. and trans., *Medieval Handbooks of Penance* (New York: Columbia UP, 1938), p.16. Compare Robert Sanderson's remark about the conscience convinced of its probity: "Since his own heart condemneth him not, neither will I." *Works*, ed. W. Jacobson, 6 vols. (Oxford, 1854), vol. 5, p.35.

assumption that casuists

> are made by Christ himselfe *judges of the Cases of Conscience*, having in
> their owne handes a *judicarie power* and authoritie, *truely* and *properly* to
> bind or loose, to remit or to retaine sinnes, to open or shut the kingdome
> of heaven. Whereas the Scripture uttereth a contrarie voyce, that Christ
> onely hath the keyes of David . . . And the ministers of God are not called
> to be *absolute Judges* of the Conscience, but onely Messengers and
> *Embassadours of reconciliation.* [10]

While the resolutions of Catholic cases were authoritative, English casuists
maintained that an individual's final decision must be his or her own.
Protestant "Embassadours of reconciliation" insured the popularity of casuistry by including the laity in the diplomacy of conscience.

Still another appeal of casuistry was its ability to address the political
and religious conflicts that beset seventeenth-century England. In the battles
among Catholics, Anglicans, Puritans, pope and monarch, foreign and do-
mestic governments, each faction warned that obedience to the other could
imperil one's soul— and in some cases, one's family, livelihood, and possessions. "Surplices became scruples and devotional practices doubts, so
that not only in moral questions, but in allied matters of ecclesiastical authority and obedience, the necessity for clear expositions of conscience, its
nature, its doubts and its perplexities was obvious." [11] Casuistry met a concrete need for guidance of the conscience; it enabled individuals to measure
their options and to govern their action when confronted with the conflicting authorities of the period.

The Reformation posed a number of cases of conscience for Donne's
contemporaries. English Catholics during the Armada threat, for example,
had to determine whether treason or disobedience of the Pope was a greater
violation. On one hand, the Papal Bull "Regnans in Excelsis" had excom-
municated Elizabeth, and had declared that those who defended her not only
sinned, but were in jeopardy of excommunication themselves. On the other
hand, allegiance to Rome meant supporting the invasion and overthrow of
their country. The vast majority of English Catholics chose in favor of
Elizabeth. [12] Patrick McGrath suggests that their reasoning is represented in

---

[10]   William Perkins, *The Whole Treatise of Cases of Conscience*, ed. Thomas
Merrill (Nieuwkoop: B. de Graaf, 1966), p.83.

[11]   H. R. McAdoo, *The Structure of Caroline Moral Theology* (London:
Longmans, Green and Co., 1949), p.65.

[12]   Indeed, the vast majority of English Catholics, early in Elizabeth's
reign, chose to attend Anglican services. The Jesuit Robert Parsons notes that,
"for ten consecutive years [1558-1568], practically all Catholics without distinction used to go to [Anglican] churches." *Letters and Memorials of Father
Robert Parsons, S. J.*, ed. Leo Hicks (London: Catholic Record Society, 1942),
p.58.

a casuistical tract which asks, "Whether catholics in England might take up arms to defend the queen and country against the Spaniards?" The author of the tract, a priest named Wright, argues that Philip's motive for attacking was political gain and not defense of the Faith. Since Christians owe political allegiance to the State and spiritual allegiance to the Church, and since Spain's chief objective was not religious, English Catholics were bound in conscience to resist a foreign aggressor. As is often true in practical theology, Wright gives decisive importance to the motive of an act, and he limits his judgment to the specific case. "He did not repudiate the papal deposing power, but he argued that *in this particular case* Catholics were not bound to obey the Pope" (my emphasis).[13] Always rooted in the occasion, casuistry enabled a concrete resolution without forcing English Catholics to betray their faith or renounce the Pope.

Wright's distinction between the political and religious motives of imperialism is tenuous. But it was an important distinction for the majority of Church-papists, or English Catholics who attended Anglican services. These "conformists" were able to avoid the fines and penal laws against recusancy by casuistically "regard[ing] their attendance as an act of political obedience rather than one of religious adherence." [14] The same distinction underlies the resolution of William Allen and Robert Persons' case concerning the Bull, "Regnans in Excelsis." According to their manual of cases written for the guidance of Jesuit priests and recusants in England, "although they are perhaps not bound to do so, Catholics may lawfully obey [Elizabeth] in everything of a purely political nature which does not involve the persecution of Catholics, at least to avoid worse evils befalling them." [15] In a period when antagonistic factions required oaths of obedience, the extent of an individual's duty to civil and ecclesiastical authorities was a common subject of casuistry. Bishop Sanderson's "Case of the Engagement" tries to reconcile a Royalist's conscience with the 1649 oath of loyalty to Parliament, and Donne's *Pseudo-Martyr* examines why English Catholics should take the Oath of Allegiance to their Anglican king. [16] Both cases argue for avoiding confrontation with the ruling powers,

---

13 Patrick McGrath, *Papists and Puritans Under Elizabeth I* (London: Blandford Press, 1967), p.277.

14 Zagorin, *Ways of Lying*, p.133. Zagorin notes that "one of the best known examples [of Church-papists] was Lord Montague, a Catholic peer who was permitted by the priest living in his household to attend the Anglican church, provided he did so from obedience to the queen and without approving the service." p.133.

15 P. J. Holmes, ed. *Elizabethan Casuistry* (London: Catholic Record Society, 1981), p.121.

16 For an excellent discussion of Sanderson's case, see Camille Wells Slights, *The Casuistical Tradition in Shakespeare, Donne, Herbert and Milton*

while taking great care that the conscience remains inviolate. For some in
seventeenth-century England, casuistry was a means of physical as well as
spiritual preservation.

Indeed, the tolerance with which Jesuit priests were advised to treat
Church-papists was born of a recognition that the politics of conscience was
extremely precarious. Moreover, today's orthodoxy could become tomor-
row's heresy. Unlike Calvin's rigid condemnation of conformist Protestants in Catholic countries, priests in England were urged to show
compassion for the "infirmity" of outward conformity. They were to admonish the guilty of their sin, but not to exclude them from Catholic rites
or services. Perez Zagorin suggests that "One explanation of the contrast
[between "Calvin's uncompromising severity" and Catholic latitude] lay in
the difference between Calvin's moral rigorism and the more humane and
flexible principles of Catholic moral theology in the direction of conscience." Another, more politically critical, explanation was that Catholic
officials were looking ahead to an end of the English Reformation, a time
when having a large Catholic constituency—and particularly a propertied
one— in place would be all-important.

> Hence while always insisting upon the obligation of nonconformity, they
> were also willing to concede a minimal accommodation to the recusancy
> laws if required for Catholic survival and especially for the survival of the
> nobles and gentlemen on whom the future of English Catholicism so
> greatly depended. Indeed, the Allen-Persons cases [of conscience] strongly
> emphasized the need for noble and wealthy Catholic families to retain their
> high position in the interests of the faith in order to be able to do it service
> after the queen's death.[17]

Casuistry, then, was a crucial instrument in the politics of conscience for
both Protestants and Catholics in early modern Europe. It was an important
factor in the international jockeying for position among nations as well as
in the self-preservation of individuals and their families.

But practical theology also provided less scrupulous means of self-
preservation. From 1580, when the first Jesuits arrived in England, equivocation and mental reservation became associated with Roman casuistry.
Both practices were intended to deceive authorities, and both could be enlisted when swearing oaths. Under the aegis of mental reservation, one could
swear to the truth of a statement while mentally denying it. The Jesuit
Campion promised his captors that his name was Butler, and then silently
added, "It is the name that I have assumed for the moment in order to avoid
persecution." [18] Similarly, equivocation allowed one to deceive an interlocu-

---

(Princeton: UP, 1981), pp.43-59.
   [17]   Zagorin, *Ways of Lying*, pp.140-141.
   [18]   Quoted in Thomas Wood, *English Casuistical Divinity During the*

tor by withholding information or misrepresenting facts. Sanderson gives several examples of this practice in his *De Juramenti Obligatione*:

> It is as if a Jesuit apprehended, should swear that he were a *Smith*, meaning that his *Name* was *Smith*; or an Apprentice commanded to tell where his Master is, should swear he died a month ago, meaning that he then *died Stockings*. . .This *Jesuitical* doctrine licenseth the Lust of Lying and Perjury unto all impious Men. [19]

While mental reservation and equivocation may have popularized casuistry for those who were able to insure their safety without betraying their allegiance, most casuists condemned the two practices. Donne likens equivocation to "a Tower of Babel. . .because therein no men can understand one another," and Juan Caramuel, a Catholic casuist, protests that "Mental reservations deprive human society of all security; they open the way to all lies and perjury; the wickedness of mendacity is not changed by calling it mental reservation, it is merely enveloping a poison with sugar and disguising vice as virtue." [20]

While most Catholic and Protestant casuists denounced mental reservation when used for "unjust deceit," both allowed its practice under restricted circumstances. Jeremy Taylor, for example, defended such dissimulation when committed in self-defense, and William Allen and Robert Persons argue that an imprisoned recusant may break his vow not to escape, if the vow was made null by silent additions to the contrary. [21] For the most part, Catholic defenses of equivocation and mental reservation were limited, cautious, and conditional, but Protestant polemicists categorically labeled both practices malign and their advocates liars. By 1679, the doctrine of mental reservation had become such a scandal that Pope Innocent XI officially condemned it. Clearly, practical theology was vulnerable to abuse, and not all

---

Seventeenth Century (London: Billing and Sons, 1952), p.49. For an illuminating discussion of dissimulation in early modern religion, see Johann P. Sommerville, "The 'new art of lying': equivocation, mental reservation, and casuistry" in *Conscience and Casuistry in Early Modern Europe*, Ed. Edmund Leites (Cambridge: UP, 1988), pp.159-184.

19   Robert Sanderson, *De Juramenti Obligatione* in *Works*, p. 202.

20   John Donne, *Pseudo-Martyr* (London: W. Stansby, 1610), p. 48; and Wood, p. 108.

21   Holmes, ed. *Elizabethan Casuistry*, p.125.   Martin Azpilcueta's *Enchiridion sive Manuale Confessariorum et Poenitentium* (Antwerp, 1566) is one of many controversial defenses of mental reservation. The work also permits equivocation when protecting oneself or one's honor and when enabling a virtuous act. For other limited defenses of mental reservation, see Juan Azor, *Institutionum Moralium* in *Quibus Questiones ad Conscientiam . . .*, 3 vols. (Lyons, 1600-1612) vol. 1, bk. 2, pp.1064-1066; vol. 3, bk. 13, pp.906-907 and Francisco Suarez, *Tractatus Quintus de Juramento et Adjuratione*, bk. 3, chaps. 9-11, in *Opera Omnia*, 24 vols. (Paris, 1859), vol. 14.

aspects of the doctrine met with approval. Indeed, by 1656, when Pascal wrote his *Provincial Letters*, casuistry had acquired the notoriety that still attends it. [22] But during Donne's life, case divinity was often a valued resource for the conscience torn between conflicting obligations. Protestant casuists, in particular, responded to the crisis of authority and interpretation that accompanied the Reformation. Their emphasis on practicality and accessibility, their role as advisors to conscience and reason, and their attention to the ethical and material problems that arose from contemporary debate insured them a wide audience in seventeenth-century England.

Antecedents and Antinomies

Case divinity was not new to early modern Europe. Benjamin Nelson observes that from 1215, when the Fourth Lateran Council required Catholics to attend confessional at least once a year, collections of cases provided valuable instruction and precedents for priests. However, confession and penance were practiced well before the Lateran decree, and in confessors' manuals dating from the sixth century one can discover a prototype of Catholic casuistry. The early manuals or penitentials provided the basis for confession, and were instrumental in enforcing church discipline and social morality. [23] They replaced the ancient system of public penance, and gave the priest absolute dominion over conscience. Published throughout Europe until the 1500's, penitentials were gradually subsumed by more case-oriented treatises of practical divinity. Renaissance casuists gave greater attention to the contingencies of an action, but their evaluative principles owed much to the penitentials.

Like case divinity, penitentials acknowledged contradictions among the

---

[22] Although Pascal's criticism of Jesuitical casuistry is partisan, there is sufficient evidence from the Catholics themselves that some Jesuits exploited case divinity. Popes Alexander VII and Innocent XI officially condemned a number of abuses, among them: "A son who has killed his father in a drunken brawl may rejoice at the fact without sin if he has come into a large inheritance thereby"; and "calumniators, witnesses and unjust judges may be murdered if there is no other way of avoiding their attacks." Quoted in Kenneth E. Kirk *Conscience and Its Problems* (London: Longmans, Green, 1927), p.118. For an account of Pascal's exaggeration in *The Provincial Letters*, see Malcolm Hay, *The Prejudices of Pascal* (London: Neville Spearman, 1962) and Albert R. Jonsen and Stephen Toulmin, *The Abuse of Casuistry: A History of Moral Reasoning* (Berkeley: Univ. of California Press, 1988), pp. 231-249.

[23] McNeill and Gamer, *Medieval Handbooks of Penance*, p.46. Subsequent references to this edition will appear in the text. For a useful and insightful discussion of earlier sources and influences on casuistry— including *Halakhah* and classical authors— see Jonsen and Toulmin, *The Abuse of Casuistry*, pp. 47-75.

civil and canon laws upon which they were founded; consequently, the manuals left final sentencing to the priest's discretion. Regino's *Of Synodical Cases and Ecclesiastical Discipline* (c. 906) concludes, "Behold, we have set in order the variant opinions of various fathers concerning the remedies of sins or the lightening of penance, leaving to the judgment of the wise priest what he may decide to be beneficial and useful to the penitent soul" (McNeill and Gamer, pp. 320-21). Although the manuals provided equation tables of sin and punishment, they encouraged the confessor to impose discipline according to the culprit rather than to the crime. The same offense committed by two people may require different treatment. Burchard of Worms' *Decretum* (c. 1008) punishes robbery with several years of penance, but adds that those who steal food because of extreme need should only fast for ten days— a somewhat redundant penalty for one who is starving. Like casuists, then, confessors' manuals adjusted judgments to circumstances. A penitential ascribed to the Venerable Bede (c. 731) explains:

> For not all are to be weighed in one and the same balance, although they be associated in one fault, but there shall be discrimination for each . . . He shall make a distinction for the character of the sins or of the men; a continent person or one who is incontinent willfully or by accident; [whether the sin is committed] in public or in secret; with what degree of compunction [the culprit] makes amends by necessity or by intention; the places and times [of offenses].   (McNeill and Gamer, p.223)

The assumption of such recommendations is that the moral status of an act may vary in different situations. As stated in the previous chapter, this assumption persisted as a staple of Reformation and Counter Reformation casuistry.

Other ways in which penitentials anticipated both Catholic and Protestant casuistry were their emphasis on the intention of an act, their care in defining terms and qualifying judgments, and their use of Biblical examples or precedents to justify decisions. In each of these practices, however, there is a difference of degree. Renaissance casuists were more scrupulous in their definitions and more prolix in their qualifications. They were likelier to draw analogies between Scripture and cases, and they were more strict in their treatment of intended offenses. To illustrate briefly the difference of degree: an English manual from the eighth century punishes anyone who intends to commit homicide, even if the murder does not occur: "He who rises up to strike a man, intending to kill him, shall do penance for three weeks; if he is a cleric, three months" (McNeill and Gamer, p.225). As noted in chapter one, Taylor, Donne, and other casuists agree that one is culpable in design as well as conduct. But Renaissance case divinity identified intention and action more closely than did penitentials. The manual just cited exacts four years of penance for killing a layperson and only three weeks for attempting to; later casuists condemned the attempt as strongly as the deed.[24]

In the evolution of practical divinity from penitentials, one can observe the influence of secular law on casuistical thought. [25] It was common for early English kings to frame their legal codes with the assistance of ecclesiastical authorities, the same authorities who developed confessors' manuals. John McNeil and Helena Gamer argue that civil law strongly influenced the Church's system of penance and, by extension, casuists' evaluation of moral dilemmas.

> In the period of the development of the penitentials, the secular laws were being codified in the Celtic and Germanic lands. While the penitentials reaffirmed those elements in the legal inheritance of the people which particularly tended to security and justice, the secular codes on their part recognized the obligatory character of the penitential discipline and lent it substantial support . . . The secular and ecclesiastical disciplines effectively supplemented each other.   (p.37)

The earliest penitentials evaluated only sins against Church doctrine, but by the sixth century, confessors' manuals included crimes against secular government. In addition, they often adopted the penalties that civil laws imposed. One such penalty was composition or monetary satisfaction paid to the family of victims. A penitential entitled *The Book of David* exacts not only a year's penance for seduction or rape, but payment of the 'dos' or brideprice set by Celtic law.[26] From its earliest manifestations, practical divinity was rooted in secular law and penal customs.

Also incorporated into penance and later into casuistical doctrine was the ancient legal practice of grading crimes according to the rank of both culprit and victim. King Ethelbert's *Laws of Kent* (c. 600) requires stricter fines for assaulting a land owner than for assaulting a peasant, and the *Laws of Canute* (c. 1030) stipulates that "in all cases, the greater a man is and the

---

[24]   Martin Azpilcueta asserts in his *Enchiridion*, p.147: "It is forbidden not only to kill or to wound, but also to intend any such harm. For, what St. Thomas says, I embrace: . . . sins of heart, word, and action are all of the same ilk" (my translation).

[25]   In *Ductor Dubitantium* (p.51), Taylor acknowledges his debt to methods of legal interpretation: "I make use of all the brocardics, or rules of interpreters; that is, not only what is established regularly in law, but what is concluded wise and reasonable by the best interpreters. Socinus, Duennas, Azo, Gabrielius, Damasus, and divers other great lawyers, attempted this way in the interpretation of the civil and canon law." For the specific rules of interpretation, see pp. 51-52.

[26]   "Composition marks an advance on the still more primitive customs of retaliation and revenge, reversion to which was frequent in the Middle Ages. The penitentials promoted the substitution of pecuniary satisfactions for revenge, thus coming to the aid of the progressive movement in customary law" (McNeill and Gamer, p.35).

higher his rank, the more stringent shall be the amends which he shall be required to make to God and to men for lawless behavior" (McNeill and Gamer, p.387). Renaissance casuists, too, weighed the position and conspicuousness of those involved in a case. They held that a person of authority who committed an offense in public was at greater fault than a commoner who made the same error in private. The rationale was that public officials set an example, and their offenses were more likely to lead others astray. In a number of their evaluative principles, then, casuists— and before them, penitentials—drew upon secular law.

But it was finally the legalism and authoritarianism of a casuistry based on penance that Protestants repudiated. The Roman doctrine of satisfaction, like composition, was essentially juristic; Reformers remonstrated that it set up a contractual relationship with God, prescribing mortification, psalms, fasting, alms, etc., in exchange for pardon. [27] While Catholic casuists and penitentials judged action by a standard of necessity or lawfulness, Reformers protested that those who "stand upon terms" with God do not serve Him "with honesty and heartiness, and they do not love him greatly; but . . . study how far they may go, and which is their utmost step of lawful, being afraid to do more for God and for their souls than is simply and indispensably necessary." [28] In addition, Protestants objected that the juristic bias of Roman casuistry led to a proliferation of technicalities and distinctions. Priests, like writers of penitentials, produced voluminous collections of precedents and sometimes bizarre cases; one confessor's manual, for example, assesses the gravity of taking communion, vomiting the Eucharist, and allowing dogs to eat the vomit.[29] Another case involves

---

[27]   McAdoo, p.10. McAdoo argues that the difference between the two Churches' doctrines of repentance is fundamental to their two systems of casuistry. Protestants conceded that penance can be an outward sign of inward contrition, but they denied its efficacy in earning pardon. While Catholic repentance involves contrition, confession, and satisfaction, Reformers insisted that true repentance not only repudiates past sins, but resolves to resist future ones (McAdoo, p. 121). Protestant casuists added to the retrospective movement of Roman penitence a forward-looking emphasis on amendment; they asserted that repentance does not end with the last assigned psalm or fast. Reformation must accompany sorrow for sin. Consequently, their cases try to anticipate moral problems and guide the perplexed conscience *before* it errs. Hensley Henson remarks that the retrospective focus of Catholic casuistry is "inseparable from the confessional . . . Not the morally perplexed are [the priest's] concern as much as the morally polluted" (*Studies in English Religion in the Seventeenth Century* [London: John Murray, 1903], p.175).

[28]   Taylor, *Ductor Dubitantium*, p.54. Subsequent citations to this edition appear in the text.

[29]   Jeremy Taylor asserts that excessive legalism only multiplies the problems of conscience. In *Ductor Dubitantium* (p. 54), he claims that when casuists "weigh grains and scruples, and give to God not more than they must needs,

yanking six hairs from a priest's head, and many manuals discuss in extraordinary detail the sexual deviations of clergy.

Rejecting the legalism of Catholic case divinity, Protestant casuists
urged a return to the individual's conscience and to Scripture. They replaced
elaborate rules and unlikely cases with general principles that were meant to
cover a wide range of experience. Taylor advises the reader of *Ductor
Dubitantium* not to "expect this book to be a collective body of particular
cases of conscience; for I find that they are infinite"; rather, he explains, "I
took my pattern from Tribonianus the lawyer, who out of the laws of the
old Romans collected some choice rules, which give answer to very many
cases that happen" (p.53). Taylor remarks that his rules are drawn from right
reason and Scripture. His resolve to simplify matters of conscience echoes a
passage from *Pseudo-Martyr*, in which Donne oppugns the "laborinths" of
Catholic casuistry:

> If . . . by some propositions propogated and deduced from those first prin-
> ciples of Nature, and Scripture, by so many descents and Generations, that
> it is hard to trie whether they doe truly come from that roote, or no, any
> Conscience. . .be straied, and dissolved, and scattered, by this remisnesse
> and vacillation, it ought rather to recollect itselfe, returne to those first in-
> grafted principles, then in this dissolute and loose distraction, to suffer an
> anxious perplexitie, or desperately to arrest itselfe upon that part, which
> their own Rules given to reduce men in such deviations, and settle them in
> such waverings, cannot assure him to be well chosen, nor deliver and extri-
> cate him, in those laborinths. [30]

The first principles to which Donne and Taylor advert are the foundation of
Protestant casuistry. For penance, legalism, and authority, Reformers sub-
stituted reason, individual conscience, and Scripture. The ramifications of
their substitution are examined more fully later in this chapter.

To return briefly to antecedents of practical divinity: not only literature
of the confessional, but also the scholastic article and the classical method
of argument 'in utramque partem' influenced casuistical reasoning. To assess the evidence of a case and to establish the most probably correct course
of action, moral theologians argued both for and against the law in question.
Their method was to reason *through* a problem, to demonstrate how one
should balance obligations, and not simply to state a solution. Contrasting
opposite opinions in order to determine the greater good was also a hallmark
of Academic analysis. The sceptic Carneades introduced argument 'in

---

they shall multiply cases of conscience to a number which no books will contain, and to a difficulty that no learning can answer." To support his criticism of
Catholic casuists for rendering "the rule of conscience infinite and indeterminable," he reports that "Menochius hath seven hundred ninety and eight
questions concerning 'possession'" (p.50).

[30]   Donne, *Pseudo-Martyr*, pp.224-225.

utramque partem' as "a practical method for establishing probabilities." [31]
The same technique characterized the scholastic article or 'quaestio dispu-
tata.' Although the scholastics were more dogmatic than the sceptics, both
investigated moral dilemmas by arguing 'in utramque partem.' A. E.
Malloch observes:

> The immediate purpose of the article is to dispel doubt, and so the title of
> an article is in the form of a question. . .Then after the statement of the
> doubt comes the invariable 'We proceed thus.' This phrase is not merely a
> declaration that the expositor is leading his audience on to the next point.
> It is rather a promise that 'thus' does the mind move to dispel doubt. The
> article itself will be a diagram of the mind in action. The article begins by
> sorting out the various conflicting arguments which, taken together, foster
> uncertainty. [32]

The method Malloch describes is remarkably similar to that of case divinity.
Like the article, casuistry attempts to enact the ratiocinative process. The
aim of both systems is not just to dispel doubt, but to show *how* to dispel
doubt.

Throughout their logical and rhetorical training, Donne and his contemporaries were instructed in casuistical reasoning. Argument 'in utramque
partem' was a common educational practice in the Renaissance. [33] Grammar
schools and universities required students to study 'declamations' or
hypotheses, which posed a moral problem, sketched its circumstances, and
drew two opposite conclusions about the case. In exercises similar to
Milton's *Prolusions*, students defended each of the conflicting opinions.
Declamations were equally common at the Inns of Court. At Thavies and
Lincoln's Inn, where Donne lived from 1591 to 1594 or 1595, students
formulated opposing judgments of legal dilemmas, raising and resolving
scruples. The study of cases of conscience was also integral to instruction in
the law. [34]

---

[31]   Patey, p.15.
[32]   A. E. Malloch, "The Techniques and Function of the Renaissance
Paradox," *Studies in Philology*, LIII, No. 1 (1956), p.197.
[33]   For a full discussion of argument 'in utramque partem' as an educational
procedure, see Joel B. Altman, *The Tudor Play of Mind: Rhetorical Inquiry and
the Development of Elizabethan Drama* (Berkeley: Univ. of California Press,
1978), pp.40-44. See also Thomas O. Sloane's account of "controversia" in
Donne, Milton, and the End of Humanist Rhetoric (Berkeley: Univ. of California
Press, 1985).
[34]   Philippe Ariès, *Centuries of Childhood: A Social History of Family Life*,
trans. Robert Baldick (New York: Random House, 1962), p.197. See also
Geoffrey Bullough, "Donne the Man of Law," in *Just So Much Honor: Essays
Commemorating the 400th Anniversary of the Birth of John Donne*, ed. Peter
Amadeus Fiore (University Park: Pennsylvania State UP, 1972), pp.57-94 *pas-
sim*.

But while casuistical reasoning was embedded in a long tradition of theological, legal, and educational methods, the florescence of case divinity did not begin until after the Reformation. Religious debate about authority and interpretation precipitated the extraordinary attention to casuistry discussed at the beginning of this chapter. Specifically, practical theology responded to the 'rule of faith' controversy, which challenged received notions of authority and raised far-reaching questions about criteria for judgment.

Central to the development of Reformed casuistry, the rule of faith crisis posed an epistemological problem: how can we justify the foundation of our knowledge? Both Protestants and Catholics agreed that Scripture is truth; their argument was how to determine whether one had correctly interpreted that truth. Catholics insisted that Scripture is obscure, and that reason alone is unable to fathom God's Word. Consequently, as Erasmus maintains in *De Libero Arbitrio*, fallen judgment needs the guidance of the Church, whose authority for interpretation derives from Scripture and tradition. [35] Protestants agreed that reason is fallible. Indeed, they argued that very fact to undermine the reliability of Popes and councils, whose interpretation of Scripture was mere opinion derived from corrupted reason. Reformers added that tradition, far from authoritative, consisted of more than a thousand years of controversy about even the most essential articles of faith. Truth, they argued, is perfect and unified; the Catholic tradition was neither. Concerning the Roman Church's claim that its interpretation of God's Word had Biblical authorization, Protestants pointed out that the controversy itself was about exegesis, and that therefore an objective criterion outside the debate was necessary. This criterion, they argued, was conscience, combined with faith. God places in each individual an undeniable conviction which authorizes the judgments of conscience.

The Catholics countered on their antagonists' own grounds: since individuals are corrupted, individual conscience and reason are unable to dispense absolute truth. Erasmus (and later counter-Reformers: Pierre Charron, Gentian Hervet, François Veron) contended that while Church authorities are subject to error, the consensus of all the orthodox faithful, the saints, scholars, martyrs, Church Fathers, bishops, popes, and councils outweighed the

---

[35] Desiderius Erasmus, "The Freedom of the Will," in *Erasmus/Luther: Discourse on Free Will*, trans. and ed. Ernst F. Winter (New York: Frederick Ungar, 1961), pp.12-20. For a more detailed discussion of the rule of faith debate and its epistemological ramifications, see chapter one of Richard Popkin's *History of Scepticism From Erasmus to Spinoza* (Berkeley: Univ. of California Press, 1979). See also chapter two of Henry Van Leeuwen's *The Problem of Certainty in English Thought 1630-1690* (The Hague: Martinus Nijhoff, 1963), and chapter three of Barbara Shapiro's *Probability and Certainty in Seventeenth Century England* (Princeton: UP, 1983).

self-professed authority of Luther or any other individual. [36] Catholics further objected that the standards of conscience and inner persuasion fostered religious anarchy; there were as many different interpretations of Scripture as there were Christians. Only the established Church could rightfully teach the ways to salvation. [37]

The rule of faith controversy established the positions that Protestant and Catholic casuists would later take in adjudicating cases of conscience. At the outset of the controversy, however, Protestant casuistry did not exist, and the debate evinced the Reformer's need to develop a system that governed actions according to the criteria they supported. In addition to charges of ethical relativism, Protestants faced the problem of guiding conscience without the sacrament of penance, the confessional, or the Catholic system of casuistry.[38] The latter, with its dependence on Church authorities as the

---

[36] "The Freedom of the Will," pp.10-20. Erasmus' concession about the fallibility of Church Fathers is expressed in casuistical terms: "I would prefer to say that at the time of the decision they acted on the evidence they had, and later practical exigencies persuaded us to modify their judgments" p.11. Concerning Catholic criticism of Protestant individualism, Alan Sinfield remarks, "Logically, Luther's demand that he be 'convicted by the testimony of scripture or plain reason' since 'it is neither safe nor honest to act against one's conscience' enabled anyone to justify any belief. The ultimate warrant for the truth of the bible could only be that the individual believer was convinced in his or her soul. However, few reformers were prepared to leave it there. . . The Althusserian assumption that religion helps to produce law-abiding subjects is substantially right in respect of early modern protestantism." *Faultlines*, p.165.

[37] Inner persuasion was indeed a knotty standard. Popkin describes the circular reasoning that supports it: "the criterion of religious knowledge is inner persuasion, the guarantee of the authenticity of inner persuasion is that it is caused by God, and this we are assured of by our inner persuasion" (p.10). The 1554 execution of Miguel Servetus dramatized Catholic claims about the subjectivity of the standard (see Popkin, pp.8-14). Inner persuasion led Servetus to preach against the doctrine of the Trinity. The same criterion convinced Calvin that anti-Trinitarianism is heresy, so he had Servetus burned at the stake. Sebastien Castellio, a Swiss Protestant, attacked Calvin in *De Haereticis*, arguing that since fallen reason dims the truth, one is unjustified in killing another for 'misinterpretation.' Ages of debate, he asserted, prove that Scripture is obscure. In a diatribe against Castellio's "scepticism," Calvin and Beza responded that religious debate is not evidence of our inability to know truth; rather, it simply shows that some interpretations are wrong. While Donne and Reformed casuists supported inner persuasion, they objected to the dogmatism of Calvin's position.

[38] Slights, p.4. In *Ductor Dubitantium* (p.47), Taylor concedes that Reformed casuists borrowed principles of law and interpretation from Catholic cases of conscience, but he adds: "we cannot be well supplied out of the Roman storehouses; for though there the staple is, and very many excellent things exposed to view; yet we have found the merchants to be deceivers, and the wares too often falsified." The authority upon which Catholic casuists base their judg-

final arbiters of truth, was inimical to Reformed standards of evaluating
judgment. Luther's burning Angelo de Clavasio's *Summa concerning the
Cases of Conscience* dramatized the Reformed attitude towards existing practical theology. Thomas Merrill observes:

> What was needed, and needed desperately, was a system of morality to
> complement Reformation dogma. The formulation of such a system would
> have enormous influence in shaping the character of English social and po-
> litical attitudes, for it would be in fact nothing less than the practical in-
> strumentation of the revolutionary changes that had already been brought
> about in theory. [39]

The following section explores how Protestants responded to the need that
Merrill describes. Defining itself against the Catholic system of applied
morality, Reformed casuistry implemented the ideology set forth in the rule
of faith controversy.

Protestant versus Catholic Casuistry:
Authority and Interpretation

Donne consistently agreed with the position of Protestant casuists in the
rule of faith controversy. Although he never devoted an entire work to the
controversy, it is possible to cull from his sermons, prose tracts, poetry,
and letters his response to most of the issues debated between Reformed and
Roman casuists. Establishing reliable criteria for judgment was at the heart
of the dispute, and on this pivotal issue especially, Donne challenged the
Catholic view throughout his works. Canon law, tradition, and Church authorities were the standards by which Roman casuists interpreted Scripture
and measured action. But Donne contended that the final arbiters of cases are
the individual's conscience and reason, guided by faith and Revelation.

---

ments is the source of their "falsified wares": "the casuists of the Roman church
take these things for resolution and answer to questions of conscience, which are
spoken by an authority that is not sufficient; and they. . .have not any sufficient
means to ascertain themselves what is binding in very many cases argued in
their canons, and decretal epistles, and bulls of Popes. . .Therefore either they
must change their principle, and rely only upon Scriptures and right reason and
universal testimonies, or give no answer to the conscience in very many cases
of the greatest concernment; for by all other measures their questions are
indeterminable. But the authority of man they make to be their foundation: and
yet. . .the doctors, whose affirmative is the decision of the case, are so infinitely
divided" (p.48).

[39] Thomas Merrill, ed., *A Discourse of Conscience* and *The Whole Treatise
of Cases of Conscience*, by William Perkins (Nieuwkoop: B. de Graaf, 1966), p.
xii. See also Thomas N. Tentler, *Sin and Confession on the Eve of the
Reformation* (Princeton: UP, 1977).

In keeping with the authoritarian tradition of penitentials, Catholic casuists asserted that canon law and Church officials can bind conscience. Donne and Reformers objected that only God has authority over conscience, and that all other lawmakers are subject to error and change. Perkins condemns as blasphemous the Pope's claim to bind conscience. His *Discourse* maintains that the authority with which God invests rulers is not equal to His own.[40] Perkins' explanation is lengthy, but it is worth quoting in full, since it summarizes casuistical attitudes towards flawed reason and law.

> Men in making laws are subject to ignorance and errour: and therefore when they have made a law (as neere as possibly they can) agreeable to the equitie of Gods law, yet can they not assure themselves and others, that they have failed in no point of circumstance. Therefore it is against reason that humane lawes being subject to defects, faults, errours, and manifold imperfections, should truly bind conscience, as Gods lawes do, which are the rule of righteousnesse. All governours in the world (by reason that to their old lawes, they are constrained to put restrictions, amplifications, and modifications of all kinds, with new readings and interpretations) upon their daily experiences see and acknowledge this to bee true which I say, saving the bishop of Rome. . . which persuades himselfe to have when he is in his consistorie, such an infallible assistance of the spirit, that he cannot possibly erre in judgment.   (*Discourse*, p.32)

The instability of law, the fallibility of judgment, and the relativity of "meaning" are central givens of casuistical epistemology. These givens, in turn, call into question fixed standards of authority. When Donne criticizes Jesuits who "thinke the Pope so much God, (for Jesuites must exceede in everything) that in him, as in God, there can bee no *Contingency*," he is criticizing the anti-casuistical view that legitimacy and authority are unqualified or universal.[41]

Similarly, in a sermon that discusses Augustine's notion of the primacy of Scriptural authority, Donne remarks,

> This the *Romane Church* pretends to embrace; but *Apishly*; like an *Ape*, it kills with embracing, for it evacuates the right *Authoritie*; The *Authoritie* that they obtrude, is the *Decretals* of their owne *Bishops*, The *authoritie*, which *Saint Augustine* literally and expressly declares himselfe to meane, is the *authoritie* of the *Scriptures*.[42]

---

40 "One of the principall notes of Antichrist agrees fitly to the Pope of Rome. *Paul* 2. *Thess.* 2.4 makes it a special propertie of Antichrist to exalt himselfe against or above all that is called God, or worshipped. Now what doth the Pope else, when he takes upon him an authoritie to make such lawes as shall binde the conscience, as properly and truly as God's lawes?" *Discourse*, p.32. Subsequent citations to the *Discourse* appear in the text.

41 Donne, *Pseudo-Martyr*, p.192.

42 *Sermons*, ed. George R. Potter and Evelyn Simpson. 10 vols. (Berkeley: Univ. of California Press, 1953-62), VI, 252.

Like the authority of officials, positive law and canon law are less binding
than the law of God, according to Protestant casuists. *Pseudo-Martyr* criticizes papists for giving equal weight to canon law and Scripture when determining cases of conscience. Donne argues that alterations of canon law
throughout history prove its fallibility.

> These Canons therefore, of so sickely and weake a constitution, that any-
> thing dejects them, cannot prevaile so much upon our consciences, as to
> imprint and worke such a confidence in them, and irremoveablenesse from
> them, as to maintaine them with the same manner of testimonie, as we
> would doe the words of God himselfe. (p.276)

Taylor agreed that canon law is not always a reliable standard of judgment.
He writes in *Ductor Dubitantium* (p.50), "The very title of the canon law
was 'Concordantia Discordantiarum,' a tying of contradictions together in
one string"; such a collection of inconsistencies, he argues, hardly merits
the absolute authority that Catholics accord it. Reformed casuists insisted
that, since fallen reason and law are fallible, neither has the jurisdiction of
Scripture and conscience.

Of course, conscience too is fallen, and Protestants admitted that their
own standard was subject to error. Nevertheless, they contended that the faculty through which God speaks to the faithful partakes of the divine.
Perkins explains in his *Discourse* (p.6), "Conscience is of a divine nature, a
thing placed of God in the middest betweene him and man, as an arbitratour
to give sentence." "Betweene him and man," conscience cannot be mediated
by another, contrary to Catholic teaching. Reformers agreed with Aquinas
that conscience consists of two parts: synteresis and conscientia; the former
is a repository of moral principles, and the latter is an agent of the practical
intellect, whereby general principles are applied to specific cases. Although
reason and conscientia are fallible, they receive direction from the Holy
Spirit and from Scripture. With such guides, conscience is the Christian's
highest authority on earth. To deny Church officials jurisdiction over conscience is not to leave the individual rudderless or wholly self-directed, since
one's final criterion for judgment is God's Word.

Reformed casuists responded to Catholic reliance on tradition with the
same arguments they leveled against canon law. While papists asserted that
the collective pronouncements of theologians should determine cases of
conscience, Protestants reiterated that Scripture is the only certain reference
for those in doubt. Like canon law, tradition is constituted of fallible and
contradictory judgments. Joseph Hall demands: "As for Oral Traditions,
what certainty can there be in them? What foundation of truth can be laid
upon the breath of man?" [43] And with similar force, Perkins protests that

---

[43]   Joseph Hall, *The Old Religion*. Vol. 9 of *The Works of Joseph Hall*. 12
vols. Ed. John Downame (Oxford: D. C. Talboys, 1937), p.376. Sanderson's

conscience cannot find final assurance in tradition:

> As for the best unwritten traditions, let all the Papists in the world answere
> if they can, how I may in conscience be perswaded that they are the word of
> God. If they say that the auncient fathers of the Primitive Church avouch in
> their writings that they are Apostolicall traditions; I answere againe, how
> shall I know and be certen in conscience that the fathers subject to errour,
> in saying so, have not erred. (*Discourse*, p.42)

The word of the Church Fathers is not the word of God; even the "ancient
fathers" are fallible, their province opinion and not truth.

Reformers further argued that common opinion was an insufficient criterion for judging moral dilemmas. Attitudes change with time and place,
they pointed out, and history has proven that concurrence on any issue is
rare and ephemeral. As Donne remarks in *Pseudo-Martyr*, common consent
is a slippery standard:

> Oftentimes, amongst them, both sides say, *This is the common opinion*,
> and who can judge it? Yea many circumstances change *the common opin-*
> *ion*: *For* (saies *Azorius* [a prominent Catholic casuist]) *it fals out often,*
> *that that which was not the common opinion a few yeares since, now is*;
> And that *that which is the common opinion of Divines in one Countrie, is*
> *not so in another.*   (p.227)

Donne adds that in matters as serious as sin and rectitude, we should measure our resolutions of cases with a more reliable criterion. Even the common consent of Church Fathers can be misleading. In "A Litanie," Donne
asks God to guide him away from the errors of "The Doctors" and to help
him distinguish between mere opinion and God's Truth. He prays "That
what they have misdone/ Or mis-said, wee to that may not adhere;/ Their
zeale may be our sinne. Lord let us runne/ Meane waies, and call them stars,
but not the Sunne" (ll.114-117). The most learned exegetes, the most pious
theologians are dim guides. Christians must apply to Revelation for en-
lightenment, or they risk sin and error.[44]

But the fallibility of Church officials, tradition, and canon law was not

---

Lectures on Conscience and Human Law, ed. C. Wordsworth (Oxford: James
Williamson, 1877), p.102, states that Scripture is Truth and has no need for "the
vain supplement of *human traditions*." And Donne concurs in *Sermons* II, 307:
"Traditions of men are not our nets; onely the Gospel is."

[44]   Confusion is another risk of relying on exegetes rather than on Scripture
itself. Donne's *Essays in Divinity*, ed. Evelyn Simpson (Oxford: Clarendon
Press, 1952), p.39, urges a return "ad fontes"; using the same metaphor of
illumination and dimness that appears in "A Litanie," Donne writes:
"oftentimes, where fewest Expositors contribute their helpes, the Spirit of God
alone enlightens us best; for many lights cast many shadows, and since controverted Divinity became an occupation, the Distortions and violencing of
Scriptures, by Christians themselves, have wounded the Scriptures more then the
Old Philosophy or *Turcism*."

the primary objection of Reformed casuists to Catholic standards for judgment. Indeed, Protestants considered all three factors in their adjudication of cases, just as Catholic casuists referred to Scripture and right reason in theirs. The chief contention between the two systems was how to apply their standards; at issue were emphasis and accountability. In Reformed casuistry, individuals were accountable for their own moral deliberation. They, and not Church appointed authorities, were the final judge of their case. According to Protestants, Roman authoritarianism excluded the laity from the process of reasoning; those in doubt consigned judgment to their priest, and thus abjured their Christian duty to participate in their own salvation. The Catholic policy left the faithful more dependent on human intercession than on God's Word.

Protestant casuists required individuals to take more responsibility for their spiritual progress and to participate personally in Christ's teaching. Taylor's *Dissuasive From Popery* reminds its audience, "We are commanded to 'ask in faith,' which is seated in the understanding, and requires the concurrence of the will." [45] Faith, understanding, and will: none of these are exercised when theologians make our decisions for us. Those who govern conduct solely by the dictates of tradition, Church officials, or canon law do not necessarily comprehend the moral principles on which they act. And according to Perkins, what is not understood cannot receive the support of conscience, which "bindeth by vertue of knowne conclusions in the mind. Therefore things that are altogither unknowne and unconceived of the understanding, doe not bind in conscience" (*Discourse*, p.17). Most importantly, understanding is essential to virtuous action. An ignorant conscience cannot do good, since rectitude depends in part on the support of conscience. Donne's *Essays in Divinity* summarizes the necessity of understanding and conscience to virtue:

> *Conscience* hath but these two *Elements*, *Knowledge*, and *Practise*; for *Conscientia presumit Scientiam*: Hee that does any thing with a good *Conscience*, knowes that hee should doe it, and why hee does it: Hee that does *good* ignorantly, stupidly, inconsiderately, implicitely, . . . does that good *ill*. *Conscience* is, *Syllogismus practicus*; upon certaine premises, well debated, I conclude, that I should doe it, and then I doe it. [46]

At best, to act without knowledge and deliberation is to do "good ill." Those who follow authority without comprehension neglect their moral duty.

One's responsibility for one's own faith, understanding, and moral

---

[45]   Jeremy Taylor, *Dissuasive From Popery*, vol. 2 in *Works*, p.799

[46]   Donne, *Essays*, p.88.   Sister M. Geraldine, "John Donne and the Mindes Indeavours," *SEL*, V, No. 1 (1965), pp.115-131, discusses Donne's belief in the interdependence of knowledge and virtue.

choices is central to Donne's "Satyre III." The poem explores criteria by which the perplexed conscience adjudicates conflicting authorities, and it advances a process of inquiry similar to that of Protestant casuistry.

Dismayed by man's disordered priorities— his worldly values and spiritual neglect— Donne exhorts in "Satyre III," "Seeke true religion." But the locus of Christ's bride is a matter of contention, and those who claim to embrace her do so with inadequate justification. The Catholic Mirreus believes that tradition is authority, and he shares with Calvinist Crants the misconception that one can know truth by outward forms. Both judge Christ's bride by her clothes. But whether her "ragges" are splendid or "plaine," they are superficial standards. The Anglican Graius blindly endorses his state's religion; like a minor whose guardian chooses for him, he submits to lawmakers and preachers who "bid him thinke" their thoughts. "Carelesse Phrygius" and Graccus are equally blind in refusing to choose any one religion. The former rejects all claims to truth, "because all cannot be good, as one/ Knowing some women whores, dares marry none." The latter accepts all without discernment. But choice is a moral imperative, and there is an urgency to Donne's admonitions: "Be busie to seeke her"; "strive so"; "therefore now doe" before reason becomes dim with "age, deaths twilight."

> Seeke true religion. O where? Mirreus
> Thinking her unhous'd here, and fled from us,
> Seekes her at Rome, there, because hee doth know
> That shee was there a thousand yeares agoe,
> He loves her ragges so, as wee here obey
> The statecloth where the Prince sate yesterday.
> Crants to such brave Loves will not be inthrall'd,
> But loves her onely, who'at Geneva'is call'd
> Religion, plaine, simple, sullen, yong,
> Contemptuous, yet unhansome. As among
> Lecherous humours, there is one that judges
> No wenches wholsome, but course country drudges.
> Graius stayes still at home here, and because
> Some preachers, vile ambitious bauds, and lawes
> Still new like fashions, bid him thinke that shee
> Which dwels with us, is onely perfect, hee
> Imbraceth her, whom his Godfathers will
> Tender to him, being tender, as Wards still
> Take such wives as their Guardians offer, or
> Pay valewes. Carelesse Phrygius doth abhorre
> All, because all cannot be good, as one
> Knowing some women whores, dares marry none.
> Graccus loves all as one, and thinkes that so
> As women do in divers countries goe
> In divers habits, yet are still one kinde;
> So doth, so is Religion; . . .   (ll.43-67)

Donne's typic characters choose their religion for insufficient reasons, but when all the reasons are combined, they form a more valid basis for judgment. As M. Thomas Hester observes, facets of each character's choice are included in the inquiry that "Satyre III" urges. Donne's recommendation to "aske thy father" where to find truth, and "Let him aske his," acknowledges the value of tradition that Mirreus espouses. Truth and falsehood are almost indistinguishable, but "truth a little elder is." By returning to the source— to the Primitive Church and Scripture— one can find the truth that Graius seeks only in current laws. And yet Graius' desire for the "onely perfect" religion is laudable, since we must "but one allow;/ And the right." Hester adds,

> Crants seems to realize that "mysteries. . .are plaine to all eyes" (88) in his preference for a religion that is "plaine," but he misapplies his criterion absurdly. . .Phrygius is full of doubt, but he does not "doubt wisely" (77), his decision to "stand inquiring right" (78) resulting only in a denial of its existence. Likewise, Graccus, who seems to understand the value of religious tolerance ("to adore, or scorn. . .may all be bad"), fails to understand that "unmov'd thou/ Of force must one, and forc'd but one allow" (69-70).[47]

Donne's object is not to discredit the religious alternatives that he represents; rather, it is to criticize inadequate standards for moral choice. As the remaining lines of "Satyre III" assert, the most important factors in discovering truth are vigilant faith and the efforts of reason.

The inquiry that Donne recommends is an arduous process, but one in which each believer must participate in order to search for the bride of Christ. Truth stands "on a huge hill,/ Cragged, and steep"; access is difficult and circuitous. In circling the hill towards truth, one approaches from all sides, just as Donne has viewed different sides of religious alternatives. The soul must "worke" at its circumambulation; the mind must endeavor to reach "hard knowledge." Protestant casuists share Donne's emphasis on labor and understanding. With a similar image of toiling, Perkins describes each Christian's duty to search for truth:

> [We must] indeavour that we may daily increase in knowledge of the word of God. . . that we might understand the wonders of his law: and withall wee must daily search the scriptures for understanding, as men used to search the mines of the earth for golde ore, *Prov.* 2.4. Lastly, we must labour for spirituall wisdome, that we might have the right use of God's word in every particular action.   (*Discourse*, p.75)

---

[47]   M. Thomas Hester, "'All Our Soules Devotion': Satire As Religion In Donne's 'Satyre III,'" *SEL*, XVII, No. 1 (1978), pp.46-7. See also Hester's chapter on "Satyre III" in *Kinde Pitty and Brave Scorn: John Donne's Satyres* (Durham: Duke UP, 1982). And see Richard Strier, "Radical Donne: 'Satyre III'" *ELH* 60 (1993), pp.283-322.

Endeavor, search, labor: Perkins' diction echoes "Satyre III." For both Donne and Reformed casuists, Christianity is an active faith, requiring the engagement of reason. Individuals are responsible for their moral choices.

Christians are also responsible for protecting the resolutions of conscience and reason: "Keepe the'truth which thou hast found." Donne urges his readers not to consign their souls to human authorities. God alone can insure salvation; the judgments of "a Philip, or a Gregory,/ A Harry, or a Martin" will not avail us at the Final Judgment. Sacrificing to earthly powers a truth held in conscience is not obedience, but "idolatrie." William Ames concurs: conscience "is immediately subject to God, and his will, and therefore it cannot submit it selfe unto any creature without Idolatry." [48] Neither Donne nor Ames disavows consulting human authority or obeying legitimate rulers; rather, they assert the superior value of God's commandments, and they contend that only He has jurisdiction over the soul. Making the same argument in his *Resolutions and Decisions of Divers Cases of Conscience*, Hall concludes, "You see then how requisite it is that you walk in a middle way, betwixt that excessive power which flattering casuists have been wont to give popes, emperors, kings, and princes in their several jurisdictions, and a lawless neglect of lawful authority." [49] Just as God's truth should be the source of our judgments, so His power is our source of authority. To stray from the source, Donne warns, is to become lost: "So perish Soules, which more chuse mens unjust/ Power from God claym'd, then God himselfe to trust."

It is appropriate that "Satyre III" never specifies which religion is the true one, since Donne's point is that the readers must decide for themselves. Throughout his career, Donne endorsed the belief of Protestant casuists that one should act in matters of conscience with "a debated and deliberate determination," and not with blind adherence to prevailing attitudes. In a sermon preached at St. Paul's, Donne warns against authoritarianism; he rebukes those who depend on what "are ordinarily received and accepted for truths: so that the end of [their] knowledge is not truth, but opinion, and the way, not inquisition, but ease." [50] Donne's criticism of authoritarianism extended to

---

[48]   William Ames, *Conscience with the Power and Cases Thereof* in *Works* (Ann Arbor: Univ. Microfilms, 1962), Bk. I, p.6.

[49]   Joseph Hall, *Resolutions and Decisions of Divers Cases of Conscience*, Vol. 12 of *Works*, p.343.

[50]   Donne, *Sermons*, IV, 222, and VI, 76. The "inquisition" that Donne recommends was critical to Reformed concepts of the self. Sinfield's *Faultlines* (pp.159-163) gives a convincing account of how Protestant self-examination, like confession in Foucault's reading, enables subjectivity—constituting the soul and establishing interiority. See also Michael C. Schoenfeldt's analysis of confession and self-construction in his illuminating *Prayer and Power: George Herbert and Renaissance Courtship* (Chicago:UP, 1991), pp.47-53.

the controversial doctrine of probabilism that Roman casuists advanced. According to Reformers, the doctrine was yet another instance of failing to perform one's moral duty.

Probabilism states that if one has the support of authority, one may disregard a law, even though conceivably there are stronger arguments and more authorities in favor of the law. In its simplest form, the doctrine grants: "We may use a probable opinion even though the contrary be more probable"; however,

> the more probable arguments which may be discounted are not the *known* but the *unknown* arguments for the law. Once you have a reasonable and weighty doubt, you need not become involved in the interminable discussions which would be necessary to weigh up the balance of probability on either side.[51]

Such, at least, was the original conception of the doctrine. But the practicality of probabilism quickly yielded to opportunism, and the theory became a notorious vehicle for moral sophistry.

Bartholomew Medina of Salamanca, a Catholic casuist, formulated the guidelines for probabilism in 1577. His intention was to offer a solution for those who must decide a case of conscience without the time or resources to weigh all arguments for and against the decision. The doctrine was to aid the overly scrupulous who were unable to act because of fear that an unanticipated argument may prove the action sinful. To circumvent such paralysis, Medina asserts, "if an opinion is solidly probable, the bare possibility that it might in the end prove less probable than its opposite need not deter us from acting upon it." [52] The definition of a probable opinion was any view sanctioned by the Catholic Church— its popes, councils, traditions, theologians, casuists. The greater the number of authorities that endorsed the view, the more probable the view was.[53] Francisco Suarez, also a Spanish casuist, stipulates that a probable opinion "must not run counter to any truth universally accepted by the Church; it must be in agreement with common sense. . .and supported by good authority; and if it has not the support of the majority of authorities, it must at all events not be an opinion generally abandoned." [54] From its inception, probabilism was an authoritarian doctrine.

Despite limitations imposed on probabilism, the theory was vulnerable

---

51   Kenneth Kirk, *Conscience and Its Problems: An Introduction to Casuistry* (London: Longmans, Green and Co., 1927), p.391 and p.393.

52   Kirk, p.392.

53   In his *Responsa Moralia* (1609), the Catholic casuist Comitolus states that when reputable authorities "are found on both sides, the opinion which the greater number of them support must be chosen." Quoted in Kirk, p.392.

54   Quoted in Kenneth Kirk, *Some Principles of Moral Theology and Their Application*, (London: Longmans, Green and Co., 1926), p.196.

to exploitation. Gabriel Vazquez, a Jesuit casuist whom Donne cites in
Biathanatos, attempted to forestall misapplication of the doctrine when he
declared that one may not invoke it at the expense of charity. And Medina
warns: "For an opinion to be probable, it is not enough that specious reasons can be adduced on its side, nor that it should have champions and de-
fenders— any error might be adjudged probable at that rate. It must be asserted by wise men and confirmed by the best arguments." [55] Nevertheless,
probabilism became a means of escaping the law and rationalizing misconduct. The most publicized abuses were those of Jesuits who taught that one
may act upon any probable opinion, despite one's knowledge of more probable arguments to the contrary. Moreover, revising Medina's stipulation
that several reputable authorities must support one's decision, some Jesuits
countenanced as probable the judgment of a single Church official, even if
the respected majority disagreed. In allowing one to choose the least probable of a number of conflicting opinions, the doctrine enabled actions that received no support from conscience. Juan Azor's *Institutionales morales*
(1600) states that one may act upon what an established authority has adduced to be lawful, even when the one's own sense of rectitude is otherwise.
In many cases, then, "we may follow a probable opinion against our best
judgment . . . No longer bound to follow his own judgment, one no longer
acts in his own right; in electing to follow a probable opinion, he assumes
a role or mask to which his self is largely irrelevant." [56]

The irrelevance of conscience to probable judgments was precisely what
Reformers objected to. By the time Protestants developed their own system
of casuistry, "Jesuitical" probabilism had eclipsed Medina's original formulation.[57] Donne remarks in a letter to Sir Thomas Lucy (c. 1607) that

---

[55] Quoted in Kirk, *Conscience and Its Problems*, p.392. Medina's restrictions were often unheeded. Taylor's *Dissuasive* (pp.797-8) lists a number of
Catholic casuists who used probabilism to legitimate sin. Among them,
"Martinus de Magistris says, To believe simple fornication to be no deadly sin,
is not heretical, because the testimonies of Scripture are not express. . .Thus the
most desperate things that ever were said by any. . .are doctrines publicly allowed; they can also become rules of practice, and securities to the conscience of
their disciples."
Abuse of probabilism became so widespread that Popes Alexander VII,
Innocent XI, and Alexander VIII imposed increasingly severe restrictions on the
doctrine.
[56] A. E. Malloch, "John Donne and the Casuists," *SEL*, II, No.1 (1962),
p.67. See also Ian Hacking, *The Emergence of Probability* (Cambridge: UP,
1975), chaps. 7-8. Among the instances of casuistical laxity condemned by
Pope Innocent XI in 1679 was the practice of allowing someone to judge a case
according to the least probable opinion.
[57] It is important to note that the Jesuits neither formulated nor initially
allowed recourse to the doctrine of probabilism. Nevertheless, as priests in the
Society of Jesus joined other advocates of the doctrine, probabilism and its

Catholic "casuists are so indulgent, as that they allow a conscience to adhere
to any probable opinion against a more probable, and do never binde him to
seek out which is the more probable, but give him leave to dissemble it and
to depart from it, if by mischance he come to know it." [58] Not only did
probabilism enable one corrupt authority to legitimate error, but it relieved
the laity from the responsibility of adjudication. It enforced opinions in
which the individual neither participated nor even necessarily believed. As
already seen, Reformers claimed that the self is disqualified from moral deliberation when external authority is the source of all decisions. Taylor
summarizes the Protestant position on probabilism: "By this principle, you
may embrace any opinion of their doctors safely . . .and you need not trou-
ble yourself with any further inquiry. . .and Christ is not your rule— but
the examples of them that live with you, or are in your eye and observation,
that is your rule." [59] Probabilism constituted yet another skirmish in the
battle between Reformed and Catholic casuists about proper criteria for
judgment.

The Protestant alternative to probabilism was probabiliorism. As its
name suggests, the Reformed doctrine required that one choose the most
probable solution to a case of conscience— that is, the solution that best
corresponds to one's understanding of Scripture. *Ductor Dubitantium*
(p.111) declares, "The greater probability destroys the less." The now familiar standards of reason, conscience, and Revelation determined whether one
act was 'probabilior' than another. Emphasizing inquiry and deliberation,
Ames writes: "everyone ought to follow that opinion which (after due diligence to search the truth) he judges to be more probable out of the nature of
the thing and the law of God compared together." [60] Protestant casuists fur-

---

abuses became associated primarily with the Jesuits.

[58]   Donne, *Letters to Severall Persons of Honour*, ed. Charles Edmund Merrill
(New York: Sturgis and Walton, 1910), p.12. For Donne's extensive knowledge
of probabilist technicalities, see *Pseudo-Martyr*, pp.229-230. Unlike most
Protestant casuists, Donne was aware of Medina's benign intentions; in *Pseudo-
Martyr* (p.230), he acknowledges that the doctrine "hath this commoditie, that it
delivers godly men from the care and solicitude, of searching out, which is the
more probable opinion." But he was also aware of the widespread abuse of
probabilism, and he joined Reformed casuists in condemning its practice.

[59]   Taylor, *Dissuasive*, p.798.

[60]   Ames, *Conscience With the Power*, Bk. 1, p.86. Again, Protestants did
not discourage consulting wise authorities about perplexed or doubtful actions.
But they did insist that the final weighing and choosing was the individual's
own. As does Donne in "Satyre III," Taylor finds greater moral value in the
search for truth than in its discovery. Indeed, Taylor acknowledges that truth can
elude fallen man; therefore, "it is not necessary that truth should be found, but it
is highly necessary it should be searched for. It may be, it cannot be hit, but it
must be aimed at." Even if one is in error, "diligence to inquire, and honesty in
consenting" determine the virtue of one's judgment (*Ductor Dubitantium*,

ther insisted that one's decision have the full persuasion of conscience. A convinced conscience needn't believe that it has arrived at immutable truth, but it must be assured that of the options discernible to fallen reason, it has chosen the one that best conforms to Biblical principles. A convinced conscience intends virtue, even if it is in error. To the Catholic objection that inner persuasion is a subjective standard, Protestants reiterated that Scripture and conscience are God's instruments; together, they create a "divine spark" which it is sin to disregard.

Despite their different priorities in assessing moral choices, Reformed and Catholic casuists agreed that probability is a sufficient basis for judgment. They recognized that absolute truth may not be within the province of fallen reason, but they maintained that grace and Revelation enabled the faithful to achieve practical assurance. Casuistry offered a method of weighing authorities, of evaluating laws and circumstances so as to guide the uncertain in righteousness, if not to guarantee deliverance from all error. Taylor remarks in *Ductor Dubitantium* (pp.36-7), "This heap of probable inducements is not of power as a mathematical and physical demonstration, which is in discourse as the sun is in heaven, but it makes a milky and a white path, visible enough to walk securely." The epistemological concessions of casuists, their constructive response to doubt, their concern with enabling action, and their belief in the importance of reason to faith and virtue attracted Donne. The following section examines Donne's response to uncertainty, and suggests that his epistemology is remarkably consonant with that of practical divinity.

Donne on Reason and Faith

Donne's works evince a continuing interest in the powers and limits of reason. More particularly, they address the role of reason in moral decisions. As poet and preacher, Donne explored how ethical deliberation is affected by imperfect knowledge, conflicting standards of truth, and contradictory laws— both civil and canon. Consider a selection of observations taken from the course of his career. The final stanza of "The Progresse of the Soule" (c.1601) concludes: "Ther's nothing simply good, nor ill alone,/ Of every quality comparison,/ The onely measure is, and judge, opinion" (ll.518-20). Seven years later, Donne argued in *Biathanatos* that moral valuation is contingent upon circumstances; the treatise explores the extent to which univocal laws can do justice to multivalent experience. In a letter written c.1610, Donne laments, "But of the diseases of the minde, there is

p.148).

no *Criterium*, no Canon, no rule; for, our own taste and apprehension and interpretation should be the Judge, and that is the disease itself." [61] Human understanding is so infirm, he adds, that even when Donne studies himself, he cannot be certain of his conclusions.

> And I still vex my self with this, because if I know it not, no body can know it. And I comfort myself, because I see dispassioned men are subject to the like ignorances. For divers mindes out of the same thing often draw contrary conclusions. . .   (p.62)

A decade later, in a sermon preached at St. Paul's (III, 360), Donne describes reason as "this poore snuff, that is almost out in thee," and in a sermon of 1626 (VII, 260), he asks rhetorically, "how imperfect is all our knowledge? What one thing doe we know perfectly?"

Clearly evident in the different periods of his life and the different genres in which he wrote, Donne's attention to epistemological problems spanned a variegated career. But while he questioned reason's ability to discover perfect truth, he never espoused the sceptic principle of permanently suspending judgment. Like casuists, his concern with epistemology was directed towards the practical end of justifying moral choice. Whether urging unmarried sex or endorsing the religious policies of his king, he strained towards mitigating doubt and enabling action.

One of the most disturbing consequences of reason's infirmity is misinterpretation of Scripture. Donne and Reformed casuists agreed that the Bible is our surest guide in moral dilemmas, but they also recognized that if our understanding is imperfect, so may be our application of God's Word. Donne observes in *Biathanatos*:

> as weake credulous Men, thinke sometymes they see two or three sunnes, when they see none but Meteors, or other apparances, so are many transported with like facility or dazeling, that for some opinions, which they mayntayne, they thinke they haue the light and authority of Scripture, When, God knowes, Truth, which is the Light of Scriptures is Diametrally vnder them, and remoued in the farthest Distance that can be.[62]

The figurative language of Revelation, the "darkness" of Christ's parables, the fact that some Biblical commands are limited to historical circumstances, while others are universal— all these add to our problems of interpreting and applying Scripture. Donne's *Essays in Divinity* addresses the problems and suggests ways to alleviate them; although the following chapter examines his suggestions, it is worth noting here, in the context of Donne's epistemology, two of his theses in the *Essays*: the importance of tolerance and the interdependence of reason and faith.

---

[61]   *Letters*, p.61. Subsequent references to this edition appear in the text.
[62]   John Donne, *Biathanatos*, ed. Ernest W. Sullivan III (Newark: Univ. of Delaware Press, 1984), pp.109-110.

Donne's professed religious tolerance is partly attributable to his belief that absolute truth eludes imperfect reason. In general, Reformed casuists claimed to share his view, their epistemological reservations making them intolerant only, they maintained, of those whom they believed to be extremists. The need for practical theology arises from the fallen legacy of uncertainty. Given that legacy, Donne and many casuists taught that dogmatism is unjustified; at the same time, they insisted that one must not abandon conviction. Anglican, Puritan, and Lutheran casuists usually agreed that in all but essential articles of faith, one should allow for inevitable differences of interpretation. Donne comments, "Christ's sheep are not always in one fold. . . that is, not in one place, nor form." [63] And the Puritan Perkins maintained that since the Bible does not specify forms of worship, there are no grounds for condemning Anglican ceremonies; "the proper practice— not just a permissible one— is to follow the usage of the Church at large, for the sake of unity." [64]

Such unity was an ideal that Donne promoted. God is the source of all religions, he argued, and the imperfections of one sect may find correction or guidance in another. Less than a year before his ordination, he wrote of the Protestant and Catholic Churches, "The channels of Gods mercies run through both fields, and they are sister teats of his graces, yet both diseased and infected, but not both [in the same ways]" (*Letters*, p.88). And in a letter to Sir Henry Goodyer, Donne expresses his belief that different sects partake variously of the same truth.

---

[63]   *Essays*, p.49. No doubt, Donne's own membership in the Anglican and Catholic Churches contributed to his tolerance of different religions.

[64]   Elliot Rose, *Cases of Conscience: Alternatives Open to Recusants and Puritans Under Elizabeth I and James I* (Cambridge: UP, 1975), p.192. The tolerance of Reformed casuists was not without exception, however. Each man would occasionally lapse into his own peculiar prejudice. Donne magnanimously states in the *Essays* (p.51): "Synagogue and Church is the same thing, and of the Church, *Roman* and *Reformed*, and all other distinctions of place, Discipline, or Person, but one Church, journeying to one *Hierusalem*, directed by one guide, Christ Jesus"; and yet he fulminated against Jesuits for years. Perkins, who was a devotee of magic before his conversion, later urged that such devotees be tortured and killed. Ames could be charitable towards Protestant sects other than his own, but he was "vehemently anti-Catholic" (Rose, p.198). For more on Donne's tolerance of Catholicism but hostility to Jesuits, see George Parfitt, *John Donne: A Literary Life* (London: Macmillan, 1989), pp.55-58. See also, Ted-Larry Pebworth, "'Let Me Here Use That Freedome': Subversive Representation in John Donne's 'Obsequies to the Lord Harrington," *JEGP*, 91, No. 1 (1992), pp.38-39 and Claude J. Summers, "The Bride of the Apocalypse and the Quest for True Religion: Donne, Herbert, and Spenser" in *Bright Shootes of Everlastingnesse: The Seventeenth-Century Religious Lyric*, eds. Claude J. Summers and Ted-Larry Pebworth (Columbia, Missouri: Univ. of Missouri Press, 1987), pp.82-84.

> You know I never fettered nor imprisoned the word Religion; not straight-
> ning it Frierly, *ad Religiones factitias* (as the Romans call well their orders
> of Religion) nor immuring it in a *Rome*, nor a *Wittenberg*, or a *Geneva*;
> they are all virtuall beams of one Sun, and wheresoever they finde clay
> hearts, they harden them, and moulder them into dust; and they entender
> and mollifie waxen. They are not so contrary as the North and South Poles;
> and that they are connaturall pieces of one circle. Religion is Christianity,
> which being too spirituall to be seen by us, doth therefore take an apparent
> body of good life and works, so salvation requires an honest Christian.
> (*Letters*, pp.25-6)

Such an inclusive definition of religion was uncommon in the wake of the
Reformation. Donne's tolerance (at least by the standards of his time) derives from his sense that if reason is imperfect, so are our grounds for condemning different formulations of truth.

   Because unaided reason cannot comprehend God's Word, it is finally
faith that assimilates religious truth. Donne held that we should "advance
faith duly above reason," and yet he believed that either one without the
other was insufficient for spiritual understanding: "Not that we are bound to
believe anything *against reason*, that is, to believe we know not why. It is
but a slacke opinion, it is not *Beliefe*, that is not grounded upon reason"
(*Sermons*, III, 357). Indeed, Donne maintained that faith is impossible
without understanding. "We beleeve nothing with a morall faith, till something have wrought upon our reason, and vanquished that, and made it assent and subscribe" (*Sermons*, III, 294). Faith and reason, then, are interdependent. The former illumines the latter; and ratiocination, with grace, leads
to faith.[65]

   Neither Donne nor Reformed casuists subscribed to rational theology,
but they did accord reason an important role in spiritual life. Just as they insisted on the personal adjudication of moral conflicts, they taught that each
Christian is responsible for studying the Reason that informs creation and
Scripture.[66] Such study is prerequisite to faith, and is a sign of regeneration.

---

   [65] Donne comments in *Sermons*, II, 308: "Grace finds out mans naturall
faculties, and exalts them to a capacity, and to a susceptiblenesse of the working
thereof, and so by the understanding infuses faith." Similarly, he explains in
Sermons IX, 357: "though faith be of infinite exaltation above understanding,
yet, although our understanding be above our sense, yet by our senses we come
to understand, so by our understanding we come to beleeve." See also Donne's
"*Elegie* On the untimely Death of the *incomparable Prince*, Henry": "For,
Reason, put t'her best *Extension*,/ Almost meetes *Faith*. . ." (ll.15-16).
   [66] Perry Miller's *The New England Mind: The Seventeenth Century*
(Cambridge, MA: Harvard UP, 1954), p.69, describes the duty of fallen reason:
"No matter how irrational the government of God may seem to his uncompre-
hending creatures, it is so only in appearance. Faith is called upon to believe,
not merely in redemption, but in the reason behind all things. The regenerated
intellect may not understand 'abstract wisdom,' but it can catch at least a glim-

Even doubt can be a religious act, one that God encourages; in a sermon that recalls "Satyre III," Donne remarks, "To come to a doubt, and to a debatement in any religious duty, is the voyce of God in our conscience: Would you know the truth? Doubt, and then you will inquire" (V, 38). The doubt that Donne describes is not a function of despair or scepticism, and the inquiry he recommends is not an arrogant prying into God's mysteries.[67] One must bring humility to the study of Scripture. However,

> it is not such a groveling, frozen, and stupid Humility, as should quench the activity of our understanding, or make us neglect the Search of those Secrets of God, which are accessible. For, Humility, and Studiousnesse, (as it is opposed to curiosity, and transgresses not her bounds) are so near of kin, that they are both agreed to be limbes and members of one vertue, *Temperance*.[68]

Although Donne recognized that understanding is limited, he also warned that ignorance is a dangerous neglect. His view of reason's role in moral decisions and in matters of faith strikingly resembled casuistical thought.

---

mering. By the very fact of being regenerated the intellect is duty-bound to strive for such a glimpse."

[67]   In *Sermons*, III, 358, Donne warns that reason should not presume upon the mysteries of faith: "when we bring this light [of faith] to the common light of reason, to our inferences, and consequences, it may be in danger to vanish itself, and perchance extinguish our reason too. . ." See also *Sermons*, IX, 245-6.

68 *Essays*, p.5. Donne is careful to distinguish between humility and ignorance; the latter, he denounces in Sermons, IV, 119: "of the ignorant God will be ignorant; not know them, that study not knowledge."

CHAPTER THREE

CASE DIVINITY AND THE ARGUMENT OF DONNE'S PROSE

The texts discussed in this chapter span more than twenty years of Donne's life. They represent three distinct periods in the author's career: his promising youth at the Inns of Court in the early 1590's, when he wrote the *Paradoxes and Problems*; his embittered years of unemployment at Mitcham, during which he wrote *Biathanatos* (1608) and published *Pseudo-Martyr* (1610); and the beginning of his profession as a preacher, when he delivered the sermon on *Esther* (c.1615), and finished the *Essays in Divinity* (by 1619). But despite differences of time, circumstances, and audience, the works have significant traits in common. In each text, Donne explores problems of knowledge, definition, and moral judgment. And in each text, he encourages the application of casuistical principles to these problems. The efforts of practical theologians to order experience and justify action engaged Donne throughout the different periods of his life.

Although neither the *Paradoxes and Problems* nor the *Essays in Divinity* is a formal case of conscience, both are concerned with the ambiguities that necessitate practical divinity. Both address, in very different ways, the fallibility of reason and language. Consequently, the two works serve as a useful introduction to Donne's most important casuistical treatises; in *Biathanatos*, *Pseudo-Martyr*, and the sermon on *Esther* 4.16, case divinity provides an anodyne to the problems set forth in the *Paradoxes* and *Essays*.

Comparison of Donne's cases illustrates that the judgments of practical theology are always contingent. Because the circumstances of each work are different, *Pseudo-Martyr* and the sermon on *Esther* arrive at opposite conclusions about suicide. In *Biathanatos*, Donne postulates numerous situations in which "selfe homicide" is laudatory, and other instances in which the act is sinful. Moreover, *Pseudo-Martyr* argues that it is sacrilege for English Catholics to disobey King James, whereas Donne's sermon applauds Esther's resolve to disregard both positive and natural laws. But while the resolutions of Donne's cases differ, the principles by which he resolves them are the same; each work subscribes to the tenets of Protestant casuistry outlined in chapters one and two. Each insists on the inviolability of conscience, and on individuals' responsibility to formulate their own moral decisions rather than rely on another's opinion. And in each case, Donne advances the casuistical theory that the province of knowledge may be probability rather than absolute truth, but that reason, guided by temperate debate, rectified conscience, and Scripture, can nevertheless arrive at a practical assurance for action.

The Wars of Truth

The *Paradoxes and Problems* dramatize the delusory powers of language and logic, powers that both delighted and disturbed Donne throughout his life. The author demonstrates how easily reason can be turned against itself as he dissociates logic from commonly held verities. Challenging appearances and the reader's expectations, the *Juvenilia* are indeed "para doxa." [1] The paradox form is particularly well-suited to Donne's probing the deficiencies of reason. Rosalie Colie observes that paradox

> is a demonstration of the problems at the limit of knowledge and of the linguistic and rhetorical problems arising from the attempt to overcome those limitations. . .Even the simplest form of paradox, the defense of a belief generally unpopular, is not really very simple, since it involves an unspoken assumption of the wars of truth, an acceptance of pluralism in the truth of sublunary situations and at the same time a conviction that truth is only one and all competing 'truths' are at best but appearances.[2]

But the *Juvenilia* prove to be a mock battleground for "the wars of truth." Donne's sophistry is so exaggerated as to become farcical. His Paradoxes do not convince the reader of their "competing 'truths'"—the merits of fatuity (VII), cowardliness (V), and discord (IX), for example; but they do force us to realize that logic, atonal and amoral, can defend what seems to be illogical. We are led to acknowledge a disjunction between reason and the existential.[3]

Frequently, Donne exposes this disjunction by exploiting the ambiguity of language. For instance, his first Paradox, "That all things kill themselves," proceeds by a series of equivocations on the word "end." At the core of his argument is the indisputable fact that all living things end in death. But Donne revises the truism to argue that death is the end, or purpose, of all living things. Treating connotation as denotation, he demonstrates the mercurial nature of language: death is a completion, completion is perfec-

---

[1]   See A. E. Malloch, "The Techniques and Function of the Renaissance Paradox," *Studies in Philology*, LII, No.1 (1956), p.193.

[2]   Rosalie Colie, "Some Paradoxes in the Language of Things," in *Reason and the Imagination*, ed. J. A. Mazzeo (New York: Macmillan, 1962), pp.109-110.

[3]   An excellent account of Donne's paradox and of his subversion of Ramist "place-logic" is Michael McCanles' "Paradox in Donne," *Studies in the Renaissance*, XIII (1966), pp.266-287.

tion, and perfection is excellence; therefore, death is the ultimate expression of excellence. Since all that is natural inclines towards its proper end, Donne concludes that all nature seeks the perfection of suicide. Self-destruction is the end/aim of even the lowest forms of life.

> Plants quickned and inhabited by the most unworthy Soule, which therfore neyther will, nor worke, affect an end, a perfection, a Death. This they spend their Spirits to attaine; this attained, they languish and wither. And by how much more they are by Mans industry warm'd and cherisht, and pamper'd, so much the more early they climbe to this perfection, this Deathe. And yf between men, not to defend be to kill, what a heinous selfe murder is it, not to defend it selfe?[4]

Donne's falsifications are patent. Reasoning as if end, perfection, and death are synonymous, he ignores the varying signification of his terms. He proves by tautology that plants desire death: "this attained, they languish and wither." That is, when they die, they die. And despite his observation that plants "neyther will, nor worke," he asserts that their failure to defend themselves against horticulture is proof of their suicide. Similarly, Donne suggests that the death of animals is volitional. Beasts, who "exceede us in number, strength, and lawles liberty," choose death over self defense against humans. Even the "galantest" of race horses "will run to their own Deathes, neyther sollicited by spurrs, which they neede not, nor by honor which they apprehend not" (p. 1). Contrary to the Aristotelian doctrine of causes, Donne contends that the final cause of life is death.

Throughout his Paradox, Donne distorts the various significances of words, deducing conclusions from one meaning and applying them to another. The final discussion of humans' suicidal impulses plays on his conflation of "aim," "end," "death," "completion" and "perfection." In seeking fulfillment, he argues, our impulses pursue their own destruction. His proof comes of literalizing different metaphorical uses of the term "kill": "Of our Powers, remembring kills our Memory. Of affections, Lusting our Lust. Of Vertues, giving kills Liberality" (p. 2). Donne equivocates that to complete or satisfy is to perfect, and to perfect is to change the disposition of a thing, thus ending its former nature:

> for after perfection immediatly followes exces: which changes the natures and the names, and makes them not the same things. If then the best things kill themselves soonest (for no perfection indures) and all things labor to this perfection, all travaile to their owne Deathe. (p. 2)

Recalling the discussion of the mean in *Nichomachean Ethics*, Donne plays on Aristotle's observation that a thing loses its identity when it suffers defi-

---

4   Donne, *Paradoxes and Problems*, ed. Helen Peters (Oxford: Clarendon Press, 1980), p.1. Subsequent page references to the *Paradoxes* will appear in the text.

ciency or excess. "It is the nature of such things to be destroyed by defect and excess, as we see in the case of strength and health," Aristotle remarks; "both excessive and defective exercise destroys the strength, and similarly drink or food which is above or below a certain amount destroys the health."[5] While the *Ethics* assert that proportion preserves a thing, Donne argues that perfection self destructs. Again, the Paradox playfully shifts its terms: interchanging end, perfection, and death, it concludes that to strive towards a proper end is to seek annihilation.

As Stanley Fish remarks of Donne's "interpretive fecundity" elsewhere, "The obvious objection to this self-propelling logic of schematic figures is that it knows no constraints and is wholly unstable; meaning can be pulled out of a suffix or out of thin air, and the linear constraints of syntax and consecutive sense are simply overwhelmed." [6] Donne's misrepresentations in the Paradox are all the more witty in that they proceed from an apparently logical structure. The Paradox opens with a pithy thesis statement that is substantiated in three parts, each part corresponding to the three souls outlined in Aristotle's *De anima*. The progression from vegetable to animal to rational souls lends a sense of order and authority to Donne's contentions. His repetition of "if-then" constructions adds to the semblance of logical sequence. And yet his assertion that the first law of nature is self-destruction, rather than self-preservation, controverts conventionally held truth. Demonstrating "the capacity of words to make connection with one another rather than with some external referent that constrains them to accuracy," Donne professes "the truth, not as it exists in some realm independent of...verbal dexterity, but as it has been established in the context *created* by that dexterity." [7] The real paradox of Donne's argument is not that "all things kill themselves," but that reason has been enlisted to destroy the rational, language to confound meaning.

The *Juvenilia*, however, are not finally vehicles of scepticism. Donne's demonstration of the deceptive powers of language and logic assumes the reader's ability to recognize specious arguments and to resist them in a dialogue with the work. In a letter written circa 1600, Donne says of his *Paradoxes and Problems*: "If they make you to find better reasons against

---

5   Aristotle, *Nichomachean Ethics* in *The Basic Works of Aristotle*, ed. Richard McKeon (New York: Random House, 1941), 1104a. See also 1106a-1107b.

6   Stanley Fish, "Masculine Persuasive Force: Donne and Verbal Power" in *Soliciting Interpretation: Literary Theory and Seventeenth-Century English Poetry*, eds. Elizabeth D. Harvey and Katharine Eisaman Maus (Chicago: UP, 1990), p.224.

7   Fish, "Masculine Persuasive Force," p.224. Fish's comments refer to "The Anagram," but his astute analysis is equally convincing when applied to Donne's similar moves in the *Paradoxes and Problems*.

them they do there office: for they are but swaggerers: quiet enough if you resist them." [8] Donne's propositions are meant to be confuted. Although they subvert customary notions of order, the result is not, as P. N. Siegal maintains, a "devastating scepticism." [9] To the extent that they provoke doubt and inquiry, the *Juvenilia* are sceptical, but they are not defeatist about the capacity of reason. Donne believes that his reader is able "to find better reasons." His sophistry calls attention to the pitfalls of the ratiocinative process so that his audience will scrutinize their own judgments and formulate counterarguments. In the letter quoted above, Donne insists that his *Paradoxes and Problems* "are rather alarums to truth to arme her then enemies." Uncontested by the reader's superior judgment, "They are not hatcht. . .they are nothings: therefore take heed of allowing any of them least you make another." To "hatch" the *Paradoxes and Problems*—to bring them to their full realization—one must refute them. Paradoxically, in their destruction by better reasons, they are finally created.

The *Juvenilia* seem far removed from cases of conscience, but even in the irreverent *Paradoxes and Problems* one can discern Donne's casuistical habits of mind. As the preceding chapters state, recognizing the defects of knowledge, while simultaneously crediting reason with corrective powers, is characteristic of casuistical epistemology. Moreover, the active participation Donne requires of the reader—his forcing us to examine methods of judgment and to "arme" ourselves against logical fallacies—is consonant with the efforts of Reformed casuists to engage their audience in the process of ethical deliberation. The insolence and humorous misrepresentations of the *Juvenilia* bear no resemblance to cases of conscience, but Donne's purpose does. One of the objectives of the *Paradoxes and Problems* is not to destroy specific opinions; rather, it is to challenge complacent submission to any opinion, whether right or wrong. Donne insists that his readers test and prove their assumptions "in an age when any thing is strong enough to overthrow [truth]." [10] Like casuists, he encourages disputation. While cases

---

[8] Quoted in Evelyn Simpson, *A Study of the Prose Works of John Donne* (Oxford: Clarendon Press, 1962), p.316.

[9] P. N. Siegal, "Donne's *Paradoxes and Problems*," *Philological Quarterly*, XXVIII (1949), p.511.

[10] Quoted in Simpson, *A Study of the Prose Works of John Donne*, p. 316. Donne's efforts to innervate his readers' judgment signal a development new to the Renaissance paradox. Traditionally a sceptical device to demonstrate the unreliability of reason, the extended paradox became a weapon against unthinking acquiescence in custom. Sir William Cornwallis prefaces his defense of inconstancy (1600): "Seinge Opinion of a litle nothinge is become soe mightie that like a Monarchesse she tyrannizeth over Judgement I have been undertaken to anatomize and confute some few of her traditions" (Peters, pp.xxi-xxii). The paradoxes of Donne and his contemporaries, unlike their classical antecedents, contest received opinion in order to "make untruth serve the cause of knowledge"

of conscience argue each side of an issue in order to determine its moral status, the *Paradoxes* present one side of a debate that incites rebuttal; the conviction underlying both practices is that disputation brings one closer to "truth."

The *Essays in Divinity* voice a similar conviction about the value of debate. Though Donne condemns the vitriolic controversies of sectarians, he maintains that our "vexation" of Scripture can be constructive and edifying. He remarks that God's Word is intentionally difficult; it contains paradoxes and problems that require the exercise of reason. Ambiguities of language and logic in the Bible militate against complacent acceptance. God exacts deliberation. "To make men sharpe and industrious in the inquisition of truth, he withdrawes it from present apprehension and obviousness." [11] Even misguided disputation can serve the cause of truth. God, Donne writes,

> is pleased that his word should endure and undergo the opinion of contra-
> diction, or other infirmities, in the eyes of Pride (the Author of Heresie and
> Schism) that after all such dissections, and cribations, and examinings of
> Hereticall adventures upon it, it might return from the furnace more refined,
> and gain luster and clearness by this vexation. (p. 57)

Through debate, and even through heretical challenges, truth is annealed.

It is significant that Donne attributes to God the same desire to exercise His "readers'" reason— to engage their active participation in Revelation— that Donne has for his own readers. Each of the works examined in this chapter manifests Donne's belief that ratiocination is not merely a condition of humanity; it is a moral responsibility. Not only must individuals choose between good and evil, but they are accountable for the reasons that effect their choice. In his 1621 Christmas sermon, Donne comments that God even requires Christians to determine the authenticity of Scripture: "God hath not proceeded in that manner, to drive our Reason into a pound, and to force it by a peremptory necessitie to accept these for Scriptures, for then, here had been no exercise of our *Will*, and our assent, if we could not have

---

(Malloch, p.196). Donne's claim to have written "alarums to truth" is similar to Anthony Munday's statement that paradoxes reveal truth by arguing for its op-posite. In his 1593 translation of Ortensio Lando's *Paradossi*, Munday com-ments that "opposed truth might appeare more cleere and apparent." See Geoffrey Bullough, "Donne the Man of Law" in *Just So Much Honour*, ed. Peter Amadeus Fiore (University Park: Penn State UP, 1972), p.66.

[11] Donne, *Essays in Divinity*, ed. Evelyn Simpson (Oxford: Clarendon Press, 1952), p.56. (Subsequent page references appear in the text.) In a sermon of 1621, Donne reiterates the importance of deliberating about religious tenets; indeed, he asserts that salvation is partly contingent upon ratiocination: "for let no man thinke that *God* hath given him so much ease here, as to save him by be-lieving he knoweth not what, or why. *Knowledge* cannot save us, but we cannot be saved without Knowledge . . ." *Sermons*, ed. George Potter and Evelyn Simpson (Berkeley: Univ. of California Press, 1953-62), III, 359.

resisted."[12] The argument continues with a list of the reasons meant to convince readers that the Bible is God's.

As stated in chapters one and two, Donne preferred Protestant rather than Catholic casuistry partly because the former insists that each individual is responsible for working out his or her own case of conscience; admittedly, one should follow the methodological paradigms that casuists set forth, but to base a decision solely on the judgments of others is to abandon reason and conscience, and therefore rectitude. Donne observes in Book One of the *Essays* that "to ly hulling upon the face of the waters, and think nothing, is a stupid and lazy inconsideration, which (as Saint *Austin* says) is the worst of all affections" (p. 13). And again in Book One, he extols the activity of Aquinas' reason: "nothing was too minerall nor centrick for the search of his wit . . . Nor doth he say this, that we should discharge our selves upon his word, and slumber in a lazy faith; for no man was ever more endeavorous then he in such inquisitions" (p. 16).

Despite Donne's emphasis on deliberation, however, his *Essays* repeatedly address the inadequacy of ratiocination. As in the *Paradoxes and Problems*, Donne exposes reason as limited, while simultaneously urging its application. Echoing lines from the most sceptical passage of his *Second Anniversary*, [13] he laments that "*Man*, who (like his own eye), sees . . . but so dimly, that there are marked an hundred differences in mens Writing concerning an *Ant*" (p. 14). The *Essays* are particularly concerned with the effect of misunderstanding on religious judgments. Donne acknowledges that conflicting interpretations of Scripture imply a disjunction between reason and truth. Such a disjunction results in epistemological anxiety and doubt about which actions are truly Christian. He attempts to obviate the destructive consequences of uncertainty (despair, intolerance, scepticism) by clarifying the roles of reason and faith, and by urging latitude in nonessentials.

As the *Essays* meditate upon the problems of interpreting and obeying God's Word, they return often to the relationship between reason and faith. That Donne was not a fideist has already been seen in the last section of chapter two. He believed that reason precedes faith, and that the two are interdependent for religious apprehension. "Understanding is the door of faith," he writes; reason must "chaff the wax" before faith "imprints the seale." [14]

---

[12] Donne, *Sermons*, III, 359.

[13] "What hope have we to know our selves, when wee/ Know not the least things, which for our use bee?/ We see in Authors, too stiffe to recant,/ A hundred controversies of an Ant" (ll. 279-282).

[14] *Sermons*, IX, 360, and *Sermons*, VII, 95. Donne asserts the interdependence of reason and faith throughout his works. He begins a verse epistle to the Countess of Bedford: "Reason is our Soules left hand, Faith her right,/ By these wee reach divinity. . ." Although reason is inferior, it leads us to, and pro-

The *Essays* remark that, although God is incomprehensible, we can glean indirect knowledge of Him through "his Image in his works" (p. 39). To study Creation is to learn of God's benevolence and power, which in turn impels us to worship and obey Him. Donne was persuaded that in the proper exercise of reason there is a nascent piety.

But he also judged reason's role in devotion to be limited. To know God, one must look beyond the Book of Nature to faith:

> But by these meditations [on Creation] we get no further, then to know what he *doth*, not what he *is*. . . .For all acquired knowledge is by degrees, and successive; but God is impartible, and only faith which can receive it all at once, can comprehend him. (pp. 20-21)

Not only does faith enable an immediate apprehension that reason can never attain, but our reception of some religious tenets by-passes reason altogether. To accept these tenets, "we are not under the insinuations and mollifyings of perswasion, and conveniency; nor under the reach and violence of Argument, or Demonstration, or Necessity; but under the Spirituall, and peaceable Tyranny, and easie yoke of sudden and present faith" (p. 16). Donne observes that miracles require such a superrational acceptance. The act of Creation, for example, "admits no arrest for our Reason, nor gradations for our discourse, but must be at once swallowed and devour'd by faith, without mastication, or digestion" (p. 54). Because it is validated by the Holy Ghost, faith is not subject to the perplexities that beset reason. "That then this Beginning *was*, is matter of faith, and so, infallible. *When* it was, is matter of reason, and therefore various and perplex'd" (p. 18). Donne insists that those who try to penetrate God's mysteries only obscure them further. Extending reason beyond its limited jurisdiction in religious matters breeds confusion and factionalism.[15]

Linguistic inadequacy compounds the problems of fallible reason. Not only are we unable to comprehend God, but we cannot even describe His at-

---

tects, faith. "For Reason is our Sword, Faith our Target [shield]. With that we prevail against others, with this we defend our selves" *Essays*, p.16. In *Sermons* IV, 119, Donne reiterates the paradox that reason supports the irrational: "Light itself is faith: but, the armour of light is knowledge; an ignorant man is a disarm'd man, a naked man." See also *Sermons*, V, 102. For a thorough discussion of Donne's Thomism and the reason/faith relationship in his works, see Terry G. Sherwood, *Fulfilling the Circle* (Toronto: Univ. Press, 1984).

15 The *Essays* admonish the reader against seeking forbidden knowledge: "there are some things which the Author of light hides from us, and the prince of darkness strives to shew to us; but with no other light, then his Firebrands of Contention and curiosity" (p.13). Donne delivers a more ominous warning in *Sermons* III, 358: "we may search so far, and reason so long of *faith* and *grace*, as that we may lose not only *them*, but even our reason too, and sooner become *mad* then *good*."

tributes. Donne examines a long list of words with which others have attempted to express the idea of God, and he proves each to be imprecise. Metaphors are also futile, but accommodated language is the closest one can come to articulating divinity. "Though God be absolutely simple, yet since for our sakes in his Scriptures he often submits himself to comparisons and similitudes, we may offencelessly (since there is nothing but himself, so large as the world) thus compare him to the world" (p. 62). Language dilutes meaning, Donne contends; it diminishes the signified. The restriction of words is nowhere more apparent than in our naming God: "thou. . .hast contracted thine immensity, and shut thy selfe within syllables, and accepted a Name from us" (p. 37). Like casuists, Donne is concerned with the *practical* consequences of linguistic inaccuracy and limited reason. The remaining pages of his *Essays* explore how the problems he has set forth affect interpretation of Scripture and, by extension, moral judgments and conduct.

Given the ambiguities of language and reason, Donne concludes that interpretation of Scripture which does not pertain to articles of faith cannot profess to absolute truth. God's Word is truth, but His creature's word is not necessarily so. William Ames concurs; in *The Marrow of Sacred Divinity* (1638?), he remarks, "Neither is there any authority on earth whereby any version [interpretation of Scripture] may be made simply authentical." [16] Since we cannot be certain that our exegesis is "authentical," Donne, Ames, and other casuists maintain that we have no authority to condemn those who posit contrary interpretations.[17] The *Essays* express a remarkable tolerance of different denominations, a tolerance born of epistemological reservations. Although Donne espouses the Anglican Church above others (and he lists *reasons* for his choice), he asserts that all religions share one foundation. Consequently, he objects to persecution among Christians for "things not essential"; he criticizes

> the severe and unrectified Zeal of many, who should impose necessity upon indifferent things, and oblige all the World to one precise forme of exterior worship, and Ecclesiastick policie; averring that every degree, and minute and scruple of all circumstances which may be admitted in either belief or practice, is certainly, constantly, expressly, and obligatorily exhibited in

---

[16]   Quoted in George L. Mosse, *The Holy Pretence* (Oxford: Basil Blackwell, 1957), p.78.

[17]   Ames comments in The Marrow of Sacred Divinity:
For in determining the controversies in Divinity, there is no visible power as it were kingly or pretorian, appointed in the Church: but there is laid a duty on men to inquire; there is bestowed a gift of discerning . . .and there is commanded a desire to further the knowledge and practice of the known truth, according to their calling, unto which is joined a promise of direction and blessing from God.

(Mosse, pp.79-80)   See also Donne's *Sermons*, II, 308.

the Scriptures; and that Grace, and Salvation is in this unity and no where else. (p. 49)

Those who claim absolute authority about nonessentials, Donne adds, usually do so by twisting Scripture to fit their purposes.

But intransigence is only one of many pitfalls in expounding Scripture. Donne lists several abuses of exegesis, and suggests ways to secure one's interpretation against gross error. His recommendations about how to read the Bible are virtually reproduced in Hall's *Resolutions and Decisions of Divers Practical Cases of Conscience*. Indeed, the *Essays* advocate many of the procedures with which casuists construe laws and "read" cases of conscience. Both Donne and Hall insist that one's understanding of Biblical directives depends on consideration of their circumstances. Paul's rebuke to the litigious Corinthians, for example, is not meant to proscribe all law suits; in judging his criticism, one must take into account the historical circumstances—the excess of suits that the Corinthians filed. Conclusions drawn in disregard of circumstances destroy the unity of Scripture: "So do they demolish God's fairest Temple, his Word, which pick out such stones, and deface the integrity of it, as neither that which they take, nor that which they leave, is the word of God" (pp.40-41). As will be seen, Donne makes the same argument in *Biathanatos* when he evaluates others' interpretations of Biblical passages that address suicide. Like casuists, he insists that the context of such passages is crucial to their meaning.

Both Donne and Hall maintain that Scripture is consistent; consequently, our reading of one passage must not contradict another. The "best way of expounding Scripture," Donne writes, is "by comparing one place with another" (p. 57). Similarly, Hall exhorts us to "a diligent sifting of the context and inference, and a careful comparing and conferring of one Scripture with another; for all truths agree with themselves, and this word of God is the sun that gives us light to see itself." [18] Limited reason can eclipse the light of Scripture, but following the safeguards of interpretation and debating difficult passages without prejudice, we can arrive at an understanding that is sufficient to guide our actions.

The defects of judgment set forth in the *Paradoxes and Problems* and *Essays in Divinity* are assumed in all casuistical deliberation. Indeed, the need for practical theology arises in part from the problems of reason and language that Donne exposes. But it remains to be seen how Donne applies to a specific case his casuistical suggestions for mitigating those problems. Moreover, it is important to consider his response to a fundamental assumption of moral theology: the relativity of law. The remainder of this chapter,

---

[18]   Joseph Hall, *Resolutions and Decisions of Divers Practical Cases of Conscience*, Vol. XII of *Works*, ed. John Downame (Oxford: D.C. Talboys, 1937), p.362.

then, explores how the methods and principles of case divinity deeply inform three of Donne's works.

Biathanatos: Moral Relativism and Moral Authority

Biathanatos advances the casuistical principle that no law, whether natural, positive, or divine, should condemn an action in disregard of circumstances. The wording of the subtitle is as conditional as the judgments that its author espouses: "A Declaration of that Paradoxe or Thesis, that selfe-homicide is not so naturally Sinne, that it may neuer be otherwise." Donne's governing assertion is that categorical arguments against suicide are both unreasonable and unjust because they fail to acknowledge that "Circumstances condition [all acts], and giue them theyr Nature." [19] Observing the interpretive methods that he would later outline in his *Essays*, Donne investigates the context of Biblical passages that seem to condemn suicide, and he compares them to other passages that condone the act. Scripture, he concludes, is far less rigorist than the prevailing conceptions of "selfe-homicide."

In his preface, Donne writes that charity obliges him to rebut the intransigence that characterizes many opinions of suicide. But *Biathanatos* is not only a defense of suicide. It is also a defense of the casuistical doctrine that we must support all our judgments with fully debated reasons; and it is an enactment of rules that practical theology recommends for moral deliberation. Although Donne's citation of a wide range of authorities is common procedure for Catholic casuists, his thesis is derived from Protestant casuistry: each person is responsible for judging the relation of general laws to particular circumstances according to the dictates of conscience and reason.

Critical evaluations of *Biathanatos* are as conflicting as the opinions about suicide that Donne cites. George Williamson asserts that the treatise is Donne's "most complete philosophical statement," while Evelyn Simpson dismisses it as one of the author's dullest works.[20] Joan Webber claims that *Biathanatos* demonstrates the inadequacy of formal logic and the weakness of reason, whereas Terry Sherwood argues it is a Thomistic defense of reason's capacity to judge complex moral problems.[21] Donne's

---

[19] John Donne, *Biathanatos*, ed. Ernest W. Sullivan III (Newark: Univ. of Delaware Press, 1984), p.120. Subsequent page references to *Biathanatos* appear within the text.

[20] George Williamson, "The Libertine Donne," *Philological Quarterly*, XII, No. 3 (1934), p.277. Simpson, *A Study of the Prose Works of John Donne*, p.179.

[21] Joan Webber, *Contrary Music* (Madison: University of Wisconsin Press, 1963), pp.5-13. Terry Sherwood, "Our Connexion of Causes," Diss. Univ. of

"defiance of law and his assertion of individual autonomy" are at "the emotional heart of *Biathanatos*," according to John Carey; conversely, Robert Ornstein writes that Donne's "arguments extend from traditional and quite respectable ethical theories." [22] William Clebsch discusses the work as a serious casuistical treatise, and Camille Slights says it is a failed satire of the methods of casuistry.[23]

One source of critical debate about *Biathanatos* is Donne's unwillingness to commit himself to a categorical rule about suicide. Although he examines at length the arguments for and against his subject, he says in the conclusion, "I abstayned purposely from extending this discourse to perticular *Rules*" (p. 145). Some readers interpret Donne's avoidance of a definitive statement about suicide as evidence of his scepticism, and still others attribute it to "his ambivalence about the lawfulness of suicide." [24] However, if Donne were to draw an absolute conclusion about "selfe-homicide," he would controvert his casuistical thesis that one must judge acts according to their circumstances. His aim is not to become yet another authority on the subject of suicide; rather, it is to demonstrate the contingency of moral judgments, and the need to weigh all sides of an issue before deciding on its moral status. In addition, Donne refrains from categorical pronouncements because he wants his readers to determine their own position. He insists throughout *Biathanatos* that his audience should discriminate among the many opinions cited, and that they should assume responsibility for their judgments rather than rely on the authority of another.

Donne's first hint of the active role that he requires of his audience is on the title page of *Biathanatos*. There he writes, "I do not profess everything to be true. But I will roil the waters for the readers' profit." [25] Because many of the arguments in *Biathanatos* are contradictory, they cannot all be true, but the veracity of Donne's references is beside the point. "Euery branch, which is excerpted from other Authors and engrafted here," Donne warns, "is not written for the Readers faith, but for illustration, and Comparison" (p. 32).[26] *Biathanatos* requires the readers to become their

---

California, Berkeley 1969, pp.143-154.

22   John Carey, *John Donne: Life, Mind and Art* (New York: Oxford UP, 1981), p.205. Robert Ornstein, "Donne, Montaigne, and Natural Law," *JEGP*, LV, No.2 (1956), p.229.

23   William Clebsch, ed. *Suicide* (Chico, California: Scholars Press, 1983), pp. ix-xvii *passim*. Camille W. Slights, *The Casuistical Tradition in Shakespeare, Donne, Herbert and Milton* (Princeton: UP, 1981), p.141.

24   Slights, p.142.

25   Clebsch's translation.

26   As in other works, Donne criticizes Catholic casuists who embrace a judgment on the basis of its advocates, rather than its substance: "Men of a weake disposition, or Lazy, or flattering, looke no further into these propositions, then from whose mouth it proceeds, or what authority it hath now, not

own casuists, choosing among conflicting laws. Like practical theologians, Donne's audience must try to dispel prejudice, extract relevant arguments from the available evidence, and reason towards a dispassioned arbitration. The author maintains that if his readers are "Siues which retayne the best onely" of the opinions presented, and if they "trust neither me nor the aduerse part, but the reasons . . . I doubt not but they may be hereby enlight'ned" (p. 32 and p. 30). Donne is more concerned with engaging his audience in the process of deliberation than with their final judgment.

Indeed, the process of moral deliberation is crucial in *Biathanatos* because there is no certain, universal rule about suicide. The opinions of classical writers, Church Fathers, casuists, and jurists are simply that: opinions. "'Controuerters often say on both sides, This is your Common opinion; And certaynely that is the common opinion in one Age which is not in another; yea in one Kingdome at the same tyme which is not in another, though both be Catholique'"(p. 69).[27] Donne observes that his sources disagree because abstract arguments cannot be resolved with certainty; however, like Protestant casuists, he insists that his readers will never make any progress "towards Peace, that is Truith," if they do not scrutinize their assumptions and debate their reasons. "Contemplatiue, and bookish men must of necessity be more quarrellsome then others, because they contend not about matter of fact, nor can determine theyr controuersies by any certayne witnesses, nor Iudges. But as long as they go towards Peace, that is Truith, it is no matter which way" (p. 31). Having no recourse to infallible judges and certain evidence, one must approach a subject from all sides, as the disputatious speaker of "Satyre III" also urges, and labor to arrive not at certainty but at a limited and practical understanding.

Donne maintains that the greatest barriers to progress towards such understanding are dogmatism and the "tyranny" of custom. Both militate against equitable decisions. "Peremptory judgements" and "uncharitablenesse" are synonymous in *Biathanatos*. Donne explains in his preface that the "burden of this custom and prescription" compels him to re-evaluate suicide. He chooses an issue about which there is not a great deal of contemporary controversy (his is the first defense of suicide published in English) in order to show that even widely accepted moral judgments are problematic and conditional.

The contingency of Donne's judgments is reflected in the style of

---

from whence it was produc'd" (p.65).

[27] Donne makes a similar observation about the relativity of positive laws to time and place: "humane Lawes by which Kingdomes are policed, be not so very neare to this Crowne of certayne Truth, and first Light (for if they were, Necessary Consequences from that Law of Nature, they could not be contrary in diuers places, and tymes, as we see Lawes to be). . ." (p.65). Like all casuists, Donne repeatedly asserts the conditional nature of legal and moral judgments.

Biathanatos. The author's conditional constructions and numerous subordinate clauses characterize the syntax of qualification found in most cases of conscience. Building his complex sentences with cumulative clauses, and weaving into them examples and exceptions that clarify his terms, Donne enacts the progressive deliberation of casuistry. Consider, for example, his view of the inspired suicide (pp. 102-103):

> If then a man after convenient and requisite, and convenient diligence, despoyled of all humane affections, and selfe interest, and *Sancto bonae Impatientiae igne exardens* ["Burning with the holy fire of good impatience"] (as *Paulynus* speakes) do in his Conscyence beleeue that he is invited by the Spirit of God to do such an act, as *Ionas*, *Abraham*, and perchance *Samson* was, who can, by these Rules, condemne this to be Sinne?

Donne's favorable conclusion, expressed in a rhetorical question, evolves from the qualifications and restrictive phrases that precede it. His sentence reproduces in miniature the casuistical process of delimiting and defining an act according to conscience, Scripture, and extenuating circumstances.

Another cause of critical disagreement about *Biathanatos* is the apparent inconsistency of Donne's attitude towards his sources. Although he criticizes servility to others' opinions, and censures "the ambages, and Multiforme entanglings of Schoolemen" (p. 102), his treatise is replete with legalistic distinctions and citations—many of them to the scholastics that he repudiates. The disparity between Donne's principles and his practices has led some readers to conclude that *Biathanatos* is a parody, and that its arguments in defense of suicide cannot be taken seriously.[28] If one considers Donne's academic audience, however, his seeming contradictions are explicable. In the preface to *Biathanatos*, he states that he has adapted his presentation to the methods of his audience in order to persuade them on their own terms. He cites numerous opinions, not to discover truth, but to convince others in the rhetorical manner to which they are accustomed.

> If therefore in multiplicity of not necessary citations, there appeare vanity, or Ostentation, or digression, my honesty must make my excuse, and compensation. . .I did the rather, because Scholastique, and Artificiall men vse this way of instructing; and I made account that I was to deale with such. (p. 32)

The scholastic form of *Biathanatos*—its many references to authorities, and its numbered subdivisions into parts, distinctions, and sections—is a consequence of Donne's attention to his readers' methods of argumentation. But just as Donne does not endorse probabilism when he advances a probabilist defense of the Oath of Allegiance for the Catholic readers of *Pseudo-Martyr*, he does not endorse in *Biathanatos* the "multiplicity of not necessary cita-

---

28   See, for example, Slights, p.144.

tions." In both instances, he meets his audience on their terms without compromising his belief that ultimately each person must be his or her own judge of moral problems.

The individual determination of moral questions, the value of debate, the relativity of ethics to circumstances, and the potentially numbing effects of custom and dogmatism are all casuistical tenets that we have seen Donne to espouse elsewhere in his works. Moreover, his comments about the conditional authority of natural, positive, and even divine law are echoed in his sermons and throughout the cases of practical theologians. Critics who divorce *Biathanatos* from the casuistical tradition misconstrue the work as an assertion of radical individualism. John Carey, for instance, cites the following passage to illustrate Donne's "defiance of law":

> No Law is so primary and simple but it fore-imagins a reason vpon which it was founded: and scarse any reason is so constant, but that Circumstances alter it. . . And he whose conscyence, well temper'd, and dispassion'd, assures him that the reason of *Selfe-preseruation* ceases in him, may allso presume that the Law ceases too, and may do that then, which otherwise were against that Law (p. 47) [29]

Far from insurgent, Donne's statement is consonant with the teaching of practical theology. Reformed and Catholic casuists agree that exceptional circumstances may render a law irrelevant to a particular case; in such a situation, the law ceases to exert a claim on conscience. As Aquinas states, neglect of such a law does not derogate from its authority in other circumstances: "He who in a case of necessity acts outside the letter of the law does not judge of the law, but of a particular case in which he sees that the letter of the law is not observed." [30] Protestant casuistry fully supports Donne's comments about the dictates of conscience; with the exception of God's word, no law is higher than one's own conscience. Hall admonishes, "Woe be to that man who shall tie himself so close to the letter of the law as to make shipwreck of conscience." [31] And Perkins writes, "What is done

---

[29]   William Ames wholly agreed with Donne's statement. In *Conscience With the Power and Cases Thereof*, from *Works* (Ann Arbor: Univ. Microfilms, 1962), Book 5, q.4, Ames writes: "The purpose and binding force of laws should not extend beyond the reason for them; so that, if the reason should come to an end, the law no longer binds."

[30]   Thomas Aquinas, *Summa Theologica*, ed. Anton Pegis (New York: Random House, 1945), II. 96. 6. In *Biathanatos* (p.47), Donne cites the passage from Aquinas in order to qualify his own comments about acting beside the law. See also Donne's *Sermons*, VI, 254: "every *forbearing* of a *Lawe*, is not an *Evacuating* of the *Law*; every *Pardon*, whether a *Post-pardon*, by way of mercy, after a Lawe is broken, or a *Prae-pardon*, by way of *Dispensation*, in wisedome before a Lawe bee broken, is not a *Destroying of this foundation*."

[31]   Hall, *Resolutions and Decisions*, p.311.

against conscience though it erre and be deceived, it is sinne in the doer."[32] Orthodox casuistry agrees with Donne's account of both law and conscience.

But Carey describes as appalling the claim that we may neglect a law when conscience advises us that circumstances have altered the reasons upon which the law was founded. "Decent citizens, in Donne's day as in ours, would be bound to find this contention appalling. If people are free to pick and choose which laws they obey, society will collapse in chaos." [33] Carey's objections would be entirely justified if Donne were not so careful to qualify the casuistical latitude he affords to individual judgment. Throughout *Biathanatos*, Donne moderates his defense of equity in general and of suicide in particular with the safe-guards of practical theology. For example, when rebutting the argument that suicide violates God's injunction against murder, he remarks:

> So as it is within the Circuit of the Command, it may allso be within the exception thereof. For though the Words be generall *Thou shalt not Kill*, we may kill beastes, Magistrates may kill Men; and a priuate Man in a iust warre may not onely kill, contrary to the sound of this Commandement, but he may kill his Father Contrary to another. (p. 116)

To argue without qualification that divine law does not always bind is to invite exploitation. But Donne tempers his observation with several casuistical restrictions. First he specifies that "It is not possible to modify divine law unless the modification itself agrees with divine law." [34] In the same section he adds, "We cannot be put to show, or plead any exemption, but when such a Case ariseth, we say that that Case neuer was within the reach of that Law" (pp. 116-117). And finally, Donne asserts that exemption can never be granted to acts committed with a lack of faith in God.

Donne is particularly careful to qualify his defense of "selfe-homicide." Early in *Biathanatos* he says that not all suicides are committed out of despair, but that those who do kill themselves without hope of God's mercy die in a state of sin. Although he adverts to many authors who justify suicide in moments of fear, pain, or pride, he remonstrates:

> as *St Aug:*, we with as much earnestnesse say. . .*That neither to auoyd temporall troubles, nor to remoue from others occasion of Sinne, nor to punish our owne past Sinnes, nor to preuent future, nor in a desire of the next Life* (where these considerations are onely or principally) *it cannot be*

---

[32] William Perkins, *A Discourse of Conscience*, ed. Thomas Merrill (Nieuwkoop: B. De Graaf, 1966), p.42. For Donne's confirmation of Perkins' assertion, see *Biathanatos*, p.102. See also *Sermons*, V, 226.

[33] Carey, pp.205-206. Disregarding the casuistical premises of Donne's treatise, Carey's comment confuses moral and positive law. For Donne's discussion (based on orthodox Protestant casuistry) of judging one's own case of conscience, see *Biathanatos*, pp.44-46.

[34] Clebsch's modernization, p.73.

Lawfull for any man to kill himselfe. But neyther *St Aug.* nor we denye but
that if there be cases, wherein the party is disinteressed, and onely, or primarily the glory of God is respected and aduanced, it may be Lawfull. (p.
77)

While Donne gives more than ample hearing to arguments and examples in
favor of suicide, his own evaluation of the act is surprisingly conservative.
He attaches more restrictions to suicide than does Joseph Hall, for instance;
in a case of conscience entitled, "Whether, and how far, a man may act towards his own death," Hall sanctions suicide if it is committed to avoid
sin.[35] As quoted above, Donne rejects such a dispensation. In the final
segment of *Biathanatos*, he concludes his discussion of Samson's death by
stating unequivocally that suicide "may be done onely, when the Honour of
God may bee promou'd by that way and no other" (p. 136).

Given Donne's limited allowance of suicide, one might well ask why
the major part of his treatise expresses the opinions of those in favor of the
act. If the answer is that the charitable impulses Donne identifies in himself
compel him to represent fairly both sides of the issue, why does he include
dubious and even absurd arguments? (When discussing fasts, he tells of an
eremite who received no food or water for twenty-two years. And to exem-
plify the casuistical principle that intention is tantamount to action in matters of conscience, he mentions a scientist who considers the flea to be
deadly, "though it neuer kill, because it endeuors it, and doth all the hurt it
can" p. 98.) [36] One explanation of Donne's ludicrous examples lies in his
description of *Biathanatos* as a paradox.

As noted earlier, Donne refers to his *Paradoxes* as "alarums to truth to
arme her." They require not only that the reader identify and resist their fallacies, but also that we formulate our own counterarguments. The point of
challenging the reader's opinion is to engage us in the process of logical
analysis. To an extent, *Biathanatos* is an "alarum to truth to arme her."
Because it argues both *for* and against received opinion, it does not strictly
belong to the paradox genre, but its purpose and methods are similar.[37] It
includes absurd examples and contradictory propositions in order to exercise
the reader's logical and moral judgment. Part 3, for instance, reiterates the

---

[35] Hall, p.323.
[36] Frank J. Warnke, *John Donne* (Boston: G. K. Hall, 1987), pp. 89-90,
ignores the playfulness and absurdity that recur in *Biathanatos* when he describes the tract as expressive of "the darkest period in Donne's career, and the
subject matter itself—the possibility of a moral justification for suicide—is re-
vealing in the extreme. . .A work of casuistical scholarship, *Biathanatos* is in-
teresting to the modern reader primarily for its illumination of Donne's spiritual
state during the most desperate period of his life."
[37] For a full discussion of the paradox genre, see Helen Peters' introduction
to Donne's *Paradoxes and Problems*.

casuistical rule that informs Donne's argument throughout: "the intent and end conditions euery action, and infuses the poyson or the nourishment, which they, which follow, suck from thence" (p. 127). Only a few paragraphs later, however, Donne writes that if good people commit suicide, then people who commit suicide must be good ("For to say, The good do it, is to say, They which do it are good" [p. 128]). The remark controverts the central assertion of *Biathanatos* that motive and circumstances determine the moral status of an act. While it may be commendable to lie in order to prevent a murder, that is not to say that all liars are virtuous. Donne forces his readers to winnow the false logic from his discourse. As in the *Paradoxes and Problems*, his contradictions demand our engagement, keeping us off balance and insuring against complaisance. Again, we are exhorted to be "Siues which retayne the best onely," to "trust neither me nor the aduerse part, but the reasons."

Reminders of our role as "Siues" are not always subtle. In a martyrology of suicides, Donne includes: Portius Latro, who killed himself in order to cure his fever; "*Hippionas* the *Poet*, [who] rimed *Bubalus* the Paynter to death with his Iambiques" (p. 50); and

> *Herennius* the *Sicilian*, [who] could endure to beat out his owne braynes against a post: and as though he had ought thanks to that braine, which had giuen him this deuise of killing himselfe, would not leaue beating till he could see and salute it. (pp. 49-50)

Combining the ridiculous with the serious, Donne compels his audience not to be "Spunges, which attract all without distinguishing" (p. 32). Moreover, his conflicting sources make it impossible for the reader not to discriminate among them. Given the conditional nature of all actions, Donne cannot prescribe answers for his audience, but "it shall satisfy me, to haue awakned them thus much, and showd them a Marke to direct theyr Meditation vpon" (p. 108). *Biathanatos* is not just about suicide, then. Like all works founded upon casuistical assumptions, it is about the contingency of law and the responsibilities of moral evaluation.

Power and Judgment in Pseudo-Martyr

Unlike *Biathanatos*, *Pseudo-Martyr* addresses a single aspect of suicide: the unwarranted self-sacrifice of English Catholics who refuse the Oath of Allegiance. Because Donne's subject is less general than in *Biathanatos*, his recommendations are more detailed, and his conclusions more emphatic. But like the treatise on "selfe-homicide," *Pseudo-Martyr* insists on the responsibility of its audience to weigh the arguments of both sides, and to reach a determination based on reason rather than on another's opinion or coercion. "And if you will suffer these things to enter your understanding and judgment," Donne writes, "I cannot doubt of your will to conforme your selves...But if you shut up that dore, and so expose yourselves, that men may possess your Will, without entring by your Judgement, they enter like Theeves at the window, and in the night." [38] A treatise about authority, *Pseudo-Martyr* begins with an admonition against authoritarianism. In keeping with the tenets of Protestant casuistry, its first appeal is to the understanding and unconstrained discrimination of its audience.

Donne's prefatory account of his conversion to Anglicanism both establishes a paradigm of judgment for his readers, and prefigures the casuistical stance he assumes throughout *Pseudo-Martyr*.[39] He relates how he "wrastled" against the prejudices inculcated in him since birth, and debated the tenets of each Church. Despite damage to his career, he delayed his decision until reason and conscience were fully persuaded.

> I used no inordinate hast, nor precipitation in binding my conscience to any locall Religion. . .And although I apprehended well enough, that this irresolution not onely retarded my fortune, but also bred some scandall, and endangered my spirituall reputation, by laying me open to many misinterpretations; yet all these respects did not transport me to any violent and sudden determination, till I had, to the measure of my poore wit and judgement, survayed and digested the whole body of Divinity, controverted betweene ours and the Romane Church. (pp. 4-5)

Throughout *Pseudo-Martyr*, Donne urges the same diligence in his readers, the same acquisition of knowledge, and unwillingness to surrender judgment to external authority.

The independent exercise of reason is particularly important to Donne's argument against obeying the Pope. According to *Pseudo-Martyr*, the Catholic Church, like its casuists, is more concerned with submission to its laws than with explaining the reasons that produce those laws.[40]

---

[38]   John Donne, *Pseudo-Martyr* (London: W. Stansby, 1610), p.18. Subsequent page references to *Pseudo-Martyr* will appear in the text.

[39]   The autobiographical passage also informs its readers that Donne is sympathetic to their difficult position. Throughout *Pseudo-Martyr*, he avoids antagonizing his audience; he presents the work as a carefully reasoned case of conscience, not a diatribe against English Catholics. Kenneth Kirk notes that the casuist's object should "be to obtain the willing and considered assent of those in whose interests [he] exerts [himself]; [he] will look not for an enforced obedience, but for a considered agreement with [his] conclusions." *Some Principles of Moral Theology* (London: Longmans, Green and Co., 1926), p.207.

[40]   Especially critical of the Jesuits' "blindnesse," Donne quotes Loyola: "let our marke be, an abdication of the will, and judgement. . .so you be carried with a blinde violence of obeying, whatever our Superiour commands" (p.132). And in a moment of humor, very rare for *Pseudo-Martyr*, Donne mocks the reflexive compliance of papists; he tells of a Catholic author who applauds the deference of Friar Reynald: "Having beene three yeres dead, when another Holy

Consequently, Catholic obedience often requires abjuration of choice and understanding, a submission that even God does not exact from His creatures. (The argument anticipates Donne's suggestion in his *Essays*: God is of the Protestant casuist persuasion that the intellect must convince the conscience before the latter can guide one to right action.) But obedience and oaths professed in ignorance are meaningless, Donne contends: "many men sweare somethings to be of the *Catholique faith,* and some other things to be *Hereticall,* in which he is so farre remooved from the knowledge of the things, that he doth not onely not understand the signification of the wordes, but is not able to sound, nor utter, nor spell them" (p. 376). A cognitive faculty, conscience cannot possibly be bound to such oaths. Those who render their superiors "blind Obedience and stupiditie" are "like the uncleane beasts; They swallow, and never chaw the cudde" (p. 173). When two superiors disagree, as do the Pope and King, one must examine the reasons for their claims and determine which has more force. *Pseudo-Martyr* undertakes such an examination. Donne's aim is a casuistical one: he attempts to educate his readers in the proper criteria for adjudicating contradictory laws.

Donne begins by identifying his argument as a case of perplexity. Two conflicting injunctions constrain English Catholics. On one hand, the Pope has deposed the King by absolving his subjects from obedience to an offender of the faith, and by encouraging subversion of James's laws against recusants. In addition, the Catholic Church promises the benefits of martyrdom (exemption from purgatory, an exalted death, etc.) for any who refuse to acknowledge the King's authority. On the other hand, James requires all subjects to swear that he is their rightful sovereign, to deny the Pope's temporal jurisdiction, and to assist in the discovery and prosecution of recusants.[41] Donne debates the claims of Pope and King in terms of their causes, circumstances, intention, and consequences— the criteria that determine rectitude or error in a case of conscience. To avoid seeming partisan, he frequently cites Catholic authorities who substantiate James's position. Like all casuists, he is concerned with the moral status of a particular act—

---

man was brought to be buried in the same Vault, [the Friar] rose up and went to the Wall, and stood upright there, that the other might have roome enough" (p.178).

41   James enacted his first Oath of Allegiance in 1606, after discovery of the Gunpowder Plot. The statute mulcted recusants of 20 pounds a month, and re-iterated Elizabeth's prohibition against Catholics in public office or university positions. In 1610, the King added a new law that required anyone 18 or older to take the Oath. But the outrage and nationalism following the Gunpowder Plot had waned, so *Pseudo-Martyr* defends an unpopular and largely unenforced statute. See J. P. Kenyon, *The Stuart Constitution: Documents and Commentary* (Cambridge: UP, 1978), pp.448-460.

in this instance, taking the Oath of Allegiance. Consequently, his treatise
focuses on three issues that immediately pertain to the problem of obedience: temporal jurisdiction, the nature of martyrdom, and the power of kingship.

Since Scripture, reason, and conscience direct all casuistical deliberation, Donne measures against the dictates of each the Pope's claim to temporal jurisdiction. He argues that nowhere does the Bible empower popes to
make citizens traitors to their king. The province of Christ's ministers is
the soul, not political aggrandizement. Jesuits, however, do not "preach
Christ, but his *Vicar*: Not his kingdome of *Grace*, or *Glorie*, but his title to
Temporall Kingdomes. . .Not Christ crucified, languishing for us under
Thorns, Nayles, Whippes and Speares, but his Vicar enthron'd, and wan-
tonly groning under the waight of his Keyes, and Swordes, and Crownes"
(pp. 153-4).[42] Despite Donne's objections that the Pope exceeds his authority, *Pseudo-Martyr* never questions the Church's spiritual jurisdiction.
Indeed, Donne asserts that "it is *spirituall Treason*, not to obey her." But he
adds:

> He therefore that can produce out of eyther of these *Authentique* sorts of
> *Records*, *Scripture* or *Church*, that is, *Text* or *Glosse*, any law, by which it
> is made either *High Treason* or *Heresie*, not to beleeve, that in my bap-
> tisme I have implied a confession, *That the Bishop of Rome is so monarch
> of the Church*, that he may *depose Princes*. . .shall drawe me into his
> mercy. (p. 181)

Since the Pope's temporal jurisdiction has no foundation in tradition, the
Primitive Church, Scripture, or the Church Fathers, it can't be considered

---

[42] Compared to the acrimony of contemporary polemics, the tone of
Pseudo-Martyr is moderate and erudite. Donne's references to the Jesuits, however, are the exception. Few passages in his works rival the virulence with
which he attacks the Society of Jesus. He objects mainly to their political
machinations (Chapter 4), equivocation (Chapter 15), and abuse of casuistry
(Chapter 8). But at times Donne's criticism is simply "ad hominem," and one is
reminded of the resentment he felt for Jesuit involvement in his brother's death,
in his mother's exile, and in other family suffering: "If therefore, as in their
Constitutions they call themselves, they be but *Cadavera*, they are either such
corrupt and putrified carcasses, as infect and envenome all places where they re-
side, or such Carcasses, as evil spirits have assumed to walk about in" (p.132).
Donne was especially bitter about the political intransigence of the Jesuits—
their support of papal deposing power and their resistance to both Elizabeth and
James; such opposition made it difficult for loyal English Catholics to occupy a
relatively safe, compromise position. In her discussion of *Ignatius His
Conclave*, Sister M. Geraldine, "John Donne and the Mindes Indeavours," *SEL*,
V, No. 1 (1965), p.120, finds Donne's enmity for Loyola unjustified and even
abnormal: "Ignatius is not a villain surely in any sense: Donne's hostility to the
Jesuits is something for the psychologists to worry about." Carey advances sev-
eral psychological theories on the subject in *John Donne: Life, Mind and Art*.

an article of faith. And martyrdom, Donne contends, is warranted only when one dies to defend an article of faith.

Donne acknowledges the powerful appeal of martyrdom in his Advertisement to the Reader. It is evident that he believes martyrdom to be a stronger incentive for recusants than any reprisals with which the King threatens them. Consequently, Donne is careful to explain the irrelevance of martyrdom to his readers' case of perplexity. He asserts the casuistical principle that "circumstances give it [self-sacrifice] all the life it hath, so that to make it obligatory or not so, depends upon them," and he demonstrates that the circumstances of English Catholics do not correspond to any definition of martyrdom (p. 226). Quoting Leo I, Donne writes: "*None of the Martyrs, saies he, had any other cause of their suffering, but the confession of the true Divinitie, and true humanitie in Christ. . .Which is neither impaired in the extent, nor corrupted in the puritie, by anything proposed in the Oath*" (p. 205). In addition, self-sacrifice should be committed only in support of a certain truth; otherwise, the act is reckless and sinful. Donne lists numerous instances of disagreement among Catholic authorities about the Church's secular capacity, demonstrating that the issue is far from certain truth. He concludes that, even among the Pope's advocates, the subject of his jurisdiction is "various and muddy." Therefore, "a hasty and unseasonable obedience to the Church, to die for her Doctrine, before she her selfe knowes what it is, have but a sower and unpleasant reward" (p. 263). Those who refuse the Oath, then, are merely criminals, not martyrs. To deny the King's authority is to endanger not only order and hierarchy, but also one's own material and spiritual welfare. Donne cites several Catholic casuists who maintain that violating a just law is an offense against God,[43] and he argues that, according to the standards of practical theology, the Oath is a just law.

All casuists agree that the aims, circumstances, and results of a law determine its legitimacy. Donne applies each of these determinations to the Oath, and systematically poses counterarguments to the Pope's objections. The intention of the Oath, he asserts, is not to persecute loyal Catholics, but to distinguish between treasonous and innocent citizens. James does not force Catholics to repudiate their faith; rather, he requires allegiance to his own and England's welfare. Echoing James's own *Triplici Nodo, Triplex Cuneus, or an Apologie for the Oath of Allegiance* (1607), Donne argues that the government is neither violating the consciences of Catholics nor punishing them for their religion.[44]

---

[43] Protestant casuists also agreed with Donne's assertion that compliance with legitimate laws is a religious duty. See, for example, Perkins' *Discourse*, pp.33-34.

[44] The argument is very similar to the official government defense of oaths of allegiance required by Elizabeth. See *The Execution of Justice in England*

> For this Oath is not offred as a Symbole or token of our Religion, nor to
> distinguish Papists from Protestants, but onely for a Declaration and
> Preservation of such as are well affected in Civill Obedience, from others
> which either have a rebellious and treacherous disposition already, or may
> decline and sinke in to it, if they bee not uphelde and arrested with such a
> helpe, as an Oath to the contrary. (p. 244)

The King is merely performing his duty as "God's lieuetenant" by defending
the country against "foraine usurpation" (p.188). The consequences of the
Oath will be to safeguard the "puritie and integrity" of the Church, and to
militate against "dangerous fluctuations and perils of shipwracke" (p.158).
With Aquinas and Carminus— both Catholic casuists—Donne remarks that
a just law is one that insures the peace and security of the State, preserves
religion, and protects the common good. The Oath of Allegiance, he
maintains, fulfills each of these criteria.

Since the Oath is legitimate, and the Pope has no certain standard to
support his temporal jurisdiction, the pivotal issue of *Pseudo-Martyr* is the
power of kingship. In all cases of perplexity, the higher authority has a
greater claim. Donne maintains that the laws of nature, reason, and
Scripture validate the King's authority; hence, it is impossible to controvert
James's law in good conscience. Homage paid to the Pope proceeds only
from our will, Donne argues, while obedience to the King proceeds from
our essential nature. "This therefore is our first Originary, naturall, and
Congenite obedience, *to obey the Prince*: This belongs to us as we are *men*;
and is no more changed in us, by being *Christians*, then our *Humanity* is
changed" (p. 173). The universality of submission to governance proves
that our obedience is a law of nature: "it is so well engrav'd in our hearts,
and naturally obvious to every understanding, that men of all conditions
have a sense of apprehension, and assurednes of that obligation" (p. 6). It is
not surprising, then, that history affords numerous examples of councils and
popes who have submitted to the decrees of kings. Religious and civil authorities share an obligation to the common good, "and to offend against
that, is to offend against rectified Reason" (p. 324). But an even greater offense is to question the power that God directly imparts to heads of state.

Pseudo-Martyr is one of Donne's strongest endorsements of the divine
right of kings. The treatise asserts that James's authority derives from God,
and therefore obedience to the King is a condition of salvation. "After God
hath infused *faith*, wee make sure our salvation by a morall obedience to the
king's Governement. . . So that *Christian* subjects need no higher power
then kings are naturally indued and qualified withall, to direct them to

---

(1583), probably written by Lord Burghley (Zagorin, pp. 191-192). For a useful
discussion of lawful allegiance, see David Martin Jones, "Sir Edward Coke and
the Interpretation of Lawful Allegiance in Seventeenth-Century England,"
History of Political Thought VII (1986), pp.321-340.

Salvation" (p. 190). While the Pope's jurisdiction is limited to the Church, the King's power encompasses all matters of state, both secular and sacred. Donne contends that a government's right to insure the security of its people extends to legislation of religion. He supports his claim by adverting to canon laws that sanction kings who declare schism treasonous: "the precedents of our owne, and other Catholicke Kingdomes, give us warrant to make seditious Doctrine *Treason*, and your owne *Canons* and *Judicature* give us example, and (if we needed it) Authoritie to proceede in that manner" (p. 166). Given the criteria that support the King's authority, there can be no doubt that the Oath is within his jurisdiction. Donne concludes that the evidence of reason, conscience, and Scripture resolves the perplexity of English Catholics, and he warns his readers not to become "pseudo martyrs" by suffering for the Pope's unfounded claims.

> So therefore a certaine and naturall evidence of a morall truth, such as arises to every man, *That to a King is due perpetuall obedience*, is better authority to induce an assurance, and to produce an oath, that the contrary is *Hereticall*, then an implicite credite rashly given to a litigious Councell, not beleeved by all Catholiques, and not understood by al that sweare to beleeve it. (pp. 376-377)

The strategy of *Pseudo-Martyr* is not simply to prove that James's authority derives from his greater power. True to the teaching of Reformed casuists, Donne assumes that no power on earth is greater than the individual's conscience, guided by Scripture. Since reason and conscience are the final determinants in ethical deliberation, Donne's strategy is to demonstrate the logical and moral superiority of the King's position.

Written for the public, and published while Donne desperately sought preferment at Court, *Pseudo-Martyr* is unequivocal in its advocacy of the King's prerogative. There is some question, however, about the conviction of Donne's pronouncements, since his private assessment of the controversy surrounding the Oath is irresolute and somewhat cynical. In a letter to Sir Henry Goodyer, dated the year before *Pseudo-Martyr* was published, Donne remarks that neither the Pope nor the King can adjudicate their dispute because the problem itself concerns their authority to judge. Consequently, an objective criterion outside the debate is necessary. But Donne does not specify what the criterion might be, or if it exists at all.

> I think truly there is a perplexity (as farre as I see yet) and both sides may be in justice, and innocence; and the wounds which they inflict upon the adverse part, are all *se defendendo*: for, clearly, our State cannot be safe without the Oath; since they professe, that Clergie-men, though Traitors, are no Subjects, and that all the rest may be none to morrow. And, as clearly, the Supremacy which the Ro[man] Church pretend, were diminished, if it were limited; and will as ill abide that, or disputation, as the Prerogative of temporall Kings, who being the onely judges of their prerogative, why may not Roman Bishops, (so enlightened as they are pre-

sumed by them) be good witnesses of their own supremacie, which is now
so much impugned?[45]

It is probable that Donne wrote *Pseudo-Martyr* with advancement in mind.
(Indeed, Walton reports that James commissioned the work, although Bald
suggests evidence to the contrary.) Annabel Patterson refers to the tract as
"that remarkable act of submission to the system." [46] But Donne's desire
for employment does not necessarily discredit the substance or methods of
the treatise. None of the arguments advanced in *Pseudo-Martyr* are contra-
dicted in Donne's later works.[47] His sermons reiterate the Pope's limited
jurisdiction, and they support laws against recusants. Moreover, the fifth
Prebend Sermon (1627) corroborates Donne's belief in the divine right of
princes, and repeats the assertion of *Pseudo-Martyr* that "it is sacriledge to
dispute the authority of a King" (p. 30). [48]

   But more important to the purposes of this study, Donne's motive of
preferment does not undermine the casuistical principles that he espouses.
As demonstrated above, a number of his prose works share the assumptions
of case divinity that pervade *Pseudo-Martyr*. Regardless of Donne's motive
in defending the Oath of Allegiance, it is problematic to dismiss the casuistical practices of one work when the same practices are repeatedly observed
in other works of unquestioned conviction. The *Essays in Divinity*, for example, agree with *Pseudo-Martyr* that ratiocination precedes ethical choice,
and that it is a sin to act without the full persuasion of conscience.
Biathanatos concurs that circumstances determine the moral status of an act;
that one should suspend preconceptions, and evaluate the arguments for and
against each side of an issue; that our responsibility for moral judgments
cannot be abandoned in deference to another's opinion. And, as will be seen,
Donne's sermon on Esther also subscribes to the casuistical methods of
Pseudo-Martyr. Both works resolve perplexity by determining the higher authority; both adjudicate contradictory laws by appealing to reason, conscience, and Scripture; and both weigh the circumstances, intention, and

---

   [45] Donne, *Letters to Severall Persons of Honour*, ed. Charles Edmund Merrill
(New York: Sturgis and Walton, 1910), p.139.
   [46] Annabel Patterson, *Censorship and Interpretation: The Conditions of
Writing and Reading in Early Modern England* (Madison: Univ. of Wisconsin
Press, 1984), p.103.
   [47] As Carey (p.33) points out, however, Donne's account of natural law in
Biathanatos, written two years before *Pseudo-Martyr*, does differ significantly
from his treatment of natural law in the later treatise.
   [48] Donne, *Sermons*, VIII,110-129. The Prebend sermon accords the King
even greater spiritual jurisdiction than does *Pseudo-Martyr*. Donne claims that
God empowers the Prince not only to legislate the religion of his own country,
but to exert any influence within his means on the religious policy of other
kingdoms. For more on royal control of religion, see *Sermons*, VI, 245 amd VI,
269.

consequences of an act in order to establish its legality in a specific case. Donne's private assessment that "both sides may be in justice, and innocence" in the Oath of Allegiance controversy makes his reliance on casuistry all the more understandable. Practical theology gives Donne's arguments in *Pseudo-Martyr* a broader causality than the occasion of the Oath or the author's need for advancement. Reaching beyond the moment of perplexity, Donne teaches by example methods of interpreting and applying any law according to the principles of case divinity.

The Politics of Casuistry in the Sermon on Esther

The sermon on *Esther* 4.16 is a model of casuistical organization and method. It follows the deliberative structure that moral theologians recommend: after delineating Esther's conflicts and establishing that hers is a case of perplexity, Donne examines first the general laws relevant to the case, then the circumstances peculiar to Esther's dilemma, and finally her contingent resolution, which serves as a guide for analogous cases. The sermon is less concerned with Esther's final decision than with her method of evaluation. Indeed, Donne never mentions the outcome of her resolution. He merely conjectures the probable success that her process of reasoning should achieve. As in *Biathanatos* and *Pseudo-Martyr*, he attempts to teach by example the procedures of moral deliberation and to demonstrate the practical value of casuistry in determining right action.

Conflicting allegiances precipitate Esther's case of conscience. The Jewish Queen of Persia learns of a pogrom that Haman plans against all Persian Jews. To prevent the attack on her nation and on God's honor, Esther must enlist her husband's support, but the King has decreed that no one, on pain of death, may address him without a summons. Positive law, the divine authority of kings, and the natural law of self-preservation militate against Esther's appeal. Against these claims, she weighs her duty to God, to her people, and to her own safety, which Haman's plot endangers. The Biblical text of Donne's sermon recounts her decision to disregard the King's decree, and her provision for the appeal. She orders that all the Jews of the city assemble, fast, and pray for her success.

> Go and assemble all the Jews that are found in Shushan, and fast ye for me, and eat not, nor drink in three days, day nor night: I also, and my maids will fast likewise; and so I will go in to the King, which is not according to the law: and if I perish, I perish.[49]

Caught among mutually hostile laws and owing divided allegiances to civil

---

[49] *Sermons*, V, 216. Subsequent page references to the sermon will appear in the text.

and religious authorities, Esther posed a familiar case of conscience for Donne's contemporaries. The sermon does not risk drawing a close analogy between the politics of her position and that of modern audiences, however; rather than make what would appear to be an overtly subversive connection between Esther's decision to resist the King's decree and the response of James' subjects to similar conflicts of allegiance, Donne insists that it is the process of judging—not the judgment itself—that his congregation should apply to their lives. His focus is on the Queen's casuistical reasoning as exemplary for all perplexed consciences. He states that the purpose of his sermon is to consider what methods of deliberation one can learn from

> this Heroical Woman, *Esther*; what she did in a perplexed and scrupulous case, when an evident danger appeared, and an evident Law was against her action; and from thence consider, what every Christian Soul ought to do, when it is surprised and overtaken with any such scruples or difficulties to the Conscience. (p. 217)

Esther is anyone, then, caught between conflicting laws, and it is casuistry that resolves her conscience and determines her action.

Having reviewed the laws at issue, Donne describes Esther's impartial evaluation of her problem. "She puts off all Passion, and all particular respects," thus grounding her decision in reason rather than sentiment or expedience (p. 217). She marshals all the facts of her case, and debates them "in a rectified and well informed Conscience." She confers with Mordecai, not for answers, but for the opinion of a virtuous man, and she measures her judgments by God's dictates. Concluding that her petition to the King is a greater responsibility,

> she neglects both that particular Law. . .and that general Law, that every Man is bound to preserve himself; and she exposes her self to an imminent, and (for any thing she knew) an unescapable death: *If I perish, I perish.* (p. 217)

Esther's disregard of positive and natural laws is justifiable only after reason and conscience persuade her that the circumstances are exceptional.

In the "divisio" of his sermon, Donne proposes to examine Esther's action in two parts: her preparation and her resolution. Each stage of her preparation generates additional cases of conscience. The first act, gathering together all Jews of the city, does not have the authorization of the State, and therefore its legality is questionable. Donne treats the problem as a case of doubt. Unlike the perplexity of Esther's appeal, no conflict of laws is involved; instead, the question is whether rules against assembly are applicable to the circumstances. To determine the moral status of the act, Donne considers the intention of legislators who forbid private convening of crowds. As casuists recommend, he compares the law's purpose with Esther's own intentions, and with the consequences of her action. Generally,

Donne concedes, prohibitions against assembly are both necessary and just. Mobs endanger the State, and whoever gathers a crowd is culpable for its disorder.

> How good soever their pretence (and perchance purpose) be, that assemble people, and discontent them, the bridle, the stern, is no longer in their hands; but there arise unexpected storms, of which, if they were not authors in their purpose, yet they are the occasioners. (p. 220)

Donne argues, however, that Esther's assembly poses no threat to the State. Rather than "discontent" the crowd, the Queen offers them hope for their safety, and orders them to humble themselves with prayers and fasting. Her action averts their despair, as well as the violence that might attend it. Consequently, she does not transgress the legislator's intention.

Donne is particularly sensitive to the religious nature of Esther's assembly. The situation would undoubtedly have reminded his congregation of contemporary laws against Catholics gathering for Mass. In what appears at first glance to be a seditious use of casuistry, Donne defends illegal worship. Unjust laws against religion, he asserts, may be broken in good conscience.[50] "In times of persecution, when no exercise of true Religion is admitted, these private Meetings may not be denied to be lawful" (p. 218). Donne defends his claim by citing an analogous case that has the support of jurists and theologians: [51]

> As for bodily sustenance, if a man could not otherwise avoid starving, the Schoolemen, and the Casuists, resolve truly, That it were no sin to steal so much meat as would preserve life; so, those souls, which without that, must necessarily starve, may steal their Spiritual food in corners, and private meetings. (p. 218)

Like most casuists, both Catholic and Protestant, Donne endorses a hierarchy of laws in which self preservation "defeats all magistry." It is lawful to steal nourishment, whether physical or spiritual, rather than starve to death.

Given the government's view of recusants, and the increasing friction between Anglicans and Puritans, Donne's statement seems imprudent, if not radical. However, like all casuists, Donne is careful to explain that his assertion is contingent upon extenuating circumstances. The exceptions with which he qualifies his statement indicate his moderate Anglican position:

> But if we will steal either of these foods, Temporal or Spiritual, because that meat which we may have, is not so dressed, so dished, so sauced, so

---

[50]   Donne's definition of unjust laws is consonant with the teaching of practical theology: "Laws against God, Laws beyond the power of him that pretends to make them, are no Laws" (p.225). For Aquinas' distinctions between binding and non-binding laws, see *Summa Theologica*, II. 96. 4.

[51]   The *Essays in Divinity* (p.68) and *Biathanatos* (p.73) make the same casuistical defense of stealing food in cases of extreme necessity.

served in, as we would have it; but accompanied with some other ceremonies then are agreeable to our taste; This is an inexcusable Theft, and
these are pernicious Conventicles. (p.218) [52]

Superficial objections to religious control (objections that Donne describes
as epicurean rather than reasonable) do not warrant disregard of the law.

In the second stage of her preparation for the appeal, Esther joins the
Jews in fasting. Once again, Donne evaluates her action in terms of casuistical principles. Indeed, his analysis is remarkably similar to Perkins' case
of conscience entitled, "How a religious Fast is to be observed?" Both
Donne and Perkins insist that fasting is an indifferent act; that is, one's intention determines whether it is constructive or misguided: "Fast with a
holy purpose; and it is a holy action" (p. 221). The proper aims of fasting
are humiliation, repentance, and prayer. Those who attempt to bargain with
God, "to satisfie his justice for sinne," are simply arrogant.[53] As Perkins
observes, fasting cannot buy merit; it "is a thing indifferent, neither good
nor evil. For though it be referred to a religious end, which is the humbling
of the soule; yet it is not good in it selfe, but onely in regard of the end."[54]
And Donne concurs: "Though fasting be not a vertue, yet it is the way to
vertue. . .look for no particular reward of it, and God shall give you a
benefit by it in the whole course of your lives" (p. 221). Because Esther's
intention is to chasten herself and her people so that their prayers will be
more acceptable to God, Donne concludes that her fast is not in error. His
discussion of Esther's preparation begins and ends with the casuistical dictum that rectitude depends not on predetermined rules of behavior, but on
the circumstances, intention, and consequences of an act.

The second half of Donne's sermon addresses Esther's resolution to disregard both positive and natural laws. Again observing the casuistical
movement from general principles to the particular case, Donne begins with
a strong affirmation of the sanctity of human laws. As in *Pseudo-Martyr*, he
asserts that kings are God's representatives; therefore, to violate their ordi-
nances is to commit sacrilege. Insofar as positive laws partake of divinity,

---

[52]   One of the reasons religious dissent was considered "pernicious," of
course, was its implications for civil disorder: "'Those which now impugn the
ecclesiastical jurisdiction [will] endeavour also to impair the temporal and to
bring even kings and princes under their censure,' Whitgift warned Queen
Elizabeth. James I summed up the anxiety: No Bishop, no King.' He feared that
if people were allowed their preferred modes of religious organization, 'Jack and
Tom, and Will and Dick, shall meet and at their pleasure censure me and my
Council and all our proceedings.'" Quoted in Alan Sinfield, *Faultlines: Cultural
Materialism and the Politics of Dissident Reading* (Berkeley: Univ. of California
Press, 1992), p.166.

[53]   William Perkins, *The Whole Treatise of Cases of Conscience*, ed. Thomas
Merrill (Nieuwkoop: B. De Graaf, 1966), p.157.

[54]   Perkins, *Whole Treatise*, p.157.

they bind the conscience. It is universally admitted, Donne maintains, that "There is in every Humane Law, part of the Law of God, which is obedience to the Superior. . .He that resists his [God's] Commission, his Lieutenancy, his Authority, in Lawmakers appointed by him resists himself" (p. 225). However, authority is hierarchical, and not all laws are equally binding. When two commands conflict, "That Law which comes from the superior Magistrate, and is in the nature of the thing commanded, highest too, that Law must prevail" (p. 226). The problem, of course, is how to determine whether "the nature of the thing commanded" is more or less imperative. But Donne's discussion of religious assembly has already taught that one should measure one's actions by the intention of the law. He applies the now familiar casuistical principle to Esther's resolution.

The purpose of the King's "retiredness, and denying of ordinary access to his person" is simply "to augment his greatness and Majesty" (p. 226). Against this "new law" is "the fix'd and permanent Law, of promoting God's glory," which Esther would transgress if she did not try to prevent the massacre of His chosen people. Since reason and conscience convince the Queen that her greater duty is to God, obeying positive law in her case would be a sin.[55] That is not to say, however, that Esther's perplexity forces her to commit sacrilege by breaking the King's rule. According to practical theology, the lesser of two conflicting laws ceases to exert its claim, so the Queen may approach her husband with impunity.[56] Donne adds that the probability of the King's clemency strengthens Esther's resolve. Although she is willing to risk death for her petition, she knows that the situation is exceptional, "and that no exception was likelier then this, That the King for all his majestical reservedness, would be content to receive information of such a dishonor done to his Queen, and to her God; she might justly think that the Law, intended onely for the King's ease, or his state, reached not to her person, who was his wife, nor to her case, which was the destruction of all that professed her Religion" (p. 227). Without knowing certainly that the king will pardon her intrusion, Esther reasons

---

[55] It is a commonplace of practical divinity that the authorization of conscience is greater than any law (natural, civil, or canon) to the contrary. As the preceding chapter notes, Donne's support of this assumption in "Satyre III" is echoed in Ames's observation that conscience "is immediately subject to God, and his will, and therefore it cannot submit it selfe unto any creature without Idolatry" (*Conscience With the Power*, Bk. I, p.6). Thus, Esther's primary responsibility is to her conscience; Donne remarks in *Sermons* III, 359: "he that sinnes against his Conscience. . .cannot be pardoned."

[56] "The precepts of God never do so jar of their nature, that it is necessary to break one of them by sin: for when a less commandment is neglected that a greater may be observed, that less commandment does cease for a while to bind, so that they who upon such an occasion neglect it are altogether blameless, that is, sin not." Ames, *Conscience With the Power*, Book 3, p.87.

that the probability is great and that, indeed, the King will want to know about Haman's threatened violence.

Esther's comment, "If I perish, I perish," introduces the sermon's final case of conscience. Donne remarks that self-preservation is a moral duty, but as in *Biathanatos*, he argues that extenuating circumstances may release one from natural law. He lists several examples of self-sacrifice that "the general stream of Casuists" condones, and he explains why Esther's risk is justifiable. One may not hazard death for dignity or reputation, "But that provident and religious Soul, which proceeds in all her enterprises as *Esther* did in her preparations. . .may also come to *Esther's* resolution, to go in to the King, though it be not according to the Law" (p. 229). Donne's emphasis here and throughout the sermon is on the process of Esther's deliberation. Her systematic observance of casuistical methods and safeguards enables her to assess the laws of her case, and gives her a probable assurance of dispensation:

> When she proceeded not upon any precipitation, upon any singular or seditious spirit, when she debated the matter temperately with a dispassioned man, . . .she was then come to that, which onely can excuse and justifie the breaking of any Law, that is, a probable, if not a certain assurance, contracted *Bona fide*, in a rectified conscience, That if this present case, which makes us break this Law, had been known and considered when the Law was made, he that made the Law would have made provision for this case. (p.226)

Like Aristotle and Aquinas in their discussions of equity, and like all casuists in their justification of acting "beside the law," Esther considers that, if the lawmaker had known of the present circumstances when formulating the law, he would have allowed for their exemption.

The sermon ends with the universal relevance of Esther's problem. Donne reiterates that the methods of case divinity exemplified in the Queen's decision are applicable to any doubtful or perplexed circumstances. By dividing Esther's actions into several cases, he has elucidated for his audience the categories and assumptions of practical divinity, and he encourages the congregation to cultivate casuistical habits of mind so that they will be prepared to adjudicate their own cases of conscience. Casuistry teaches not only one's legitimate relation to specific laws, but also the practical application of Christianity to all experience. Donne remarks that the greatest instance of casuistry is the New Testament dispensation. By the old law, humans were eternally damned, but Christ, incarnating God's mercy, became the exceptional circumstance that altered the law against humanity. Even God's decrees, then, admit exceptions: "that Law of denying sinners access, and turning his face from them, is not a perpetual, not an irrevocable

Law" (p. 229).[57] Consequently, Donne concludes, if we imitate Esther, if we learn from casuistry how to direct our actions, fortify our conscience, reform our reason, temper our emotion, and rectify our lives, we may believe that we are exceptions to the general law of damnation.

Thus, casuistry affords hope for salvation as well as resolutions of immediate dilemmas. The Esther sermon, *Biathanatos*, and *Pseudo-Martyr* all treat practical theology not merely as a legal resource, but as a "modus vivendi." Although cases of conscience are always occasional, their objectives extend beyond the moment of doubt or perplexity to the interpretation and application of Christian principles in all actions. With the guidance of reason, conscience, and Scripture, casuistry enables one to order experience despite diffidence about reason's ability to perceive absolute truth. Practical theology cannot eradicate the epistemological problems raised in Donne's *Essays* and *Paradoxes and Problems*, just as a judicatory cannot eradicate crime; uncertainty and reprobation are, especially for Reformed casuists, givens of humanity. But practical theology can mitigate one's anxiety about justifiable action by mediating between apparently conflicting truths. Casuistry implements moral law, and casuistical habits of mind direct one in the ways of salvation.[58]

In my introduction to chapter one, I suggested that studying Donne's prose within the context of case divinity reveals a theoretical and methodological continuity in the author's career. More specifically, such a study discloses Donne's enduring identification with Protestant casuistry. From his forcing us to evaluate received opinion in the *Paradoxes and Problems* to his criticism of dependence on others' judgments in *Biathanatos* and *Pseudo-Martyr*, Donne allies himself with the Protestant notion that each person is

---

[57] In his first sermon preached to King Charles (1625), Donne reiterates that God's laws are not unyielding: "*God* would not bee beleeved, in denouncing of Judgements, so absolutely, so peremptorily, as to bee thought to speake unconditionally, illimitedly. . ." (*Sermons*, VI, 260). My reading of casuistical principles in Donne's sermons is indebted to Jeanne M. Shami's work on related issues: "Donne on Discretion," *ELH* 47 (1980), pp.49-66 and "Donne's Protestant Casuistry: Cases of Conscience in the Sermons," *Studies in Philology* LXX (1983), pp.53-66.

[58] Renaissance casuists share Donne's conviction that, properly employed, practical theology can be a vehicle of salvation. Robert Sanderson, for example, writes: "When all is done, positive and practique Divinity is it must bring us to Heaven: that is it must poise our judgments, settle our consciences, direct our lives, mortify our corruptions, increase our graces, strengthen our comforts, save our souls." *Works*, ed. William Jacobson (Oxford: UP, 1854), II, 105.

responsible for making his or her own moral decisions. Dispassioned counsel from someone outside a case can be valuable, but it has less authority than one's own conscience, and it should be only one of many factors that effect judgment. The counsel of practical theologians is no exception. Even in the exhortatory *Pseudo-Martyr*, Donne's relation to his audience is advisory rather than prescriptive. His object in all the cases is to teach by example the methods of casuistical evaluation, not to dictate specific actions. Throughout the prose works discussed above, Donne's point of departure is the casuistical principle that circumstances determine our relation to any law. As the following chapter will argue, the same principle, resonant with epistemological and ethical complications, is operative in the *Songs and Sonets*.

CHAPTER FOUR

"IN THAT THE WORLD'S CONTRACTED THUS": CASUISTRY AND BEYOND IN THE *SONGS AND SONETS*

Unlike most of Donne's prose works, his lyrics play with and exploit the assumptions of case divinity, posing casuistical problems and then abusing the latitude afforded to individual judgment. The same problems of reason and law that necessitate practical theology necessitate many of Donne's arguments in both prose and verse, but while the prose invites close comparison to the methods of casuistry, the poems often adapt rather than adopt casuistical formulae. This chapter considers Donne's casuistical response to problems of action, interpretation, definition, and authority in the *Songs and Sonets*. The study begins with brief discussions of poems that share methodological or interpretive concerns with practical theology, but that are not fully integrated cases of conscience. Even when Donne does not structure his arguments precisely according to case divinity, he addresses the same questions of authority and judgment, impermanence and uncertainty, private and public responsibilities that casuists address. The remainder of the chapter includes close readings of several poems that assert the relativity of law and that invoke principles of case divinity in order to justify an anomalous course of action. Like Dwight Cathcart, I suggest that Donne's speaker assumes the role of casuist when confronted with the conventional objections of his interlocutor or reader. But unlike Cathcart, I argue that casuistical efforts to resolve legal and moral conflicts in the lyrics are finally unsuccessful. The speaker fails to relieve tensions among opposing points of view, because he forces practical theology beyond its conditional limits. He claims for himself an absolute authority that casuistry is unable to accommodate.

For example, in "A Valediction forbidding mourning," "The Canonization," and "The Sunne Rising," the speaker sets up his defense in casuistical terms— i.e., his circumstances are extenuating or involve conflicting laws that require special consideration—and he argues that the conventions by which his audience determines right action are merely relative. His primary concerns are to vindicate his motives and to define the exceptional status of his situation so that he may claim a casuistical dispensation. Donne's persona must contend not only with customary determinations against his position, but also with the linguistic and epistemological problems of advancing his own criteria for action. Once he secures a hearing for his case by asserting the conditional nature of law and ethics, however, he has no absolute standard with which to justify his position. The same principle that validates his exceptional claims potentially threatens them: that is, altered or exceptional circumstances may in turn nullify his dispensation. Because his frame of reference is not Scriptural, the speaker cannot achieve the certain authorization towards which he strains. Faith in God's directive truth alleviates the tensions that conflicting laws generate in moral theology; casuists can measure their judgments against an absolute ethic. But Donne's speaker refers right action to fallible reason and secular criteria. His authority is of his own construction— whether it is sophistic logic or exceptional love— and therefore is as subject to defects and omissions as any other human authority. Given his casuistical premise about the inadequacy of culturally constructed laws and conventions, his arguments are ultimately unresolved because he cannot establish that his position is more probable than that of his audience without measuring both against certain truth.

In all three poems mentioned above, the speaker tries to authorize his claims by substituting love for religion as the measure of truth. He and his lover will be canonized as love's saints; unlike the "sublunary" affections of the "laity," their union is eternal, perfect, transcendent. And yet the love that Donne's persona exalts is by nature fallible; its source is human, and therefore the speaker judges his case by a flawed standard. Exchanging a Scriptural rule of faith for an amatory one, he argues from uncertain premises. Moreover, he is aware of his tenuous grounds: at the heart of the speaker's protestations that his love is absolute is the perceived threat of alteration. Critics have often noted Donne's preoccupation with impermanence and infidelity, just as they have noted the poet's rendering of sexual love in sacred terms. But few readers have examined the tensions that result when the speaker's efforts to invest love with religious authority are undercut by his sense that fallen love is mutable. Donne's persona embraces casuists' belief in the contingency of right action because it affords him the opportunity to challenge convention; but he substitutes love for the casuistical standard of judgment, and is unwilling to accept the conditional nature of his criterion. When he claims more than the provisional authority that casuistry enables, he compounds the tensions that precipitate his argument.

The tensions in case divinity result not only from the initial problem of judgment, but also from the disjunction between law and atypical circumstances of the individual. Such tension manifests itself in the syntactical and logical complexity of cases of conscience, as their authors define and argue towards the recommended action. Likewise, as Donne's speaker attempts to defend his unconventional or illegal point of view, a similar tension is evident in his irregular metrics ("She'is all States, and all Princes, I,/ Nothing else is"), paradox ("Our two soules therefore, which are one"), hyperbole ("Princes doe but play us; compar'd to this,/All honor's mimique; All wealth alchimie"), and dramatic argumentation ("For Godsake hold your tongue, and let me love").[1] As is true in cases of conscience, the speaker's style reflects the strain of his anomalous stance. I suggest, then, that Donne's adaptation of casuistical paradigms in a number of the *Songs and Sonets* informs the modes of expression and the argumentative evolution of his poems. But in claiming that the verse is casuistical, I do not mean to imply conversely that cases of conscience are "metaphysical," although they do have logical and rhetorical traits in common with Donne's poetry. The unorthodox demands that Donne makes on practical theology—his founding judgments on secular rather than Scriptural criteria, and his efforts to draw unconditional conclusions from its conditional sanctions—distinguish his verse from orthodox cases of conscience.

In addition, I do not want to assert the influence of practical divinity in the *Songs and Sonets* to the exclusion of other traditions. Lovers who are "Inter-assured of the mind" are casuistically exempt from conventional responses to separation, but they are also Neoplatonic lovers. Indeed, their participation in the Ideal is what makes them exceptional. As critics have shown, Petrarchism, Ramism, and rhetorical humanism, to name only a few traditions, inform the argument of Donne's lyrics.[2] Judith Scherer Herz has wisely admonished against "readings that seek to explain the poems by importing full-scale ideological systems that often ignore the individual poem in the interest of the comprehensive theory." [3] What I propose is not a totalizing approach to the *Songs and Sonets*. My focus on the poems is necessarily limited, but if my reading is born out, casuistry proves yet another facet of the richness and complexity of Donne's verse.

---

1   John Carey, *John Donne: Life, Mind and Art* (London: Faber and Faber, 1981), p.191, astutely notes that the threat of change and the instability of contradictions pressurize Donne's verse: "Donne's rhythms give a sense of metrical norms being underscored or overridden, in order to cope with the stresses of the instant. A similar adjustment to the exigencies of circumstance is suggested by his multiple stanza forms— he uses forty-six different forms in all, and only two of them more than once. Every endeavor required a new shape."

2   See, respectively: Donald Guss, *John Donne: Petrarchist* (Detroit: Wayne State UP, 1966; Rosemond Tuve, *Elizabethan and Metaphysical Imagery* (Chicago: UP, 1972); Thomas O. Sloane, *Donne, Milton, and the End of Humanist Rhetoric* (Berkeley: Univ. of California Press, 1985).

3   Judith Scherer Herz, "'An excellent Exercise of Wit That Speaks So Well of Ill': Donne and the Poetics of Concealment" in *The Eagle and the Dove: Reassessing John Donne*, eds. Claude J. Summers and Ted-Larry Pebworth (Columbia, Missouri: Univ. of Missouri Press, 1986), p. 5.

"So incorporated into the body of the world":
Donne's Casuistry and the Lover's Constructed Self

Case divinity was peculiarly suited to two conflicting impulses in Donne. On one hand, the poet felt a powerful need to belong, to participate in a community of shared values and endeavors. On the other hand, he insisted on his exceptionality to the rule, on his uniqueness and separation from common assumptions. As David Norbrook observes, "He constantly seeks to put his feet down on the ground, to become part of a society from which he feels alienated. And yet he desires also to maintain a critical distance, a standpoint outside the existing social order from which he can criticize it."[4] Donne's use of the phoenix image in two poems exemplifies his ambivalence. The speaker of *The First Anniversary* laments that individualism has fractured the world. Traditional structures of order and authority are

> ...all in pieces, all cohaerence gone;
> All just supply, and all Relation:
> Prince, Subject, Father, Sonne, are things forgot,
> For every man alone thinkes he hath got
> To be a Phoenix, and that there can bee
> None of that kinde, of which he is, but hee.   (ll.213-218)

To assert one's uniqueness is to undermine social coherence.

And yet the same assertion is used to justify eschewing the world in "The Canonization." The latter poem advances love above mundane achievements and argues that one of love's virtues is its unique autonomy. "The Phoenix ridle hath more wit/ By us, we two being one, are it." The phoenix, an emblem of self-perpetuity, and the speaker's exceptional love are both their own "just supply." Implicit in the poem's defense of separation from the world is the very claim that fractures social unity in *The First Anniversary*; the speaker wants to assert that "there can bee/ None of that kinde, of which he is, but hee." Donne's desire for integration and his defense of particularity were both fundamental to his contradictory self-construction. This section suggests that the two conflicting impulses found a sympathetic hearing in casuistry.

In 1608, Donne wrote to Goodyer that the highest titles and distinctions are meaningless unless those who hold them "be so incorporated into the body of the world, that they contribute something to the sustentation of the whole."[5] Donne himself sought such an incorporation into the body of

---

[4]   David Norbrook, "The Monarchy of Wit and the Republic of Letters: Donne's Politics" in *Soliciting Interpretation: Literary Theory and Seventeenth-Century English Poetry*, eds. Elizabeth D. Harvey and Katharine Eisaman Maus (Chicago: UP, 1990), p. 6.

[5]   John Donne, *Letters to Severall Persons of Honour*, ed. Charles Edmund

the world. For fourteen years after his secret marriage to Ann More, however, his efforts to secure employment and to take an active part in society were unavailing. "I would fain do something," he confides in Goodyer; "to this hour I am nothing, or so little, that I am scarce subject and argument good enough for one of my own letters." [6] The nothingness that comes of isolation echoes through Donne's letters and sermons. Again in 1608 he wrote, "to be no part of any body is to be nothing." And in a sermon preached at Paul's Cross, he warns, "he that will be *nothing* in this world, shall be nothing in the next." Assimilation into society was not simply a financial necessity for Donne. It was a spiritual obligation with eternal consequences. Those who refuse to participate in the community violate both social and divine order: "idle and unprofitable persons; persons of no use to the Church or to the State," Donne observed in 1626, disrupt "the order that God hath established in this world." [7]

Although Donne believed that pursuing a vocation was a moral duty,[8] his need to be part of the social order was not limited to employment. John Carey argues that Donne's apostasy produced a life-long sense of dislocation, and David Chanoff suggests that Donne strongly missed the universal range of vision and communion that the Catholic Church had offered him.[9] Certainly, Donne's efforts to unify opposites in his poetry and prose reflect a preoccupation with conjunction; critics have often remarked

---

Merrill (New York: Sturgis and Walton, 1910), p.44.

[6] *Letters*, p.44. In the years between his marriage in 1601 and his ordination in 1615, Donne did have one opportunity to enter public life. Sir Edward Phelips, Master of the Rolls, secured for Donne a parliamentary seat from Taunton in 1614. However, the position proved to be both disappointing and disconcerting. Embroiled in controversy over parliamentary privileges, monopolies and impositions, the "Addled Parliament" had the distinction of being the first in history to pass no legislation. In addition, Commons fiercely criticized James' Scottish favorites, Lord Hay and Somerset, whom Donne had sought as benefactors, and whom he could not afford to offend. After three months of wrangling among Commons, Lords, and King, James imprisoned four MPs and dissolved both Parliament and Donne's hopes for political advancement. For more on Donne's futile months as an MP, see R. C. Bald, *John Donne: A Life* (Oxford: UP, 1970), pp.284-9.

[7] John Donne, *Sermons*, ed. George R. Potter and Evelyn Simpson (Berkeley: Univ. of California Press, 1953-62), VII, 149. In a letter written to Goodyer c.1610, Donne describes himself as "rather a sicknesse and disease of the world then any part of it" (*Letters*, p.51).

[8] See *Sermons*, VII, 149: "every man should embrace a Calling, and walk therein; they who do not so, pervert God's order."

[9] David Chanoff, "Donne's Anglicanism," *Recusant History*, 15 (1980), p.163: "He was separated from Catholicism, but the Catholic commitment to order, authority and corporate worship was part of his soul. . . Donne struggl[ed] to place himself, and especially his religious experience, within a social milieu."

on his "yoking" east and west, body and soul, sacred and profane. The same
drive towards conjunction is evident in his claim that two lovers become
one entity. In "The Dissolution," "Song: Sweetest Love," "The Extasie,"
"Loves infinitenesse," and "The good-morrow" (among others), the speaker
asserts that he and his lover are both physically and spiritually integrated.
The poems describe love as an absolute belonging, an "equall communion
and Identity" that anticipates Donne's portrayal of beatitude; in a sermon
preached near the end of his life, Donne envisioned that in Heaven

> there shall be no Cloud nor Sun, no darkenesse nor dazling, but one equall
> light, no noyse nor silence, but one equall musick, no fears nor hopes, but
> one equall possession, no foes nor friends, but one equall communion and
> Identity, no ends nor beginnings, but one equall eternity.[10]

Like love, which is "mixt equally" in "The good-morrow," and "so alike,
that none doe slacken, none can die," Heaven resolves difference and disjunction.[11] For Donne, communion was blessedness.

And yet at times, Donne resists belonging to the collective order. His
Songs and Sonets often pit the speaker against the rest of society. In "The
Anniversarie," for example, Donne's persona insists that he and his lover
are independent from "All other things." Their love, defined against the cor-
ruptible world, is uniquely unalterable, uniquely blessed. A supernatural
union exempts them from the forces of time, change, and decay that prey in
nature. Theirs is a spiritual entitlement that only Heaven can match: "Here
upon earth, we'are Kings, and none but wee/ Can be such Kings." Even the
slight qualification, "Here upon earth," disturbs Donne's emphatic speaker,
who in three stanzas uses the absolute "all" six times (recalling the equally
insistent "nothingness" of Donne's self-description in his letters). He seems
to regret that in Heaven they will no longer be unique:

> And then wee shall be throughly blest,
> But wee no more, then all the rest.
> Here upon earth, we'are Kings, and none but wee
> Can be such Kings, nor of such subjects bee.   (ll. 21-24)

It is only in contradistinction to the rest of the world that the speaker finds
the greatest value. Only as an exception does he find his fullest self expression.[12]

---

[10] *Sermons*, VIII, 191.

[11] Or so Donne's speaker would like to believe of love. As I argue later, the
claims of invulnerable mutuality that the speaker makes for himself and his
beloved are often undercut by his anxieties about impermanence, uncertainty,
and the pressures that the outside world exerts. Love's "one equall communion
and identity," however, are no less ideals for being unattained in the poems.

[12] For a related discussion of Donne's "anti-worlds," see David Aers and
Gunther Kress, "Vexatious Contraries: A Reading of Donne's Poetry," in

But his exceptionality is inevitably expressed in terms of the orthodoxies that he claims to resist. A number of the *Songs and Sonets* defend the lovers' entitlement— their legitimacy and jurisdiction— by way of comparison with absolutist images and hierarchical principles that the speaker disingenuously disparages ("Princes do but play us"). Even as Donne's persona insists on his singularity, we recognize what Stephen Greenblatt discovers in the course of writing *Renaissance Self-Fashioning*:

> no moments of pure, unfettered subjectivity; indeed the human subject itself began to seem remarkably unfree, the ideological product of the relations of power in a particular society. Whenever I focused sharply upon a moment of apparently autonomous self-fashioning, I found not an epiphany of identity freely chosen but a cultural artifact. If there remained traces of free choice, the choice was among possibilities whose range was strictly delineated by the social and ideological system in force.

The speaker's straining towards autonomy is always itself constrained by the values and discourses against which he tries to distinguish himself.[13]

Donne's desire for social integration and his insistence on singularity seem to pose an irreconcilable paradox. But casuistry offers a practical response to the two impulses. Itself an exercise in paradox,[14] casuistry seeks a morally acceptable relation between the unique individual and the community's norms. It recognizes the need for collective order and shared standards of conduct, and at the same time, it accommodates legal and ethical judgments to the exception. (Recall Perkins' description of practical theologians as "Embassadours of reconciliation.") With a casuistical dispensation, the individual perpetuates culturally established principles of justice from which the community derives order and authority, while simultaneously securing for herself exemption from the letter of the law. For instance, Esther's resolve to petition the King was in disregard of positive law, but paradoxically, her decision was a just one. Seemingly subversive, her noncompliance was casuistically sanctioned. The same principles of reason and rectitude that legitimate social authority empowered Esther's action. In the largest sense, then, she participated in the social order. Uniting equity and

---

Literature, Language, and Society in England, 1580-1680 (Dublin: Gill and Macmillan, 1981), p. 57.

[13] Stephen Greenblatt, *Renaissance Self-Fashioning* (Chicago: UP, 1980), p. 256. See also Jonathan Goldberg, *James I and the Politics of Literature: Jonson, Shakespeare, Donne, and Their Contemporaries* (Baltimore: Johns Hopkins Press, 1983), pp. 111-112.

[14] As Dwight Cathcart observes (*Doubting Conscience* [Ann Arbor: Univ. of Michigan Press, 1975], p.35), casuistical decisions are often paradoxical, in that they "justify committing an act that in other circumstances has been known to be a sin." Given Donne's penchant for welding contradictions, it is not surprising that he was drawn to a process of inquiry that legitimates paradoxical reasoning.

law, practical theology provides a means of addressing conflicts between public and private claims—conflicts that recur in Donne's poetry and in his fractured self-construction.

But how does case divinity satisfy Donne's impulse to "be so incorporated into the body of the world, that he contributes to the sustentation of the whole"? The aim of casuistry is not simply to rescue the individual from unfair constraints of the law. Certainly, the individual benefits from equitable dispensations, but the community also benefits in that moral law is refined and enlarged for future reference: resolutions of cases become precedents for analogous dilemmas. Camille Slights rightly observes that "While professing the uniqueness of each case, the casuist must also try to create a model resolution that will apply to the problems of many men. [Casuists] attempt to universalize while preaching particularity. . . ." [15] In defending the individual, they also provide direction and instruction for others. Donne was drawn to this dual design of casuistry, partly because it allows the individual a politically acceptable alliance with the community, but primarily because it endows the individual with authority by making him or her a standard for subsequent cases. A number of Donne's personae seek such an authority. The most notable examples are in "The Sunne Rising" and "The Canonization," which are examined in casuistical terms later in this chapter. But even in poems that are not casuistically motivated— "Twicknam garden" and "Valediction of the booke," for instance— the amatory speakers present themselves as models of instruction and standards of judgment for other lovers. In their role as paradigms, they "contribute something to the sustentation of the whole."

In "Twicknam garden," Donne's unrequited persona finds no correspondence— either in women or nature— between outward signs and internal states. He laments that it is impossible to determine a woman's truth by her appearance or behavior:

> Alas, hearts do not in eyes shine,
> Nor can you more judge womans thoughts by teares,
> Then by her shadow, what she weares.   (ll.23-25)

The speaker claims that, unlike women's tears, his are genuinely expressive of love, and so he offers them as a touchstone for others, as a standard for measuring interiority.

> Hither with christall vyals, lovers come,
> And take my teares, which are loves wine,
> And try your mistresse Teares at home,
> For all are false, that tast not just like mine.   (ll.19-22)

---

[15]   Camille Wells Slights, *The Casuistical Tradition in Shakespeare, Donne, Herbert and Milton* (Princeton: Univ. Press, 1981), p.63.

Twicknam garden is "True Paradise" lost (1.9), but the speaker's eucharistic tears will restore truth to a world of uncertainty and deception. Donne's religious diction lends his persona a divine authority that flirts with impiety. He depicts his passion— like Christ's suffering— as a testimony of love and truth. Line 22 is reminiscent of Christ's cry in *Lamentations* 1.12: "Behold and see if there were any sorrow, any tears like mine." Donne's hyperbolic speaker presents himself as a standard of judgment that benefits mankind, if not womankind. Despite his Messianic pretenses, however, the speaker is fallen ("I have the serpent brought") and mortal ("her truth kills mee"). Like any authority other than Scripture, his is transitory.

Donne's persona in "Valediction of the booke" claims a more enduring authority. He proposes that in his absence, his lover should write a history of their love, a kind of Scripture that will serve as a model for posterity. Compiled from "our manuscripts, those Myriades/ Of letters, which have past twixt thee and mee," the book will contain all love's learning. It will be a definitive reference:

> Thence write our Annals, and in them will bee
> To all whom loves subliming fire invades,
> Rule and example found.   (ll.12-14)

The book described is very like a collection of cases of conscience. A compendium of general principles and illustrative examples, it will include cases on the religious, legal, and political ramifications of love. More specifically, the book has traits in common with Catholic cases. Written "In cypher. . .or new made Idiome" (1.21) rather than in the vernacular, it will be mediated by the ordained: "Wee for loves clergie only'are instruments" (1.22). In the hands of the laity—the lawyers and politicians of stanzas 5 and 6—the book will suffer the same misinterpretation and misapplication that Catholic casuists feared their cases would suffer if they were made available to the public.[16] The speaker predicts that the laity will abuse the lovers' Scripture, reading their own experiences into the book and rationalizing their own dubious practices. "In this thy booke, such will their nothing see,/ As in the Bible some can finde out Alchimy" (ll.53-4). That is, lawyers and politicians will infer principles that are not in the "Annals," just as alchemists erroneously identify their science in Scripture. Like any collection of cases, the book will be subject to misapplication, but it will nevertheless endure as a standard for love's clergy; "as long-liv'd as the elements," it will preserve love's learning for the initiated. Above all, the book establishes the speaker and his lover as paradigms, as "rule and example"; it universalizes their particular experience, and provides direction and

---

16   See John T. McNeill and Helena Gamer, ed. and trans. *Medieval Handbooks of Penance* (New York: Columbia Univ. Press, 1938), p.4.

instruction for "all whom loves subliming fire invades."

Thus, "Valediction of the booke" and "Twicknam garden" illustrate the speaker's concern with achieving an authoritative status that legitimates his experience in social terms. Casuists share the speaker's concern; in their resolutions are "Rule and example found" for subsequent cases. Recognizing the potential antagonism between individuality and social coherence, practical theologians try to effect a mutually beneficial reconciliation between the two. But while Donne's claim to an instructive authority over analogous cases is consistent with casuistical policy, the criterion with which he establishes his authority is not. Investing love with an absolutism that only Scripture possesses, his speaker refuses to admit that circumstances can ever change his rule of faith. In "The Sunne Rising," he insists that "Love, all alike, no season knowes, nor clyme,/ Nor houres, dayes, moneths, which are the rags of time." He contends that his love is exceptional— and therefore exempt from conventional expectations— because it is immutable.[17] Since neither time, separation, nor even death can alter love, its exemption is also immutable. Donne's persona attempts to push casuistical accommodation beyond its conditional bounds. He strains towards a permanence in human experience that practical theology does not (cannot) recognize.

"The Anniversarie" similarly asserts love's immunity from time. Although the poem is not a case of conscience, it represents some of the anxieties that draw Donne to casuistical analysis in other poems; it demonstrates the need to control experience in the face of uncertainty and inevitable change. Written to celebrate the passage of one year since "thou and I first one another saw," the poem paradoxically claims that time is meaningless to lovers:

> All other things, to their destruction draw,
> Only our love hath no decay;
> This, no to morrow hath, nor yesterday,
> Running it never runs from us away,
> But truly keepes his first, last, everlasting day.   (ll. 6-10)

Asserting love's immortality is a stock Petrarchan move, but in "The Anniversarie" it acquires a strange urgency. The speaker's protestations of permanence are interwoven with references to destruction, decay, graves, corpses, death, tears, divorce, treason, and "True and false feares." Donne's

---

17 (For a detailed account of casuistical manipulation in "The Sunne Rising," see pp.110-120 below.) That love and the beloved not change is a persistent concern of Donne's amatory speaker, just as "Loves sweetest Part, Variety" is a favorite topic of his rakish persona. "A Feaver" describes the apocalyptic consequences for the world if "thou, the worlds soule, goest," (l.9) but denies that either sickness or death can alter the beloved's essential nature: "Thy beauty,'and all parts, which are thee,/ Are unchangeable firmament" (ll. 23-24).

persona betrays a disturbing awareness of impermanence and a consequent reaching for absolutes: eternity, oneness, uniqueness, and particularly the absolute authority of kingship. As in "The Sunne Rising," kings figure in every stanza. Monarchy is an appropriate emblem for one who insists that he and his lover are unequaled; indeed, the speaker claims even greater authority than temporal princes, who cannot rival love's power: "none but wee/ Can be such Kings, nor of such subjects bee." Not only are kings peerless, but their pronouncements are Law, and Donne's persona— so conscious of disintegration— tries unsuccessfully to appropriate monarchical control. He maintains that the lovers are sovereign in their control over each other, and yet they are subject to *true* fears as well as false ones. As in other lyrics, Donne's persona insists on "a mastery that is never more fragile than at those moments when it is most loudly proclaimed." Beneath the poem's hyperbole is a poignant need simply to assure that the speaker and his lady are "safe." [18] And even that safety is expressed precariously, in the form of a rhetorical question:

> Who is so safe as wee? where none can doe
> Treason to us, except one of us two.
> True and false feares let us refraine,
> Let us love nobly,' and live, and adde againe
> Yeares and yeares unto yeares... (ll.25-29)

It is peculiar solace that only one's beloved can turn traitor. Even if the speaker flatly denied the threat of treason—and he does not—the mere mention of treason suggests its possibility. Despite his absolute claims ("Only

---

[18]   Stanley Fish, "Masculine Persuasive Force: Donne and Verbal Power" in *Soliciting Interpretation* p. 229. The poignant references to safety and fear may well have biographical resonance. John Carey (p.92) observes that the speaker of "The Anniversarie" is not married to his beloved, since "Two graves must hide thine and my coarse." While Carey dismisses conjecture about the woman's identity in the poem, Ilona Bell, "'Under Ye Rage of a Hott Sonn and Yr Eyes': John Donne's Love Letters to Ann More," in *The Eagle and the Dove: Reassessing John Donne*, ed. Claude J. Summers and Ted-Larry Pebworth (Columbia: Univ. of Missouri Press, 1986), pp. 46-47, argues that "Donne wrote 'The Anniversarie' for Ann More when her name was still More." Donne's secret affair with Ann was potentially ruinous and surely caused both lovers fears about their safety (fears that were realized when Donne was imprisoned for eloping) as well as uncertainty about their future together. During his clandestine courtship, Donne must have identified with the speaker's description of love as dissociated from "All other things"; the poet's life, like his writing, was troubled with the conflicts between public and private imperatives that casuists attempt to reconcile. That Donne's social status was lower than Ann's was one of several obstacles to their marriage, and may account for the repeated allusions to love's ennobling power in "The Anniversarie"; regardless of their worldly rank, the lovers are "Prince enough in one another." For Donne's fears about the possibility of Ann's "treason," see Bell, pp.41-45.

our love hath no decay"; "none but wee/ Can be such Kings"), Donne's persona is unable to convince *himself* of love's immutability. "Let us love
nobly" is an exhortation to emulate those kings he earlier claimed they
were. And while he exults in the first stanza that love "no to morrow hath,
nor yesterday," in the final lines he counts the years that remain "till we at-
taine/ To write threescore," the full span of life designated in the Bible. By
the end of the poem, love's permanence and absolutism have become ideals
rather than accomplished facts. Nevertheless, the speaker still reaches: "This
is the second of our raigne."

If Donne's persona reaches for absolute authority, control, and perma-
nence in "The Anniversarie," he reaches for and grabs them in "The Sunne
Rising." The speaker of Donne's anti-aubade argues towards the same
paradigmatic position that the speakers of "Twicknam garden" and
"Valediction of the booke" seek. And as already noted, the poem shares with
"The Anniversarie" a desire for immunity from time and change. But "The
Sunne Rising" differs significantly in its approach: Donne structures his arguments according to the principles and methods of case divinity, producing
a witty parody that illustrates how the term "casuistical" acquired its pejora-
tive connotations.

In "The Sunne Rising," Donne's speaker exploits casuistical directives
in order to sanction his goal of uninterrupted pleasure. He argues that conventional laws of behavior— arising at daybreak and pursuing distinction in
worldly activities— do not apply to lovers, who possess all value and
distinction in each other. He constructs a mock case of conscience in which
duties of the external world conflict with those of the internal world, and he
endeavors to prove that love exerts a greater claim. According to the principles of case divinity, he must compare the purpose and consequences of each
conflicting obligation, and he must define the lovers' circumstances in order
to determine how they constitute an exception to general laws of conduct.
As will be seen, the speaker's manipulation of casuistical sanctions transforms his futile enterprise of commanding the sun into a sophistical coup.
He 'proves' not only that the lovers may remain in bed with impunity, but
also that their doing so enriches the sublunary world with new criteria of
value. Much of the speaker's wit derives from his dressing the specious case
in the legal and moral terms of practical theology.

Donne's argument advances through a tangle of contradictions and re-
versals. Opening with a malediction forbidding morning, his persona wants
to banish the sun from his bedroom. But the poem ends with an invitation
to "Shine here to us," and the tone shifts from contempt ("Busie old foole")
to solicitude ("Thine age askes ease"). In the second stanza, the speaker invokes the differentiations of time that he disavowed in lines 9 and 10, and
although "Love. . .no season knowes," there are still "lovers seasons" (1.4).
Another contradiction, one that acquires new significance as the argument

progresses, occurs when Donne terms the sun both "unruly" and "pedantique." Moreover, the first stanza dissociates the lovers from the world; the speaker repudiates mundane distinctions and measurements, claiming that love is "all alike." But the second stanza attributes to love the world's highest distinctions of wealth and title, and the third stanza transforms the lovers into the world itself. A closer look at Donne's argument shows that his playful forging of casuistical assumptions helps account for such tonal and logical shifts.

Since neither sentiment nor appetite warrants the casuistical dispensation that he needs in order to stay in bed, the speaker pretends to be caught in a moral dilemma of conflicting obligations. Perplexity is the category to which practical theologians assign such a dilemma (as in *Pseudo-Martyr* and the sermon on *Esther*), and perplexity can be resolved only by determining which claim has greater force.[19] Because the sun is both an agent of quantification— demarcating hours, seasons, and climates— and instigator of the day's pursuits, the speaker personifies it as the legislator of conventional laws of activity and measurement. Against the sun's summons to arise, the speaker poses love's obligations. "All alike," love and its laws of behavior conflict with the sun's laws of change and difference. The distinctions that the world seeks in its diverse activities are already conjoined in the lovers; consequently, their duties are to remain together and cultivate the value that proximity enables. In the course of the poem, Donne's persona contracts the sun's province from public summoner to private sanctioner, just as moral theologians contract the focus of general law to the individual.

The speaker begins by reproving the sun for violating its jurisdiction.

> Busie old foole, unruly Sunne,
> Why dost thou thus,
> Through windowes, and through curtaines call on us?
> Must to thy motions lovers seasons run?
> Sawcy pedantique wretch. . . (ll.1-5)

Differentiation is the sun's domain. Its motion measures change, and it regulates a society whose hierarchies of title, vocation, and age ("Schoole boyes," "prentices," "Court-huntsmen," and "the King") depend upon the same laws of differentiation that the sun occasions. But love's law, the speaker remonstrates, is unification; its calling is the beloved. The con-

---

19   William Perkins, *A Discourse of Conscience*, ed. Thomas Merrill (Nieuwkoop: B. De Graaf, 1966), p. 11, explains: "When two commandements of the morall law are opposite in respect of us; so as we cannot doe them both at the same time; the lesser commaundement give place to the greater, and doth not bind or constraine for that instant." See also Jeremy Taylor, *Ductor Dubitantium*, Vol. XII of *Works*, ed. Alexander Taylor (London: Longman, Brown, Green and Longman, 1855), I, 5, viii; and Aquinas, *Summa Theologica*, ed. Anton Pegis (New York: Random House, 1948), I. 2. 101.

stancy of the speaker and his lover makes them unique and exempts them
from the activities that time regulates. Consequently, the sun exceeds its authority when it enjoins them to arise at daybreak. It ignores the casuistical
rule that legislators must accommodate laws to exceptional circumstances.
In its narrow-minded insistence on convention, the "pedantique" sun is re-
miss, not the lovers. Justice is sacrificed to rigorism, according to casuists,
when law-makers are "over straitlaced, and too much wedded to syllables";[20] Donne's persona argues that the "Busie old foole" makes such a
sacrifice of justice when it intrudes on the lovers.

Paradoxically, the pedantic sun is also unruly. It is "sawcy" in both
Renaissance uses of the term: lewd, and insolent to superiors. An unruly
voyeur, it spies on the lovers through their bedroom curtains. And since the
speaker later argues that love exerts a greater claim in his case of perplexity,
the sun is also unruly for infringing on a higher law. In calling the sun im-
pertinent, the first line of the poem anticipates the speaker's casuistical
strategy: his objective is not only to establish that lovers are exempt from
the convention of arising at daybreak, but also to prove that their remaining
in bed is of greater merit, and therefore a higher obligation, than are the
world's matutinal activities.

To defend love's superiority, Donne's persona depicts as insignificant
the activities that the sun instigates. In a list of those over whom the sun
does have jurisdiction, the speaker trivializes society's pursuit of wisdom,
wealth, title, and authority by reducing its practitioners to dilatory school
children, recalcitrant apprentices, gossiping courtiers, and an idle king.

> . . . goe chide
> Late Schoole boyes, and sowre prentices,
> Goe tell Court-huntsmen that the King will ride   (ll.5-7)

The list of characters progresses hierarchically from school boys to king before culminating in the bathetic line, "Call countrey ants to harvest offices."
Juxtaposing the king to insects deflates the dignity of rank, and the reference
to harvest offices of ants recalls and further diminishes the offices that society 'harvests.' As Perkins states, "The necessitie of the lawe ariseth out of
the necessitie of the good end thereof." [21] According to Donne's persona,
the sun's demands and the activities to which the world attaches value result
in little that is good.

Having repudiated the world's endeavors and its criteria of value, the
speaker attempts to prove love's greater worth in stanza two. He begins by
belittling the sun's power, thus playing on his own casuistical claim to a

---

[20]   Joseph Hall, *Resolutions and Decisions of Divers Practical Cases of
Conscience*, Vol. XII of *Works*, ed. John Downame (Oxford: D. C. Talboys,
1937), p.368.
[21]   Perkins, *Discourse*, p. 34.

'stronger' law.

> Thy beames, so reverend, and strong,
> Why shouldst thou thinke?
> I could eclipse and cloud them with a winke (ll.11-13)

The separation of love and the world begun in stanza one is now a veritable divorce. To emphasize his autonomy from the mundane conventions that the sun enforces, Donne's persona reifies the metaphor of the lovers' microcosm, and likens himself to a separate world with the power to eclipse the sun. Further, his suggestion in line 15 that the woman's eyes might blind "thine" is more than a Petrarchan tribute; it implies that she is a stronger sun, one that has the jurisdiction (unlike the speaker's "unruly" interlocutor) to compel him to 'rise' to love's activities. But the speaker's insistence on exemption from sublunary rules comes perilously close to solipsism when he threatens simply to shut his eyes; eclipsing the sun may dramatize his claims to a greater law, but refusing to acknowledge the sun's demand would only stultify his defense. And if the speaker were truly able to disregard the pressure of convention, he'd never have felt the need to vindicate his position.

Significantly, Donne's persona does not carry out his boast, explaining, "I would not lose her sight so long" (l.14). If he denies the sun by 'winking,' he will literally lose sight of his lady; more importantly, if he denies the standards of differentiation that the sun personifies, he will deprive himself of any evaluative means of comparing and championing love's greater claims. He can measure love only in terms of the distinctions that he has disparaged throughout the first half of the poem.[22] Consequently, the volta at the end of line 14 signals a reversal in the speaker's argument: the second half of the poem restores the value of social distinctions. Once trivialized, kings and the world's "harvest" (now promoted

---

[22] John Carey observes: "If lovers can be supreme only by being called kings, then kings are still supreme. The private world is valued only as it apes the public" (p.109). The inadequacy of language to express the ideal is a recurrent topic in Donne's works. He remarks in his *Essays in Divinity*, ed. Evelyn Simpson (Oxford: Clarendon Press, 1952), p.44, that to name is to know: "Whether *Nomen* be *Novimen*, or Notamen, it is still to make known." But since reason is fallen and language corrupt, we can neither name nor know perfection. The speaker of "A Valediction forbidding mourning" marvels, "But we by a love, so much refin'd,/ That our selves know not what it is" (ll.17-18), and "The Relique" ends, "All measure, and all language, I should passe,/ Should I tell what a miracle shee was" (ll. 31-32). At best, the sublime can be discussed only in terms of known experience, and as Donne's persona discovers in "The Sunne Rising," accommodated language devalues the ideal. Any superlative includes its lesser degrees. See *Essays*, p.21 for the same inadequacy of language to describe God.

to a harvest of "spice and Myne") are expressive of love's properties. Once "all alike," love is now defined in terms of divisions: geographical ("both the'India's"), chronological (all that the sun sees between "to morrow late" and "yesterday"), and hierarchical divisions ("those Kings whom thou saw'st"). "The counter-world is ultimately bound within the discourse of the poem." [23] But while the speaker has altered the terms of his exceptional status, he has not rendered his case any less exceptional. On the contrary, love is greater than the sum of its newly acknowledged parts; it synthesizes the power, wealth, and luxury of all the rulers, gold, and spices that are dissipated throughout the earth.

> Looke, and to morrow late, tell mee,
> Whether both the'India's of spice and Myne
> Be where thou leftst them, or lie here with mee.
> Aske for those Kings whom thou saw'st yesterday,
> And thou shalt heare, All here in one bed lay   (ll. 16-20).

While Donne's persona asserts in stanza one that he and his lover are exempt from the convention of arising at daybreak and cultivating worldly values, by stanza three he argues that they are the locus of value itself. All that society profits by and esteems is embedded in the bedded lovers ("All here in one bed lay"). Since the world's benefits are only simulacra of love's paradigm, conventional criteria of value must be amended: the speaker and his lover become society's gauge of distinction, and not vice versa. "Princes doe but play us; compar'd to this,/ All honor's mimique; All wealth alchimie." Together, the lovers hypostatize the Ideal; consequently, they have a greater obligation to remain in bed than to arise and pursue the counterfeit distinctions of wealth and honor. Their pretended case of perplexity is thus resolved: love's law exerts a greater claim than does the unruly sun.

But clearly Donne's witty resolution is not "honestly" come by. His persona pushes to an extreme the casuistical accommodation of exceptional circumstances in order to argue for an ontological reversal that makes love the standard for a dimly analogous world. Moreover, he reasons speciously from adjunct to subject— from 'love constitutes all the world's value' to 'love constitutes all the world'— in order to transform the reified microcosm of lines 11-13 into the macrocosm around which the sun revolves. The new ontology allows the sun the same retirement that the speaker is allowed: the sun must illuminate the world, but since love constitutes a superior world, the sun can fulfill its responsibility simply by shining on the lovers. Like them, it can combine duty and pleasure by remaining in the

---

[23]   Helen Carr, "Donne's Masculine Persuasive Force" in *Jacobean Poetry and Prose: Rhetoric, Representation, and the Popular Imagination*, ed. Clive Bloom (London: Macmillan, 1988), p. 105.

bedroom.[24]

> Thou sunne art halfe as happy' as wee,
> In that the world's contracted thus.
> Thine age askes ease, and since thy duties bee
> To warme the world, that's done in warming us.
> Shine here to us, and thou art every where;
> This bed thy center is, these walls, thy spheare.   (ll.25-30)

And of course the sun *does* illuminate them. It has done so throughout the poem. But its originally censorious beams are now invested with new significance. Casuists allow immunity from the law as long as one can prove "the undoubted tolerance by authority of [the law's] neglect." [25] By 'obeying' the speaker's command to "Shine here to us," the sun not only tolerates the lovers' neglect of conventional activities, but it also ratifies love's claim to a stronger law. According to the speaker's terms, the sun's shining is an endorsement of love's new ontology. Like most cases of conscience, the poem ends with a revised law that is tailored to specific circumstances, and that has the sanction of authority.

But the authority that sanctions the speaker's conclusions is as bogus as the logic from which the conclusions are deduced. Much of the speaker's sophistical wit results from his personification of the sun as "lex loquens." Throughout the poem, he appeals to the sun as his judge, attributing to it the faculties for weighing evidence ("Looke, and...tell mee"; "Aske for...And thou shalt heare") and the casuistical ability to determine exceptional circumstances. Although every one of his imperatives directs the sun to do exactly what it always does, the speaker treats its natural shining as a rational response. His arguing with and pretending to 'persuade' an insentient object dramatizes one of the many characteristics of casuistry that is vulnerable to abuse: the moral theologian must be his or her own objective judge.[26] The law or convention against which one argues cannot refute one's fallacies. Cases of conscience are private deliberations in which the

---

24   Line 25 has the only overt mention of pleasure in the poem. Since intention is crucial to justifying an action, the speaker avoids the obvious issue of sensual gratification, and wittily defends remaining in bed as a moral duty. Jeremy Taylor observes: "That is the prevailing ingredient in the determination which is most valued, not which most pleases; that which is rationally preferred, not that which delights the senses" (*Ductor Dubitantium*, I, 2, Rule 5).

25   Kenneth E. Kirk, *Conscience and Its Problems* (London: Longmans, Green, 1927), p.270.

26   As established in chapter two, conscience and reason should appeal to Scripture, and if necessary, the opinions of reputable authorities when making a moral judgment. But reason is fallible. And although "conscience is of a divine nature, a thing placed of God in the middest between him and man, as an arbitratour to give sentence," it can be erroneous or, in the unscrupulous, inaudible (Perkins, *Discourse*, p.6).

individual must argue both sides of a dilemma. If he is predisposed towards one side (remaining with his lover, for example), he might present the counterarguments with all the force of mute sunshine.

It is appropriate that the speaker addresses a Ptolemaic sun. Donne was well aware of "the new philosophy," and his self-conscious sophistry is all the more apparent in that it assumes a cosmology that has been called into doubt. (Once again, the speaker's 'judge' is as false as his arguments.) But more importantly, the orbital hub of the Ptolemaic sun is earth, and contracting the sun's center from all of humanity to only the lovers is emblematic of casuistry's contracting the general law to the necessities of the individual. The same contraction of public to private is evident in the speaker's imagery. In stanza two, for example, kings and kingdoms, gold and spices crowd into the lovers' bed. Vast distances ("both the' India's") are telescoped into one room. Even when Donne's persona dispatches the sun to compare the public and private worlds, his repetition of "here" redirects its focus to the lovers: "lie here with me'; "Shine here to us"; "And thou shalt heare, All here in one bed lay." The Ptolemaic sun must orbit the lovers because "the world's contracted" to them. Arguing that even the laws of astronomy must be amended in his case, the speaker burlesques casuists who redirect the focus of general law to particular circumstances.

The casuistical terms in which the speaker casts his argument are delightfully false from the start. By pretending to be caught in a case of perplexity, he can exploit the equitable sanctions of casuistry and at the same time posture as one who is concerned, not with defending sensuality, but with submitting to a higher law. The audience is encouraged to believe that his motive— that all-important factor in the judgment of moral theologians— is piety, rather than gratification. Part of the humor of "The Sunne Rising" is that its elaborate and complex argument is simply a disguise for the speaker's motive of pleasure. The speaker's greatest abuse of casuistry, however, is his attempt to make love a permanent and universal standard. He enlists the principles of case divinity without endorsing the Scriptural criterion that gives them their authority. Moreover, while casuistry proceeds by qualification, the speaker insists on absolutes: "all States, and all Princes"; "All honor's mimique; All wealth alchemie"; "All here in one bed lay." Finally, casuists attempt to mitigate the conflict between general law and anomalous situations without violating the integrity of either. But Donne's persona tries to dispel all conflict by becoming the law itself, like the kings to whom his attention returns in every stanza.

To observe that the speaker distorts casuistical principles, however, is not to say that casuistry does not inform his arguments. Like any parody, Donne's poem is 'similar with a difference'; that is, it recalls its casuistical model closely enough to play upon the contrast. Donne poses a mock case of conscience, but his premises are rooted in legitimate assumptions of case divinity: general laws are not always applicable to idiosyncratic experience; moral precepts are not always consonant, and when they conflict, the lesser obligation ceases to bind; ignoring a law is justified when authority tolerates its neglect. Despite their misapplication, casuistical formulae are central to the speaker's argument.

In addition, structural principles of case divinity inform "The Sunne Rising." Donne's poem follows the tripartite structure of cases of conscience. Moral theologians first identify the general laws relevant to their problem. Next they consider the conditions that individuate the case. In this second stage, they define the terms of the conflict in light of extenuating or exceptional circumstances; rather than address their subject in the abstract, they investigate concrete examples of the operation of each law. And finally, if the application of existing rules proves to be inadequate or unjust, moral theologians formulate a new law that accommodates the unusual configuration of circumstances. The same process of deliberation structures Donne's poem. His persona defines the conflict between love's laws and the conventions that the sun represents in the first stanza. In doing so, he establishes that his dilemma is one of perplexity. To determine which law constitutes the greater obligation, he compares the value of each. And, as demonstrated above, he formulates a new law that is appropriate to the terms of the case—as he has defined them. He judges that love's rule exerts a greater claim than does the world.

The speaker's tone alters with his manipulation of casuistical reasoning. Although the burden of justification is his, he addresses the "sawcy" sun as if it, and not he, is culpable. His explosive beginning and indignant epithets are more offensive than defensive. But the speaker's bravado— his threat to "eclipse" the sun and his spondaic boast that "She'is all States, and all Princes, I,/ Nothing else is"— is merely a smoke screen for the witty fallacies that he promotes under the aegis of moral theology. Until the final stanza, his tone has none of the impartiality that casuists require. Once he proves love's autonomy, however, he becomes more temperate. The last five lines of the poem are the largest block of verse to scan regularly. No longer a meddlesome voyeur, the sun affords a tacit validation of the speaker's claims. Consequently, Donne's persona expresses in even iambs his concern for the aged sun. With the shift of tone, he feigns the restraint that is a desideratum of practical theologians.

Donne's parody of casuistical procedures ends by inverting even the customary objective of casuists: the final achievement of a case of conscience is that it enables action, but the final achievement of "The Sunne Rising" is that it enables *in*action. Neither the lovers nor the sun should rise. (In other respects, of course, the speaker will "rise" to love while staying in bed.) Ironically, the speaker's exploitation of case divinity and his ontological transformation simply confirm, in effect, the status quo. The action at the end of the poem is exactly what it was at the beginning. The sun still shines, the lovers remain in bed, and society still awakens to its quotidian endeavors. But the speaker has invested each of these circumstances with new significance by manipulating casuistical sanctions. And in the process, he has delivered an extravagant compliment to his lover.

It is possible that the lover to whom he delivered the compliment was Ann More. Although dating many of the *Songs and Sonets* is problematic and conjectural, a number of critics have inferred that "The Sunne Rising" was written after Donne's marriage to Ann in 1601. William Zunder and Arthur F. Marrotti, for example, argue that line 7 ("Goe tell court-huntsmen that the King will ride") alludes to King James and his well-known penchant for the hunt.[27] Moreover, the conflict in the poem between public duties and private affections, between the political world and the lovers' microcosm, recalls the conflict in Donne's own affair with Ann. By seventeenth-century standards, their elopement was both politically and socially subversive. Ilona Bell points out that marrying a minor without her father's consent challenged "the patriarchal social structure on which all the country's laws were founded." [28] That Donne was a member of the middle class, while Ann was of the gentry, further undermined "the hierarchical norms of the time."[29]

Donne's elopement and his subsequent dejection about being socially exiled dramatize the two conflicting impulses described earlier: his assertion of independence and exceptionality, and his need to be incorporated into the body of the world, particularly the political world of power and position for which he was groomed at university, at the Inns of Court, under the military command of men who were themselves placed near the vertex of power, and as secretary to Sir Thomas Egerton, a central figure in Elizabethan and Jacobean government. Donne's opposition to cultural constraints on love, along with his political ambition to "contribute something to the sustentation of the whole," resonate in "The Sunne Rising." As already seen, the poem establishes a new order that places love at the center of the generative power from which Donne was excluded. Elevating love above socio-political demands, "The Sunne Rising" playfully enacts the defiance of authority

---

[27]   William Zunder, "The Poetry of John Donne: Literature, History and Ideology" in *Jacobean Poetry and Prose*, p. 85; Arthur F. Marotti, *John Donne: Coterie Poet* (Madison: Univ. of Wisconsin Press, 1986), pp.156-7.

[28]   Bell, p.44.

[29]   William Zunder, *The Poetry of John Donne: Literature and Culture in the Elizabethan and Jacobean Period* (Sussex: Harvester Press, 1982), p.42.

that Donne's marriage expressed, and it invests the lover's motives with a legitimacy that they were never accorded in fact. The poem justifies love in terms of the same political order and structures of power that Donne's elopement was seen to subvert. His persona wittily challenges the value of social status and power only to appropriate them and to claim the crowning position in the political hierarchy. Exploiting casuistical accommodation, he argues for a new definition of authority, claiming that his exceptional love constitutes the standard against which political structures and social values should be measured.

Thus, the intensely private love that left Donne politically dispossessed becomes in "The Sunne Rising" a touchstone for public power and prestige: "Princes doe but play us; compar'd to this,/ All honor's mimique; All wealth alchemie." In Donne's world, the poet's unruly marriage resulted in his exclusion from governmental office, but in the world of the poem, it is the lover who excludes, discredits, and commands representatives of authority. A political outsider, Donne could only watch from a distance the privileges and privileged at court, but in his poem, the *sun* is the outsider, a voyeur of the privileged lovers. Such a reversal is particularly striking when one considers that the sun was a Renaissance emblem of sovereignty. "In the reign of James I, the image was used to promote the absolutist pretensions of the monarchy." [30] The speaker's efforts to undermine the sun's authority, then, appear to be an assault on absolutism. William Zunder remarks that Donne's poem shatters the idea of sovereignty "and with it the principle of social hierarchy." [31] I would argue, however, that in the speaker's fantasy of power, the political structures remain intact; the difference is that they derive their authority from the lovers and not the sovereign sun. As the preceding pages have suggested, Donne's persona manipulates casuistical sanctions in order to appropriate rather than subvert monarchical control. His objection is not to absolutism; instead, it is to the subordination of his absolutist love to the lesser claims of a "Busie old foole." With wit that dazzles the sun, he usurps that kingly figure's power, constructing his own "Monarchy of wit."

If not in fact, then in fiction, the poet achieves an authoritative status that legitimates his love in social and political terms. His comic abuse of casuistical principles enables him to legislate his own gratification, to arbitrate the conflicting desires for integration and uniqueness that distinguish his self construction. His persona forges a new hierarchy in which lovers govern rather than obey society's laws of value and conduct. With a witty reversal of Donne's own experience, love becomes the means whereby the speaker and his beloved are "so incorporated into the body of the world, that

---

[30] Zunder, p.39.
[31] Zunder, p.41.

they contribute something to the sustentation of the whole."

"The sustentation of the whole":
Position and Opposition in "The Canonization"

The preceding section has argued that two casuistical objectives particularly engaged Donne: allowing expression of the individual's singularity, while allying the individual with the community by treating his or her case as an instructive precedent for analogous dilemmas. "The Canonization" is one of Donne's most extravagant parodies of these objectives. As in "Twicknam garden," "Valediction of the booke," and "The Sunne Rising," the speaker asserts his exceptional status, and at the same time claims that in his resolution are "rule and example found" for subsequent cases. Hyperbole distinguishes the argument of all four poems, but perhaps the most exaggerated construction of love's authoritative paradigm occurs in "The Canonization." The poem begins with a disjunction between public norms and private action, and the speaker is confronted with an essentially casuistical dilemma: individual integrity and conventional expectations seem mutually exclusive. The interlocutor's implied admonishment against abandoning the world provokes Donne's persona to counter that his exceptional love is of greater value, both to himself and to the community, than mundane achievements. His is "a patterne of. . .love" (l.45) that will enrich and instruct others. The speaker remonstrates that he and his lover are not "idle and unprofitable persons" who disrupt "the order that God hath established in this world," and whom Donne was to condemn in the 1626 sermon mentioned earlier. Rather, they are a distillation of "the whole worlds soule" (l.40), with the power to restore order when others' love becomes "rage." As exemplars, they "contribute to the sustentation of the whole."

The perplexity that besets Donne's persona in "The Canonization" is very like the conflict addressed in "The Sunne Rising." Society's values and obligations are set in opposition to those of love, and the speaker must establish which claim exerts greater force. The resolution of his case is contingent on his definition of love; to justify his aberrant point of view, he must define love's superior qualities. And yet this crucial act of defining proves to be the speaker's most perplexing problem.[32] Constituted of para-

---

[32]   The problem is also a source of perplexity for Donne's critics. As Marotti remarks (p.161), readings of the poem usually hinge on the third stanza's definition of love. Few passages in the *Songs and Sonets* have inspired such disparate and wide-ranging interpretations. For an impressive array of critical responses to Donne's "bewildering set of conceits," see Marotti, pp.161-164. For a discussion of nomination in "The Canonization," see Thomas Docherty, *John Donne, Undone* (London: Methuen, 1986), pp. 173-175.

doxes, his love is both carnal and spiritual, consuming and renewing, material and "mysterious." Neither language nor logic can comprehend its qualities. In trying to articulate an experience that eludes reason and familiar categories, the speaker encounters the same difficulties that Donne meets with when describing God in his *Essays*. Since language and reason are fallen, the *Essays* observe, we are unable to describe or to understand God as He is; consequently, we must resort to similitudes, speaking of Him in terms of the world that we do know. God "may not be directly and presently beheld and contemplated. . .[so] we must seek his Image in his works." [33] Finding in the world the image of that which is unknowable or inexpressible enables indirect understanding. Accordingly, the speaker of "The Canonization" attempts to describe his ineffable love in accommodated terms of the world: flies, tapers, the eagle, dove, phoenix, etc. Throughout, the exempla are both evaluative and definitional. "Call her," "Call us," he begins the stanza in which his own "calling" or describing of love eludes precision. To establish the superior moral status of a relationship that is finally "mysterious," the speaker necessarily relies on analogies.

Defining experience, evaluating an action or point of view so as to determine its moral status, is one of the primary functions of casuistry. The problems of definition that confront Donne's persona in "The Canonization" are familiar to practical theologians, who recognize that language is both limited and mercurial. As already seen, Joseph Hall objects to lawmakers who are "over straitlaced and too much wedded to syllables," and he insists that our evaluation of any experience should be in terms of its context.[34] Donne's speaker argues similarly that his auditor's criticism of neglecting worldly pursuits fails to take into account the nature of the lovers' experience and their relation to society. A closer look at the poem shows that, as the speaker gathers exempla to illustrate the opposing values in his case, he builds to a definition of love that can be expressed only in terms of the religious sublime. Although judged "unfit" by worldly values, the martyred lovers possess "the whole worlds soule" in each other; love's saints, they embody the ideal against which earthly lovers measure their actions. As in a number of the *Songs and Sonets*, Donne's persona wittily argues his case

---

[33]   Donne, *Essays in Divinity*, p.39.
[34]   William Ames concurs that definitions of an act must be rooted in its circumstances. *De Conscientia* defines the "Jesuitical" practice of mental reservation, for example, as "lying" and "false witness." However, Ames concedes that under certain conditions, false implication is allowable and should not be termed lying. "It is sometimes lawful, so long as truth is not violated, to utter words from which in all probability the hearers will draw a false inference. This is not lying, nor false witness, but merely giving others an opportunity of making a mistake, with a view not to their committing sin, but rather to their avoiding it." Quoted in Kirk, p.205.

by treating love as an unassailable rule of faith.

The dramatic first stanza of "The Canonization" immediately establishes the perplexed terms of the poem. A worldly acquaintance, whose values are illustrated in the dismissive list of activities in lines 4-7, has criticized the speaker's absorption with love, urging him not to neglect social and economic advancement. Participation in society is a moral duty as well as a means of aggrandizement, and the lovers' preoccupation interferes with both. The speaker's explosive response betrays his defensiveness, but it also conveys his conviction. Donne's persona argues with the force of inner persuasion; and as Aquinas maintains in his *Summa Theologica*, one of the first principles of moral law is that we must follow a convinced conscience, "even though impartial criticism holds that the conscience is 'erroneous.'"[35] By casuistical standards, the speaker's inner persuasion outweighs his social obligations, although he still must prove the grounds of his conviction.

> For Godsake hold your tongue, and let me love,
> Or chide my palsie, or my gout,
> My five gray haires, or ruin'd fortune flout,
> With wealth your state, your minde with Arts improve,
> Take you a course, get you a place,
> Observe his honour, or his grace,
> Or the Kings reall, or his stamped face
> Contemplate, what you will, approve,
> So you will let me love.   (ll. 1-9)

Significantly, the speaker makes no attempt to deny his auditor's criticism. Indeed, his response to the implied reproach is to confirm his isolation by insisting on being left alone with his love. His imperatives to "hold your tongue, and let me love," and to do "what you will. . ./So you will let me love" express a fundamental unconcern with what the auditor would have him do. Listing the activities that society judges worthwhile, Donne's persona is dismissive and even contemptuous: contemplate coins, bow to title, "take" and "get." Central to his case of perplexity is a clash of values—those of the world, which are based on taking and getting, and those of love, which he claims are resolutely uninvolved with acquisition, social status, or materialism.

Stanza two further suggests the speaker's disregard for his interlocutor's standards. Lines 10-18 imply that the pursuit of wealth, glory, and honor results in "warres," competition, lawsuits, and quarrels. In this context of predatory ambition, Marotti remarks, "the allusion to the current plague

---

[35] Aquinas, *Summa Theologica*, 1.2.19. Quoted in Kenneth E. Kirk, *Some Principles of Moral Theology* (London: Longmans, Green and Co., 1926), p.179.

calls forth the usual moral framework in which this phenomenon was interpreted—that of God's punishing man for his sins and enormities."[36]
Recalling the casuistical dictum that "The necessitie of the law ariseth out
of the necessitie of the good end thereof," Donne's persona depicts no "good
end"; to the endeavors that his auditor deems a "necessitie." As the preceding
chapters note, practical theologians judge cases of conscience by evaluating
both the consequences of an act and the intention of the agent. In Donne's
sermon on *Esther*, for example, nearly all of the Queen's decisions would
have been unjustifiable under different circumstances; but given that they
neither intended nor caused injury, and given Esther's conviction of their legitimacy, her resolutions were laudable. Accordingly, in the second stanza
of "The Canonization," the speaker protests that the consequences of his
love are benign, whereas the products of worldly values are not. His list of
the activities that engage society— many of them forms of aggression— is
disparaging. Claiming not to impinge on those who share his auditor's
values, Donne's persona insists that his love causes no injustice or
"injuria"; the grounds for legal actions posed in lines 11-15 are absurd.

> Alas, alas, who's injur'd by my love?
> What merchants ships have my sighs drown'd?
> Who saies my teares have overflow'd his ground?
> When did my colds a forward spring remove?
> When did the heats which my veines fill
> Adde one more, to the plaguie Bill?
> Soldiers finde warres, and Lawyers finde out still
> Litigious men, which quarrels move,
> Though she and I do love.   (ll. 10-18)

The defense of love in stanza two is not only that it does not obtrude on
public affairs, but that there is no legal case against it. The social consequences of the speaker's love are benign.

Early in the poem, it is clear that the speaker's argument is against
conventional standards and activities. But his repudiation is not limited to
socio-economic conventions. In stanza two, he invokes the stock Petrarchan
claim that lovers' emotions (the sighs, tears, colds, and heats of lines 11-
14) have macrocosmic effects—only to *deny* those effects. No "teare-floods,
nor sigh-tempests" injure the world: merchant ships and property values remain afloat. Insisting that his case is exceptional, Donne's persona chafes at
poetic as well as social conventions. And Petrarchism is not the only poetic
tradition he invokes in order to disavow. Marotti rightly notes that the
speaker's belligerent self-defense at the beginning of the poem "has its roots
in the impudently anti-social stance of the youthful Ovidian libertine whose
only moral response to the society that criticizes his behavior is to charge

---

[36]   Marotti, p.161.

that the supposedly normative public world is itself deeply flawed." [37] But Donne's persona disaffirms the conventional Ovidian position when, in the last stanzas, he projects love back into the community, offering a corrective for the flawed society against which he has defined himself and his lover. This final gesture is neither "antisocial" nor "libertine"; attempting to bridge the distance between his ideal love and the world of aggression and materialism, or "rage," the speaker invalidates the expectations that the Ovidian convention raised. Even the standard neo-Platonic description of love as spiritual and sublime inadequately represents the speaker's experience, since consuming passion (figured in the flies and tapers of stanza three) also distinguishes his relationship with the beloved. Throughout "The Canonization," Donne introduces conventions only to break out of them. His doing so reinforces the speaker's casuistical assertion that his uncommon love cannot be expressed in conventional terms— whether poetic, philosophical, or social conventions.

For the most part, the first two stanzas of the poem treat only one side of the speaker's perplexity. They represent the auditor's values, and they minimize the moral force of his demands on the lovers. In stanza three, Donne's persona attempts to define love so as to establish its greater worth in his case of perplexity.

> Call us what you will, wee'are made such by love;
> Call her one, mee another flye,
> We'are Tapers too, and at our owne cost die,
> And wee in us finde the'Eagle and the dove.
> The Phoenix ridle hath more wit
> By us, we two being one, are it.
> So, to one neutrall thing both sexes fit.
> Wee dye and rise the same, and prove
> Mysterious by this love.   (ll.19-27)

As occurs between each stanza of "The Flea," Donne's auditor interjects his opposing point of view between lines eighteen and nineteen. Stanza three begins in response to his implied objection that passion is consuming and destructive. Like "the taper-fly which burns itself to death by approaching a flame," the lovers sacrifice themselves to a misdirected desire.[38] Again, the speaker does not deny his interlocutor's accusation ("Call us what you will"), but gradually he turns the charge to his advantage. Admitting that passion consumes the lovers— "We'are Tapers too"— he adds that it also brings about their resurrection and peace, both of which are suggested by the eagle and the dove. His pun on "die" plays with the popular notion that in-

---

[37]   Marotti, p.161.
[38]   John T. Shawcross, *The Complete Poetry of John Donne* (Garden City, New York: Anchor, 1967), p. 97, n.20.

tercourse shortens one's life, and suggests a more benign meaning of love's destructiveness than the auditor had posed. Moreover, "At our owne cost die" reiterates that no one else is "injur'd by my love," and the subsequent lines assert that the "cost" of love is not death, but regeneration— both physical and spiritual. If the speaker and his lover are self-immolating, they are also self-renewing, like the phoenix which is reborn from its ashes and which is an emblem of the risen Christ. Critics often differ as to the precise significance of the eagle, dove, and phoenix, thus demonstrating that the speaker's attempts to figure the ineffable or mysterious are themselves cryptic and equivocal. But whether the figures connote righteousness and mercy, vigilance and peace, constancy or the Trinity, most readers concur that they impart to love a superior moral status. This status assures love's greater claim in the speaker's case of conscience.

It is significant that interpretations of Donne's exempla in stanza three so frequently diverge. The speaker maintains that his "mysterious" love transcends understanding, and so the exempla with which he attempts to render that experience are "multivalent, ambiguous, and fundamentally *resistant* to interpretation." [39] His efforts to define love through analogy result in contradictions and "ridles." Paradoxically, the summary description of love is that it is indescribable: "Wee. . .prove/ Mysterious by this love." Like religious mysteries, the speaker's experience is incomprehensible. And like some religious truths, it can be known only through divine revelation—the revelation that earthly lovers beg at the end of the poem. Ironically, it is impossible to translate the "patterne" by which the speaker and his lover are vindicated.

Thus Donne's persona transforms into a sacred mystery the self destructive passion that his auditor denounces. The transformation proceeds by witty puns on sexual "death" and rekindling, and it reaches its outrageous climax in the final couplet's comparison of intercourse with the mystery of Christ's crucifixion and ascension: "Wee dye and rise the same, and prove/ Mysterious by this love." The speaker's hyperbole makes a travesty of his casuistical pretensions. He parodies practical theologians who look to Scripture for analogies that may illuminate their cases. And hardly observing the reasonable impartiality that case divinity requires, he ascribes to love the transcendent and unquestionable authority of religious mysteries. Stanzas four and five further develop the idea of love's mystic value; they depict the speaker and his lover as saints who die for their belief and who,

---

39   Marotti, p.163. Marotti argues convincingly that the analogies in stanza three are "*resistant* to interpretation," but his explanation for the ambiguity differs from my own. He maintains that Donne scrambles the argument simply to prove his intellectual superiority over his socially superior coterie of readers (see pp.163-5).

though condemned during their lives, will be canonized after death. With
characteristic extravagance, Donne's persona envisions that posterity will
venerate his miraculous union— just as the Church commemorates the
miracles of its saints.

> Wee can dye by it, if not live by love,
> And if unfit for tombes and hearse
> Our legend bee, it will be fit for verse;
> And if no peece of Chronicle wee prove,
> We'll build in sonnets pretty roomes;
> As well a well wrought urne becomes
> The greatest ashes, as halfe-acre tombes,
> And by these hymnes, all shall approve
> Us *Canoniz'd* for Love.
>
> And thus invoke us; You whom reverend love
> Made one anothers hermitage;
> You, to whom love was peace, that now is rage,
> Who did the whole worlds soule extract, and drove
> Into the glasses of your eyes
> So made such mirrors, and such spies,
> That they did all to you epitomize,
> Countries, Townes, Courts: Beg from above
> A patterne of your love!   (ll. 28-45)

Love is the province of poetry rather than history. Donne's distinction in
stanza four draws on the familiar Renaissance argument that poetry can represent the ideal, teaching virtue and delighting its audience, while history is
"captived to the truth of a foolish world."[40] Although the speaker's love is
"unfit" to be chronicled with the exploits of kings and soldiers— the
wealthy and powerful whom he disparages in the first two stanzas— it is
the appropriate subject of hymns and lyrics. His distinction hallows love.
The auditor's values are mired in an imperfect world, but love is able to realize a divine ideal. Claiming that he and his lover are "fit for verse," the
speaker recalls Sidney's assertion that poetry offers a "perfect pattern" of
whatever is fit "to be called and accounted good. Which setting forward and
moving to well-doing indeed sets the laurel crown upon the poet as victori-

---

[40]   Sir Philip Sidney, *Defense of Poesy*, ed. Lewis Soens (Lincoln, Nebraska:
Univ. of Nebraska Press, 1970), p.22. In his *De Dignitate et Augmentis
Scientiarum*, Francis Bacon develops Sidney's distinction between history and
poetry. The former, he remarks, is confined to what *is*; the latter, however,
expresses what should be. "Poesy conduces not only to delight but also to
magnanimity and morality. Whence it may be fairly thought to partake of the
divine nature; because it raises the mind and carries it aloft, accommodating the
shows of things to the desires of the mind, not (like reason and history)
buckling and bowing down the mind to the nature of things." *The Philosophical
Works*, ed. John M. Robertson (New York: E. P. Dutton, 1905), p.440.

ous, not only of the historian, but over the philosopher. . ." [41] Setting love's truth in verse, Donne's persona will be victorious over "the truth of a foolish world," which both history and his interlocutor purvey. Like the lyrics that commemorate them, the lovers will inspire and instruct future generations, providing a "patterne" or rule of faith that "all shall approve." The speaker's argument is not simply that love exerts a greater claim in this particular case of perplexity, but that his particular love is the standard of value itself.

But casuistry, dependent on circumstances and analogy, cannot produce the kind of universal canon that the speaker claims to embody. Only God's Word provides such a "patterne." Endowing love with the authority that practical theologians ascribe solely to Scripture is a hallmark of Donne's casuistical parodies in the *Songs and Sonets*. As in "The Sunne Rising," the speaker of "The Canonization" argues that love is the pattern of value, and thus constitutes a greater obligation than his auditor's demands. To establish whether an unorthodox course of action is a legitimate exception to the rule, casuists instruct that one must define the terms of the conflict in light of any extenuating circumstances. Comically subverting this instruction, Donne's persona suggests that the very impossibility of defining love proves its exceptional status: his union with the lady is an ineffable mystery, and like all miracles, it derives its legitimacy from God. The poem's extravagant assertions are all the more witty in that they proceed from the cautious and reasonable methods of case divinity. Like casuists, the speaker evaluates the conflicting claims in his perplexity, considering the purpose and consequences of each in terms of the circumstances that individuate his case. The consequences of preferring love to the world, he maintains, are beneficial to all. He and his lover will remain "one anothers hermitage," and they will serve as a pattern to enlighten the benighted world. Exploiting casuistical accommodation, Donne's persona transforms his own pleasure into a moral imperative that "all shall approve."

Ironically, the speaker arrives at his unqualified conclusion— "all shall approve/ Us *Canoniz'd* for Love"— by way of the qualifying language that distinguishes casuistical reasoning. The repeated "ifs" in stanza four are typical of argumentative concessions in cases of conscience. Seeming to amend his assertion that "Wee dye and rise the same," Donne's persona concedes in line 28 that if love cannot provide for his beloved and him in life (as the auditor has argued), it can immortalize them after death. And although theirs may not be the immortal "legend" of statesmen, their preservation in verse will be no less permanent. Not public monuments, but private lyrics will publicize their love. When future generations read the speaker's poetry, his hymns to a miraculous love, then "by these hymns, all shall approve/ Us

---

41   Sidney, p.20 and p.23.

Canoniz'd." As in "The Flea" (ll.23-7), Donne's persona triumphs through apparent concessions to his interlocutor's point of view. At the beginning of stanza four, he seems to dignify his auditor's standards: the lofty tombs, hearse, and chronicles that commemorate public figures dwarf the "pretty roomes" that memorialize the private lovers. But by the end of the poem, the speaker and his beloved are neither insignificant nor anonymous. They are exemplars for all lovers. Far from yielding any ground, Donne's concessions are illusory and strategic.

Thus "The Canonization" begins with society's disapproval of the lovers, and ends with universal adulation of them. The speaker contrives this dramatic shift of perspective by manipulating casuistical assumptions about the relativity of right action. He champions love above conventional activities, and in the process appropriates all the fame, glory, and honor that he disingenuously scorned in the first two stanzas. Like "The Sunne Rising," the poem recalls Donne's own dramatic decision to challenge social norms and marry Ann. The reference to "my ruin'd fortune" hints at the consequences of Donne's decision. But in "The Canonization," such a decision results in the lover's apotheosis rather than his ruin. Significantly, the speaker's means of vindication is his poetry: "And by these hymns, all shall approve/ Us *Canoniz'd* for Love." Donne's own poem is just such a hymn. By distorting casuistical principles and methods, it ascribes to love the moral and social legitimacy that the poet's marriage lacked. In verse, the love of both Donne and his persona can triumph over the historical world of "warres, . . .Litigious men," and ruinous marriages. "The Canonization" indeed "sets the laurel crown upon the poet as victorious, not only of the historian, but over the philosopher."

"The uncertainty of Humane affairs":
"A Valediction forbidding mourning"

As in "The Sunne Rising," the speaker of "A Valediction forbidding mourning" adduces casuistical arguments to defend unconventional behavior and to establish that his case is exceptional. But unlike Donne's persona in "The Sunne Rising," he does not base his defense on the perplexed opposition between public and private obligations; he does, after all, respond to the world's demands by leaving his lover.[42] Instead, the speaker of the valedic-

---

[42] Izaak Walton, *The Life of Dr. John Donne* (London: Oxford Univ. Press, 1973), p.42, reports that Donne wrote the valediction for Ann in 1611, before accompanying Sir Robert Drury and Lord Hay on a diplomatic mission abroad. Walton is not always a reliable source, but whatever the cause of the speaker's departure, it is apparent that he will "obliquely runne" (1.34) a course that is not directly related to his love. Unlike Donne's persona in "The Sunne Rising," he

tion fashions his defense as a case of doubt. Such cases argue that customary judgments are inapplicable to singular or extenuating events. (Recall, for instance, Donne's justification of Esther's unauthorized religious assembly.) The valediction poses a case of doubt in which the speaker examines why conventional responses to separation are inappropriate to the two lovers. Advancing the casuistical proposition that the significance of an act— in this case, parting— depends on its circumstances, he attempts to define a proper attitude towards departure. His spiritual union with the woman, he maintains, makes the circumstances of his departure exceptional; though parted physically, they will remain together metaphysically, and therefore will not be subject to the fear and uncertainty of absence. The speaker casuistically defends the paradox of both leaving and staying by redefining separation in terms of his uncommon love. But while insistent on the relativity of action and definition to circumstances, he is unwilling to admit the same contingency in his love. With the celebrated compass figure, he attempts to place the lovers in the unconditional realm of mathematical certainty. As I will argue, Donne's persona once again reaches beyond his casuistical premises for an absolute in human experience that practical theology cannot support. As always, this straining the bounds of casuistry belies a self-conscious straining or anxiety in the speaker's own position. Although he casts he argument in terms of religious faith, his own faith in the lovers' union, and particularly in her constancy, is far less "Inter-assured of the mind" than he claims. The tension in the poem is evident, in part, in the speaker's pushing casuistry beyond its conditional bounds.

Uncertainty and loss are the effects of separation against which the valediction argues. It seems counterproductive, then, that the poem opens with a deathbed scene. And yet the scene is uncommonly peaceful; it depicts death as imperceptible, transitional rather than final. Donne's persona chooses the apparently incongruous example of death in order to make his casuistical argument more forceful: circumstances determine our judgment of even the most extreme experience. For the virtuous, dying is not an occasion of loss or alarm. The faithful are assured that separation of body and soul is not to be feared; indeed, they gently urge "their soules, to goe." [43] Certain of spiritual continuity, they "passe mildly away"—so mildly that it is difficult to discern the moment of their death.

---

cannot argue that the world outside his love exerts no claim on him.

[43]   Donne makes the same point in a Lenten sermon of 1622/3 (*Sermons*, IV, 331): "Now a good man is not the worse for dying, that is true and capable of a good sense, because he is established in a better world." Consequently, "To mourne passionately for the love of this world, which is decrepit, and upon the deathbed, or immoderately for the death of any that is passed out of this world, is not the right use of teares" (p.341).

> As virtuous men passe mildly'away,
> And whisper to their soules, to goe,
> Whilst some of their sad friends doe say,
> The breath goes now, and some say, no.
>
> So let us melt, and make no noise,
> No teare-floods, nor sigh-tempests move,
> T'were prophanation of our joyes
> To tell the layetie our love.   (ll.1-8)

The opening comparison of parting lovers to dying, virtuous men places separation— of body from soul and of the speaker from his beloved— in a moral context. Donne's persona argues that the lovers should "make no noise" because they are as unthreatened by the parting of their souls (that is, of each other) as virtuous men are. It is a commonplace of the amatory lyric that lovers become the keepers of one another's soul. As "Song: Sweetest love" protests, "When thou sigh'st, thou sigh'st not winde,/ But sigh'st my soule away" (ll. 25-6). Similarly, the opening analogy of "A Valediction forbidding mourning" suggests that the two lovers possess each other's soul: when the two are separated, each experiences a kind of death, since each soul departs with the beloved. And yet commonplace reactions to such a death— the Petrarchan "teare-floods" and "sigh-tempests" of stanza two— are unworthy of the speaker and his lover. Theirs is a transcendent connection in which conventional expressions of sadness are not only unwarranted, but impious. As in "The Canonization," Donne's persona asserts his exceptional status in religious terms, a strategy that is key to his argument against mourning.

The deathbed analogy also implies that to mourn is to admit a lack of faith in their love. Those who are virtuous need not grieve at parting. The speaker urges in his interlocutor a response that bespeaks the conviction of her love, and that is appropriate to their hieratic station. Distinguishing them from the "layetie," he claims it would be a kind of sacrilege ("prophanation of our joyes") to admit fear and uncertainty. Central to his argument is the casuistical premise that meaning is contextual—that circumstances determine the significance of their separation. As Perkins maintains, "the workes of men of what dignitie soever, are not to be esteemed by the shew and outward appearance of them, but by the minde and condition of the doer." [44] Donne's persona reasons that the "minde and condition" of the lovers call for a re-evaluation of his departure in terms that take account of their atypical union. Like practical theologians, he is concerned more with the intention or state of mind that colors an act than he is with the "outward appearance" of parting. The governing assertion of his case of doubt is that

---

[44] William Perkins, *The Whole Treatise of Cases of Conscience*, ed. Thomas Merrill (Nieuwkoop: B. de Graaf, 1966), p.109.

mourning is inappropriate, and the opening analogy dramatizes his point of view. The first two stanzas establish the casuistical strategy with which the speaker will analyze and define the lovers' case: his analogy demonstrates that extenuating circumstances invalidate commonly held interpretations of departure. The simile places separation in a context of uninterrupted assurance, and it introduces principles of case divinity that justify the lovers' exemption from conventional responses to parting.

While the speaker cannot deny that he is leaving his beloved, he does deny that their moving apart portends any change in their love. In the third stanza, he remarks two kinds of movement— earthly and celestial— and he observes that each is attached with entirely different significance.

> Moving of th'earth brings harmes and feares,
> Men reckon what it did and meant,
> But trepidation of the spheares,
> Though greater farre, is innocent.   (ll.9-12)

The portentous motion of line 9 anticipates the harms and fears of earthly affections in the following stanza; the parting of "sublunary lovers" is as threatening as the parting of the earth, of which their souls are "elemented." But to superlunary lovers, more "refined" than their earthly counterparts, separation is as "innocent" as the moving of the spheres. The speaker's description of earthquakes acknowledges that what is not understood causes fear ("Men reckon what it did and meant"), and so throughout the poem he is concerned that his lover understand the nature of their separation. That she has no cause for fear or mourning is the central issue of his case of doubt. To resolve the case, he must prove that their love is not subject to the loss that absence ordinarily occasions. So in stanzas four and five, he distinguishes their love from common affections, arguing that their intimacy does not depend on physical communication. Consequently, he asserts, the significance of their absence is diminished.

> Dull sublunary lovers love
> (Whose soule is sense) cannot admit
> Absence, because it doth remove
> Those things which elemented it.
>
> But we by'a love, so much refin'd,
> That our selves know not what it is,
> Inter-assured of the mind,
> Care lesse, eyes, lips, and hands to misse.   (ll.13-20)

The speaker's contrast of sublunary love to that which is "Inter-assured of the mind" provides evidence for his case of doubt. Defining his love against the norm, he contends that the effects of separation are qualitatively different in each case, and therefore so should be the responses. Absence causes the laity to mourn because only sensuality sustains their love. But the "refined" mutuality of the speaker and his beloved is not dependent on the senses. In a case of conscience that examines the moral ramifications of grief, Perkins observes that "the sorrow of the mind, must be measured by the... estimation of the thing for which we sorrow." [45] With similar reasoning, Donne's persona argues against sorrow in parting lovers who "Care lesse" about the absence of eyes, lips, and hands. He claims that what is estimable about their love is their interassurance of the mind, a quality that separation cannot interrupt. That is not to say, however, that sexuality is of no consequence to the speaker. They may "Care lesse" about the physical than do "Dull sublunary lovers," but if they didn't care at all, the argument of the poem would be unnecessary. The sexual diction in Donne's compass conceit— "stiffe," "growes erect," "comes home," and "firmnes"— affirms that the lovers' union is not solely disembodied. It is unique, but not wholly abstracted. [46]

It is not until the speaker has defined the exceptional qualities of his union with the beloved that he can justify his casuistical redefinition of separation in the sixth stanza. [47] Given a love as secure as the souls of virtuous men, certain of spiritual continuity, and unrestricted to the senses, separation becomes not "A breach, but an expansion." Significantly, the two departing souls of the first stanza are now one. Having evaluated both love and leave-taking in terms of his anomalous case of doubt, Donne's persona has revised his original account of the lovers' relation. The opening analogy admitted that separation was a kind of death— albeit an untroubled one— because each lover departed with the other's soul; but given the evidence of their spiritual union in the intervening stanzas, the second analogy recasts their relation as a mingling rather than an exchanging of souls. As in "The Extasie," love "Interinanimates two soules," creating a "new soule. . .whom no change can invade." [48]

---

[45]   Perkins, *Whole Treatise*, p.104.

[46]   See A. B. Chambers, "Glorified Bodies and the 'Valediction: forbidding Mourning,'" *John Donne Journal*, 1, No.1 (1982), p.14 and p.19, n. 46. It is a critical commonplace that fusing physical and spiritual love is characteristic of Donne; see, for example, A. J. Smith, "No Man Is a Contradiction," *John Donne Journal*, 1, No. 1 (1982), pp.21-38.

[47]   To be sure, the speaker remarks that their love is indefinable— "our selves know not what it is"—-but his comment nonetheless suggests the super-rational, ineffable qualities of their union. Such attributes are consistent with the religious terms in which Donne's persona has cast their love from the start. Inter-assurance of the mind is like the inner persuasion of faith; both are a guarantee against ultimate loss.

[48]   Love, these mixt soules, doth mixe againe,
       And makes both one, each this and that. . .
       When love, with one another so
       Interinanimates two soules,

Our two soules therefore, which are one,
Though I must goe, endure not yet
A breach, but an expansion,
Like gold to ayery thinnesse beate.   (ll.21-24)

The stanza incapsulates the casuistical argument of the poem. Judging the significance of his departure by the uncommon circumstances of his love ("Our two soules. . .are one"), the speaker arrives at a redefinition of separation that is appropriate to his particular experience. His evaluation conforms to the teaching of practical theologians that "definitions should not be reached *a priori*, but only in relation to the verdicts of actual consciences reflecting upon concrete situations." [49] The logical connectives, careful qualifications, and amplification of the sixth stanza form a rational structure for its paradoxical claims that two are one and that parting is not a disruption. As A. E. Malloch notes, paradox forces one to realize "that knowledge is dramatic, i.e., that it is proportional to each historical scene." [50] Donne's paradox, born of casuistical premises, forces the beloved to realize that the meaning of separation is dramatic; in the lovers' "historical scene," it means a rarefaction, "Like gold to ayery thinnesse beate." [51] The simile of softened gold recalls the melting lovers of stanza two. It suggests that their union is "elemented" of the same qualities that characterize the element of gold: purity and indestructibility.

All three similes of "A Valediction forbidding mourning," including the compass analogy of the last three stanzas, ascribe to love the capacity to admit changing circumstances without itself changing at the same time. Though its bodily form changes and dies, the departing soul does not; though beaten gold becomes attenuated "to ayery thinnesse," its re-formation does not alter its constituent parts.[52] Similarly, the areas circumscribed

---

That abler soule, which thence doth flow,
Defects of lonelinesse controules.
Wee then, who are this new soule, know. . .
("The Extasie," ll.35-6; 41-5)

[49]   Kirk, p.381.
[50]   A. E. Malloch, "The Techniques and Function of the Renaissance Paradox," *Studies in Philology*, LIII, No. 1 (1956), p.202.
[51]   Gold beaten to airy thinness is an apt analogue of casuistical procedure. Case divinity does to the law what beating does to gold (and what separation does to Donne's lovers): rather than cause a disruption or "breach" of the law, casuistry enables an "expansion" of the letter of the law; it encompasses the exceptional and the unanticipated within the spirit of the law.
[52]   For a scrupulously detailed study of alchemy, astrology, astronomy, and theology in the poem, see John Freccero, "Donne's 'Valediction: Forbidding Mourning,'" *English Literary History*, 30, (1963), pp.335-376. For a related discussion of alchemy and the theology of glorified bodies, see Chambers, pp.1-20.

by the legs of a compass may change, but the legs are always coextensive, their movement is always commensurate, and when describing a circle, their relation to each other is constant. Donne's departing speaker admits his own changing circumstances; like the outer leg of a compass, he "far doth rome," and he will "obliquely runne." But as already seen, he insists throughout the poem that such changes cannot affect the union with his lover. If Walton is correct in assigning the composition of the valediction to 1611, however, another of Donne's poems written in the same year makes the opposite claim for both love and lovers. *The Second Anniversary* asserts the radical impermanence of all experience on earth, and it denies the possibility of either physical or spiritual continuity in love.

> Poore couse'ned cose'nor, that she, and that thou,
> Which did begin to love, are neither now.
> You are both fluid, chang'd since yesterday;
> Next day repaires, (but ill) last daies decay.
> Nor are, (Although the river keep the name)
> Yesterdaies waters, and to daies the same.
> So flowes her face, and thine eies, neither now
> That saint, nor Pilgrime, which your loving vow
> Concernd, remaines; but whil'st you thinke you bee
> Constant, you'are howrely in inconstancee.   (ll.391-400)

Not only the laity's love is subject to decay. Change is ineluctable, even for the saints and pilgrims of love. It is the threat of such impermanence, and of the uncertainty that accompanies change, that the speaker of "A Valediction" seeks to invalidate in his concluding simile.

The speaker's argument that the significance of separation depends on "the minde and condition of the doer" assumes the instability of interpretation, the contingency of meaning; his assumption about both judgment and experience is one that practical theologians share. But while Donne's persona embraces casuistical relativity to justify his unconventional response to separation, he refuses to admit that his love is subject to the same experiential instability. Drawing on the conviction of the faithful in his first analogy, and the certain evidence of metallurgy and geometry in the second and third analogies, he describes his relation with the beloved in terms of religious and scientific truths. With the compass image, he seeks mathematical verification that their union is certain and constant. Donne shared his speaker's sense that one must look to mathematical demonstrations for unconditional certainty. In a letter of 1613, he remarks, "Except Demonstrations, (and perchance there are very few of them) I find nothing without perplexities." [53] Attempting to remove his love from the casuisti-

---

[53]   Quoted in Edmund Gosse, *The Life and Letters of John Donne* (New York: Dodd, Mead and Co., 1899), II, 16.

cal realm of perplexity and relativity, Donne's persona says of the lovers' souls:

> If they be two, they are two so
> As stiffe twin compasses are two,
> Thy soule the fixt foot, makes no show
> To move, but doth, if the'other doe.
>
> And though it in the center sit,
> Yet when the other far doth rome,
> It leanes, and hearkens after it,
> And growes erect, as that comes home.
>
> Such wilt thou be to mee, who must
> Like th'other foot, obliquely runne.
> Thy firmnes makes my circle just,
> And makes me end, where I begunne.   (ll. 25-36)

Kenneth Kirk observes that "Casuistry works by choosing incontrovertible examples of a law, and then applying them by analogy to parallel cases."[54] An incontrovertible example of commensurateness, the compass demonstrates how two entities function as one— and by analogy, how the lovers' movement is always congruent. As do casuists, the speaker defines what is personal, qualitative, and unconventional (his love) in terms of what is understood and undisputed. Likening the lovers to an instrument that delimits and contains movement, he attempts to defuse the uncertainty and change that movement threatens. The compass image is only one of several indications of his need to control experience and contain movement in the poem. From the first stanza, he urges stillness: "make no noise,/ No teare-floods, nor sigh-tempests move"; he urges containment of the emotions and containment of the lovers from the rest of the world: "T'were prophanation of our joyes/ To tell the layetie our love." [55] The circles that the compass

---

54   Kirk, p.159.
55   The speaker wants to control not only the lovers' responses, but also any knowledge of the lovers that the laity might draw from their behavior. The first stanza's appeal for the quietude of one whose dying breath is imperceptible to others recalls the almost paranoic self-containment urged in Donne's verse letter, "Sir, more then kisses":
Be thou thine owne home, and in thy selfe dwell. . .
And in the worlds sea, do not like corke sleepe
Upon the waters face; nor in the deepe
Sinke like a lead without a line: but as
Fishes glide, leaving no print where they passe,
Nor making sound; so, closely thy course goe,
Let men dispute, whether thou breathe, or no.   (ll.47-58; my emphasis)
The verse letter warns that to allow others knowledge of yourself is to enable them to corrupt you; it is to lose control of your identity and of your experience.

draws contain the lovers' experience, and the speaker's final line, "And makes me end, where I begunne," suggests that the poem itself is a kind of circle, ending with the religious certainty of the faithful that begins the first stanza.

But the speaker's claims of certainty and permanence, his defining love in terms of mathematical demonstration and in terms of the circle's endless containment, are undermined by his earlier casuistical assertion about the instability of experience and interpretation. Contending first that judgment and action are relative, and then that love is absolute, Donne's persona engenders a contradiction that he is unable to resolve logically. The immunity from future alteration, the enduring control and containment that he wants to ascribe to his love, are impossible, given the casuistical terms on which he has built his case. As Robert Sanderson maintains, "A mathematical certitude, which is manifest by Demonstration, and impossible to be false, is in vain to be expected in morals, by reason of the infinite variety of Circumstances, and uncertainty of Humane affairs. . ." [56]

The mathematical assurance that Donne's persona wants to claim for his union with the beloved is, according to casuists, beyond the capacity of human love. Only God's truth is absolute and unalterable. That is not to say, however, that case divinity disallows analogies between uncertain experience and that which is unquestioned, or between the human and non-human world. While the certitude towards which the speaker strains is "in vain to be expected in morals," his use of the compass figure is not inconsistent with casuistical practices. Indeed, practical theologians often support their judgments with the evidence of analogies drawn from disparate areas of knowledge. As Jeremy Taylor explains:

> But in the discourses of conscience, whatsoever is right reason, though taken from any faculty or science, is also of use and efficacy. Because whatever can guide the actions or discourses, or be the business or conduct, of any man, does belong to conscience and its measures; and what is true in any science, is true in conscience. . . Because the questions of conscience do relate to all matters, therefore to these all arts and sciences do minister.[57]

Donne's compass analogy, then, may be an appropriate image of his lovers' congruence, but the certainty and permanence with which his persona wants to attribute love are the exclusive domain of a religious rule of faith.

Despite his protestations of assurance, the speaker is well aware of the

---

As already noted, the lovers' identity in Donne's valediction is defined in contradistinction to the rest of the world.

[56] *Bishop Sanderson's Lectures on Conscience and Human Law*, ed. C. Wordsworth (Oxford: James Williamson, 1877), p.243.

[57] Jeremy Taylor, *Ductor Dubitantium*, p.51.

pressure exerted by "the infinite variety of Circumstances, and the uncertainty of Humane affairs." Indeed, the last stanza suggests that he is as in need of assurance as his mourning lover is. The conventional valedictory speaker consoles his interlocutor with pledges of his constancy, as Donne's persona does in "Song: Sweetest Love" and "A Valediction of my name, in the window." The speaker of the latter poem tells of "*my* firmnesse," and promises that his love will not change with their separation: "so shall all times finde *mee* the same" (my emphases). But in "A Valediction forbidding mourning," it is "*Thy* firmness" that concerns the speaker; his compass conceit focuses on the woman's behavior in his absence. She will remain faithfully "fixed," making "no show/ To move." She will "in the center sit," contained and unchanging, her only movement correspondent with his. While Donne's persona in "Song: Sweetest Love" insists that he will be even more reliable than the sun (ll. 916), the emphasis in "A Valediction forbidding mourning" is on the beloved's reliability: "Such wilt *thou be* to me." The speaker seems to be assuring himself, more than his lover, that while he obliquely runs she will remain static and constant. Recognizing "the uncertainty of Humane affairs," he nevertheless seeks in love an assurance that transcends "the infinite variety of Circumstances."

Casuistry is unable to admit the mathematical certainty that Donne's persona seeks, but it does provide for the guarantee of faith. The end of the valediction looks towards that guarantee. The compass conceit depicts not only the reunion of lovers, but also the reunion of souls in God.[58] Despite his efforts to define and rationally represent their love, the speaker suggests that it is finally faith that "makes my circle just,/ And makes me end where I begunne." A symbol of both God and the soul,[59] the circle image returns us to the beginning of the poem; line 36 is self-referential, an ending that directs our attention back to the opening lines "where I begunne." And the opening lines, recall, are of a deathbed scene. Rare in the *Songs and Sonets*, the scene is one of untroubled contradictions: extremity but mildness, certain death and equally certain continuance, sadness and infinite assurance. Like the separation of lovers, death is constituted of contradictions whose tensions are relieved by faith. Donne's valediction suggests that neither earthly love, nor wit, nor poetic virtuosity can relieve his contradictory claims of relativity and absolutism. Only faith, the final guarantee of casuistical adjudication, can encompass such perplexities. To judge any case of

---

58   See Marotti's discussion of "A Valediction forbidding mourning," p.177.

59   Donne's verse letter, "To the Countesse of Bedford," describes circles as "types of God" (1.46). For the religious significance of circle imagery in Donne, see Louis Bredvold, "The Religious Thought of Donne in Relation to Medieval and Later Traditions," in *Studies in Shakespeare, Milton, and Donne* by members of the English Department of the University of Michigan (New York: Haskell House, 1964), pp.230-231.

doubt against God's unchanging truth, a mere type of which is the beloved's "firmnes," is to measure action with a certain rule of faith.

Arthur Marotti remarks: "As the most religious of the valedictions, 'A Valediction: forbidding mourning' touches the boundary between Donne's secular and sacred verse."[60] I would add that the poem also touches the boundary between works in which Donne cleverly overreaches the casuistical principles that he invokes and works in which he makes legitimate use of those principles by acknowledging that they derive their authority from faith in God's Word and not from human constructions. To the first group of works belong the poems discussed earlier in this chapter. The second group includes *Pseudo-Martyr, Biathanatos*, and the sermon on *Esther*. Both groups demonstrate that it is only with reference to God's directive truth that the tenets of case divinity are able to mitigate problems of reason, law, and ethical choice. When Donne enlists casuistical arguments in the *Songs and Sonets* without measuring his claims against a certain standard, the results are near-radical relativity and hyperbolic individualism, traits that other critics have described as libertinism, scepticism, and naturalism. While Donne's misappropriation of casuistical principles only compounds the conflicts in his verse, the poet's witty distortion of casuistry contributes to the humor and complexity of his secular lyrics.

---

60   Marotti, p.177.

CHAPTER FIVE

CONCLUSION

It is understandable that casuistry flourished after the Reformation. A system of moral inquiry that explores how to verify knowledge, how to measure judgment, and how to justify action, it offered a constructive response to the turmoil over authority and interpretation. But the questions of epistemology and theology that casuistry addresses are not historically restricted to the cases of "a Philip, or a Gregory,/ A Harry, or a Martin." Indeed, in the 1970's a distinguished group of Catholic and Anglican clergy held a series of conferences on moral theology in the modern church community. The issues discussed are remarkably familiar.

> Anglicans were made aware that many Roman Catholic theologians were shifting from a moral theology based on natural and canonical law to one founded on scriptural teaching as its basis. This revealed a very similar structure to that of traditional Anglican moral theology. Instances of convergence were: the basing of moral theology on Scripture. . . emphasis on the normative role of charity and on response and responsibility; the frequent use of the category of the disciple rather than that of the penitent...Divergence was felt to exist in that Anglicans stress the process of moral reasoning as opposed to what seemed to them to be morals by decree. It was considered that there was a need for an investigation of the nature and role of the magisterium in this field, and of the interrelation of conscience, freedom, and authority.[61]

Donne would have been delighted with the convergences described above. They agree with his teaching on the centrality of Scripture and on moral responsibility. They also draw nearer to his ideal of unity. But the remaining divergence concerns what Donne held to be the most important issue in casuistical debate: emphasis on "the process of moral reasoning as opposed to . . . morals by decree." The issue has arisen throughout this study. It informs Donne's objections to the legalism inherited from penitentials, to the authoritarian basis of probabilism, and to criteria for judgment that are external to the morally deliberating self. Donne fully shared the belief of Reformed casuists that "Truth is to be weighed by argument, not by testimony." [62] He maintained that inquiry, understanding, choice, and

---

[61] H. R. McAdoo, "Anglican/Roman Catholic Relations" in *Rome and the Anglicans*, ed. Wolfgang Haase (New York: Walter de Gruyter, 1982), pp.232-3.

[62] Jeremy Taylor, *Ductor Dubitantium*, Vol. 3 of *Works* (London: Henry

conviction are moral duties. In conjunction with faith, they are acts of worship: "He praises not God, he prays not to God, he worships him not, whatsoever he does, if he have not considered it, debated it, concluded it, to be rightly done, and necessarily done." [63]

The value of casuistry for Donne was that it teaches one how to "stand inquiring right" in a world where "truth and falshood bee/ Neare twins." One can read Donne's works as an exercise of his responsibility to inquire, to weigh truth by argument, to recognize the indeterminacy of language and the instability of law (which always produce in Donne's works opportunities for playfulness and/or anxiety), and to forge his own moral judgments in the face of conflicting precepts and opinions. My study has proposed such a reading.

Epistemological, ethical, and legal perplexities, pressurized by Reformation debate over authority and interpretation, were of deep concern to Donne. From as early as "Satyre III" through the sermons, he applied to those problems (whether playfully or in earnest) the methods of practical theology. Donne's engagement with the motives and recommendations of casuistry spans his varied career and signals in his writing a pervasive concern with epistemological and interpretive instability. More specifically, he subscribed to the Reformed system of case divinity. His letters and prose works frequently object to the legalism and authoritarianism of Catholic casuists, and they denounce the Jesuitical practices of equivocation, mental reservation, and probabilism. But Donne consistently endorses the views of Reformed casuists. He shares their conviction that all individuals are morally accountable for the reasons that inform their actions; that Scripture is truth, and that conscience, guided by faith, is the final arbiter in applying truth to experience; that we must constantly test our assumptions and reappraise both law and authority in terms of particular circumstances; and that while we may not be able to achieve mathematical certainty in ethics, we must nevertheless weigh all discernible arguments for and against an act and choose the course that conscience and reason believe is most conformable to Biblical teaching. As this list of tenets suggests, the evaluation that Reformed casuists encourage is characterized by argumentativeness, immediacy, intellection, and sensitivity to contradictory claims. These characteristics are also hallmarks of Donne's style and method. Thus, one of my objectives has been to relate the dramatic movement and narrative practices in Donne's verse and prose to his use of casuistry in addressing ethical problems.

In addition to demonstrating how casuistry informs the argument of

---

Bohn, 1844), p.118.

[63] John Donne, *Sermons*, ed. George R. Potter and Evelyn Simpson (Berkeley: Univ. of California Press, 1953-62), I, 278.

specific texts, I have been concerned with *why* practical theology was of such interest to Donne. Chapters two and three explore ways in which his epistemology corresponds to that of casuistry, and chapters three and four argue that the aims and assumptions of case divinity appealed strongly to his fractured self construction. Finding "nothing without perplexities," Donne was drawn to casuists' constructive responses to doubt and to their methods of ordering experience in the face of uncertainty and inevitable change. Practical theology does not offer a cure-all for problems of judgment. It cannot entirely abolish the tensions generated between conflicting laws or between public and private obligations. Nor could it provide Donne with more than a provisional, localized answer to the uncertainties and apprehensions of "my riddling, perplexed, labyrinthical soule." [64] But casuistry can achieve a temporary compromise among contradictions; in Donne's words, it facilitates "a probable, if not a certain assurance, contracted *Bona fide*, in a rectified conscience." [65] Occupying a middle ground between scepticism and dogmatism, case divinity acknowledges the pressure of paradox and the ambiguity of truth— problems that engage Donne throughout his works; at the same time, it enables one to impose form on uncertainty, to reason towards practical answers to moral conflicts, and to justify action despite doubts about one's ability to perceive absolute truth.

My discussion of Donne and casuistry has been integrally involved with their historical contexts. In delineating the positions on reason, law, and interpretation that Donne shared with practical theologians, I have located him in contemporary debate about the limits of knowledge, the rule of faith, and valid criteria for judgment. Religious and political controversies in late Renaissance England precipitated the pressing need for, and the enormous popularity of, case divinity during Donne's lifetime. As the most prominent figures of power— King, Pope, and later in the period, members of Parliament— jockeyed for greater jurisdiction, each called into question the very basis of the other's authority. Ironically, the more absolute their conflicting claims of authority became, the more they forced individuals to judge for themselves the *limits* of another's jurisdiction over their own experience. The perplexity of allegiance, combined with Protestant emphasis on self-reflective determination of moral dilemmas, led the laity to assume increasing authority for their own actions—led them, in other words, to become their own casuists. While both James and the Pope claimed to be the highest authority on earth, Reformed casuists taught that no authority was greater than the individual's understanding of Scripture. During Donne's life, practical theology was the resource of moderates and conservatives, but its elevation of conclusions drawn in conscience over institutionally medi-

---

[64]   Donne, *Sermons*, VIII, 332.
[65]   *Sermons*, V, 226.

ated truths was potentially subversive.

> What was dangerous about casuistry, ultimately, is that its inescapable in-
> volvement in political and ideological conflicts— which by the sixteenth
> century had percolated into quotidian antagonisms— problematized the
> culture's received truths, making their immanent character susceptible to
> interpretation as an arbitrary construct . . .

While Donne recognized, and exploited, the "destabilizing effect of casuistry," Lowell Gallagher suggests that most of the author's contemporaries
were "evidently unwilling or unable to see that what they practiced for the
sake of conscience and its nominally stable truths was producing a context
of ideological and interpretive instability that might be beyond their power
to contain." [66] Indeed, as Alan Sinfield remarks, Protestant emphasis on
conscience and the individual finally undermined established social structures
in the seventeenth century:

> Protestantism proved itself accessible to both dissidence and control. . .
> Nevertheless, the changes of the seventeenth century were ultimately at the
> expense of Calvinism. It proved inadequate to the historical situation—to
> the extent, in fact, that it actually became a stimulant to heterodoxy and
> dissidence. Briefly, its social theory, based on notions of stability, order,
> and unanimity in religious and political purposes, could hardly accommo-
> date the social mobility that it helped to cause. . .[S]ince Protestantism
> contained elements of disintegration as well as social cohesion, it could
> not be held inert by the powerful forces that informed it.[67]

It would be fruitful to consider more specifically how casuistical "elements
of disintegration as well as social cohesion" contributed to the "dissidence"
and "social mobility" of the English Revolution. Indeed, the role of casuistical principles in the breakdown of traditional institutions of authority later
in the period is an important subject for further study.

Also a matter for further consideration is the assimilation of casuistical
tenets into other intellectual movements of the seventeenth century.
Practical theologians' assessment of reason and certainty is echoed in the
Royal Society's science of probabilities and in the writing of William
Chillingworth and other latitudinarians. Although Sanderson maintains that
mathematical certainty is impossible in ethics, he adds, "nevertheless, a certain logical certitude may oftentimes be had of the Intention of the Law-

---

[66] Lowell Gallagher, *Medusa's Gaze: Casuistry and Conscience in the
Renaissance* (Stanford: UP, 1991), p.4 and p.11.
[67] Alan Sinfield, *Faultlines: Cultural Materialism and the Politics of
Dissident Reading* (Berkeley: Univ. of California Press, 1992), pp.174-176. See
also Keith Thomas, "Cases of Conscience in Seventeenth-Century England" in
Public Duty and Private Conscience in Seventeenth-Century England, eds. John
Morrill, Paul Slack, and Daniel Woolf (Oxford: Clarendon Press, 1993), pp.42-
43.

maker." [68] The tentative "logical certitude" that casuists believe is within reason's power has a great deal in common with the latitudinarian concept of moral certainty. And the limited but practical assurance of case divinity becomes the goal of English scientists later in the century. I maintain, then, that casuistry was not an isolated system of inquiry, nor was its influence confined to Donne. The extent to which casuistical assumptions permeated political, scientific, and philosophical movements after Donne's death is a promising field of study.

---

[68] *Bishop Sanderson's Lectures on Conscience and Human Law*, ed. C. Wordsworth (Oxford: James Williamson, 1877), p.243.

A SELECTED BIBLIOGRAPHY

Aers, David and Gunther Kress. "Vexatious Contraries: A Reading of Donne's Poetry." In *Literature, Language, and Society in England, 1580-1680.* Dublin: Gill and Macmillan, 1981, 49-67.

Agrippa, Henricus Cornelius. *The Vanity of Arts and Sciences.* Ann Arbor: Univ. Microfilms, 1975.

Allen, Don Cameron. *Doubt's Boundless Sea: Skepticism and Faith in the Renaissance.* Baltimore: Johns Hopkins UP, 1964.

Altman, Joel B. *The Tudor Play of Mind: Rhetorical Inquiry and the Development of Elizabethan Drama.* Berkeley: Univ. of California Press, 1978.

Ames, William. *The Works.* Ann Arbor: Univ. Microfilms, 1962.

Andreasen, N. J. C. *John Donne: Conservative Revolutionary.* Princeton: UP, 1967.

Aquinas, St. Thomas. *Summa Theologica.* Ed. Anton Pegis. New York: Random House, 1945.

Ariès, Philippe. *Centuries of Childhood: A Social History of Family Life.* Trans. Robert Baldick. New York: Random House, 1962.

Aristotle. *The Basic Works of Aristotle.* Ed. Richard McKeon. New York: Random House, 1941.

Augustine. *Against the Academics.* Trans. John O'Meara. Westminster, Maryland: The Newman Press, 1950.

Aveling, J. C. H. "The English Clergy, Catholic and Protestant, in the 16th and 17th Centuries." In *Rome and the Anglicans: Historical and Doctrinal Aspects of Anglican-Roman Catholic Relations.* Ed. Wolfgang Haase. New York: Walter de Gruyter, 1982.

Aveling, Hugh. *The Handle and the Axe: The Catholic Recusants in England for Reformation to Emancipation.* London: Blond and Briggs, 1976.

Azor, Juan. *Institutionum Moralium.* Vol. 1 In *Quibus Questiones ad Conscientiam . . .* 3 vols. Lyons, 1600-1612.

Azpilcueta, Martin de (Navarrus). *Enchiridion sive Manuale Confessariorum et Poenitentium.* Antwerp, 1566.

Bacon, Francis. *De Dignitate et Augmentis Scientiarum.* In *The Philosophical Works.* Ed. John M. Robertson. New York: E. P. Dutton, 1905.

Bainton, Roland. *Castellioniana: Quatre Études Sur Sébastien Castellion Et L'Idée de La Tolérance.* Leiden: E. J. Brill, 1951.

Baker, Herschel. *The Wars of Truth.* Cambridge, Mass: Harvard UP, 1952.

Bald, R. C. *John Donne: A Life.* Oxford: Clarendon Press, 1970.

Battenhouse, Roy W. "The Grounds of Religious Toleration in the Thought of John Donne." *Church History*, XI, No. 3 (1942), 217-248.

Baxter, Richard. *A Christian Directory: or, A Summ of practical theologie, and cases of conscience. Directing Christians, how to use their knowledge and faith.* Ann Arbor: Univ. Microfilms, 1970.

Bell, Ilona. "'Under Ye Rage of a Hott Sonn & Yr Eyes': John Donne's Love Letters to Ann More." In *The Eagle and the Dove: Reassessing John Donne.*

Ed. Claude J. Summers and Ted-Larry Pebworth. Columbia: Univ. of Missouri Press, 1986, 25-52.

Bethell, S. L. *The Cultural Revolution of the Seventeenth Century.* London: Dobson Books, 1963.

Bettenson, Henry, ed. *Documents of the Christian Church.* Oxford: UP, 1967.

Bossy, John. "The Character of Elizabethan Catholicism." *Past and Present,* 21 (1962), 39-59.

Bredvold, Louis I. "The Naturalism of Donne in Relation to Some Renaissance Traditions." *Journal of English and Germanic Philology* , 22 (1923), 471-502.

_____ "The Religious Thought of Donne in Relation to Medieval and Later Traditions." 197 in *Studies in Shakespeare, Milton, and Donne, by Members of the English Department of the Univ. of Michigan* (New York, 1952), 193-232.

Brodrick, James. *The Economic Morals of the Jesuits.* London: Oxford UP, 1934.

Brodsky, Claudia. "Donne: The Imaging of the Logical Conceit." *English Literary History,* 49 (1982), 829-848.

Brués, Guy de. *Les Dialogues.* Ed. Panos Paul Morphos. Baltimore: Johns Hopkins UP, 1953.

Bullough, Geoffrey. "Donne the Man of Law." In *Just So Much Honor.* Ed. Peter Amadeus Fiore. University Park: Penn. State UP, 1972.

Carey, John. *John Donne: Life, Mind and Art.* New York: Oxford UP, 1981.

Carr, Helen. "Donne's Masculine Persuasive Force." In *Jacobean Poetry and Prose: Rhetoric, Representation, and the Popular Imagination.* Ed. Clive Bloom. London: Macmillan, 1988, 96-118.

Carrithers, Gale. *Donne at Sermons: A Christian Existential World.* Albany: State Univ. of New York, 1972.

Cathcart, Dwight. *Doubting Conscience.* Ann Arbor: Univ. Michigan Press, 1975.

Chamberlin, John. *Increase and Multiply.* Chapel Hill: Univ. of NC Press, 1976.

Chambers. A. B. "Glorified Bodies and the 'Valediction: forbidding Mourning.'" *John Donne Journal,* 1, No. 1 (1982), 1-20.

Chanoff, David. "Donne's Anglicanism." *Recusant History,* 15, No. 3 (1980), 154-167.

Chillingworth, William. *The Religion of Protestants, A Safe Way to Salvation.* In *Works.* London: A. Churchill, 1704.

Cicero. *Academica.* Trans. H. Rackham. Cambridge, Mass: Harvard UP, 1967.

Clebsch, William A., ed. *Suicide. By John Donne.* Chico, California: Scholars Press, 1983.

Coffin, Charles Monroe. *John Donne and the New Philosophy.* New York: The Humanities Press, 1958.

Colie, Rosalie. *Paradoxia Epidemica: The Renaissance Tradition of Paradox.* Princeton: UP, 1966.

_____ "The Rhetoric of Transcendence." *Philological Quarterly,* XLIII (1964), 145-170.

_____ "Some Paradoxes in the Language of Things." In *Reason and the Imagination: Studies in the History of Ideas 1600-1800.* Ed. J. A. Mazzeo. New York: Columbia UP, 1962.

Cunningham, James. "Logic and Lyric." *Modern Philology,* XI (1954), 33-41.

Deman, Thomas. "Probabilisme." *Dictionnaire de Théologie Catholique*, vol. XIIIA, cols. 437-97. Paris: Letouzey et Ané, 1936.

Diogenes Laertius. *Lives*. Cambridge, Mass: Harvard UP, 1950.

Docherty, Thomas. *John Donne, Undone*. London: Methuen, 1986.

Donne, John. *Biathanatos*. Ed. Ernest W. Sullivan III. Newark: University of Delaware Press, 1984.

___ *Essays in Divinity*. Ed. Evelyn Simpson. Oxford: Clarendon Press, 1952.

___ *Letters to Severall Persons of Honour*. Ed. Charles Edmund Merrill. New York: Sturgis and Walton, 1910.

___ *Paradoxes and Problems*. Ed. Helen Peters. Oxford: Clarendon Press, 1980.

___ *Poetical Works*. Ed. Herbert Grierson. Oxford: Oxford UP, 1929.

___ *Pseudo-Martyr*. Ann Arbor: Univ. Microfilms, 1967.

___ *Sermons*. 10 vols. Eds. Evelyn Simpson and George R. Potter. Berkeley: Univ. of California Press, 1953-62.

Dubrow, Heather. "'No Man is an island': Donne's Satires and Satiric Traditions." *Studies in English Literature*, XIX, No.1 (1979), 71-83.

Dubrow, Heather and Richard Strier, Eds. *The Historical Renaissance: New Essays on Tudor and Stuart Literature and Culture*. Chicago: UP, 1988.

Eire, Carlos M. *War Against the Idols: The Reformation of Worship from Erasmus to Calvin*. Cambridge: UP, 1986.

Ellrodt, Robert. *L'Inspiration Personelle et l'Esprit Du Temps Chez Les Poètes Métaphysiques Anglais*. 3 vols. Paris: Librairie Jose Corti, 1960.

Empson, William. "Donne and the Rhetorical Tradition." *The Kenyon Review*, XI (1949), 571-587.

___ "Donne the Spaceman." *The Kenyon Review*, XIX (1957), 337-399.

Erasmus, Desiderius. *Collected Works*. Ed. Craig Thompson. Toronto: UP, 1974-82.

Febvre, Lucien. *The Problem of Unbelief in the Sixteenth Century: The Religion of Rabelais*. Trans. Beatrice Gottlieb. Cambridge, Mass.: Harvard UP, 1982.

Ferry, Anne. *The "Inward" Language: Sonnets of Wyatt, Sidney, Shakespeare, Donne*. Chicago: UP, 1983.

Fish, Stanley. "Masculine Persuasive Force: Donne and Verbal Power." In *Soliciting Interpretation: Literary Theory and Seventeenth-Century English Poetry*. Eds. Elizabeth D. Harvey and Katharine Eisaman Maus. Chicago: UP, 1990, 223-252.

___ *Self-Consuming Artifacts*. Berkeley: Univ. of Calif. Press, 1972.

Flynn, Dennis. "The 'Annales School' and the Catholicism of Donne's Family." *John Donne Journal*, 2, No. 2 (1983), 1-9.

___ "Donne's Catholicism: I." *Recusant History*, 13, No. 1 (1975), 1-17.

___ "Donne's Catholicism: II." *Recusant History*, 13, No. 3 (1976), 178-195.

___ "Irony in Donne's Biathanatos and Pseudo-Martyr." *Recusant History*, 12, No. 2 (1973), 49-69.

Foucault, Michel. *Discipline and Punish: The Birth of the Prison*. NY: Vintage, 1979.

Freccero, John. "Donne's 'Valediction Forbidding Mourning.'" *English Literary History*, 30, No. 4 (1963), 335-376.

Friederich, Reinhard H. "Strategies of Persuasion in Donne's Devotions." *A Review of International English Literature*, 9, No. 1 (1978), 51-70.

Gallagher, Lowell. *Medusa's Gaze: Casuistry and Conscience in the Renaissance*. Stanford: UP, 1991.

Gardner, Helen, ed. *John Donne: A Collection of Critical Essays*. New Jersey: Prentice Hall, 1962.

Geraldine, Sister M. "John Donne and the Mindes Indeavours." *Studies in English Literature*, 5, No. 1 (1965), 115-131.

Goldberg, Jonathan. *James I and the Politics of Literature*. Baltimore: Johns Hopkins UP, 1983.

Gosse, Edmund. *The Life and Letters of John Donne*. 2 vols. New York: Dodd, Mead and Co., 1899.

Gottlieb, Sidney. "Elegies Upon the Author : Defining, Defending, and Surviving Donne." *John Donne Journal*, 2, No.2 (1983), 23-38.

Graff, Gerald. "What Has Literary Theory Wrought?" *The Chronicle of Higher Education*, Feb. 12, 1992, A48.

Grant, Edward. "Hypotheses in Late Medieval and Early Modern Science." *Daedalus*, 91 (1962), 599-616.

Greenblatt, Stephen. *Renaissance Self-Fashioning*. Chicago: UP, 1980.

Grennen, Joseph E. "Donne on the Growth and Infiniteness of Love." *John Donne Journal*, 3 (1984), 131-139.

Guss, Donald. *John Donne, Petrarchist*. Detroit: Wayne State UP, 1966.

Haase, Wolfgang, Ed. *Rome and the Anglicans: Historical and Doctrinal Aspects of Anglican-Roman Catholic Relations*. New York: Walter de Gruyter, 1982.

Hacking, Ian. *The Emergence of Probability*. Cambridge: UP, 1975.

Hall, Joseph. *The Old Religion*. Vol. 9 of *The Works of Joseph Hall*. 12 vols. Ed. John Downame. Oxford: D.C. Talboys, 1937.

___ *Resolutions and Decisions of Divers Practical Cases of Conscience, In Continual Use Amongst Men*. Vol. 12 of *The Works of Joseph Hall*. 12 vols. Ed. John Downame. Oxford: D.C. Talboys, 1937.

Hallie, Phillip. *Scepticism, Man, and God*. Middletown: Wesleyan UP, 1964.

Hay, Malcolm. *The Prejudices of Pascal*. London: Neville Spearman, 1962.

Haydn, Hiram. *The Counter-Renaissance*. New York: Grove Press, 1950.

Henson, H. Hensley. *Studies in English Religion in the Seventeenth Century*. London: John Murray, 1903.

Herz, Judith Scherer. "'An excellent Exercise of Wit That Speaks So Well of Ill': Donne and the Poetics of Concealment." In *The Eagle and the Dove: Reassessing John Donne*. Eds. Claude J. Summers and Ted-Larry Pebworth. Columbia, Missouri: Univ. of Missouri Press, 1986, 3-14.

Hester, Thomas. "'All our Soules Devotion': Satire as Religion in Donne's 'Satyre III.'" *Studies in English Literature*, 18, No. 1 (1978), 35-55.

___ "The 'Bona Carmina' of Donne and Horace." *Renaissance Papers: The Southeastern Renaissance Conference*, 1976.

___ *Kinde Pitty and Brave Scorn: John Donne's Satyres*. Durham: Duke UP, 1982.

___ "The Satirist as Exegete: John Donne's 'Satyre V.'" *Texas Studies in Language and Literature*, 20, No. 3 (1978), 347-366.

Hicks, Leo, Ed. *Letters and Memorials of Father Robert Parsons, S. J.* London: Catholic Record Society, 1942.

Hill, Christopher. *Century of Revolution*. NY: W. W. Norton, 1966.

___ *The Collected Essays of Christopher Hill: Religion and Politics in Seventeenth-Century England*. Amherst: Univ. of Mass. Press, 1986.

Holmes, P. J. Ed. *Elizabethan Casuistry*. London: Catholic Record Society, 1981.

___ *Resistance and Compromise*. Cambridge: UP, 1982.

Howell, Wilber Samuel. *Logic and Rhetoric in England 1500-1700*. Princeton: UP, 1950.

Huntley, Frank Livingstone. "Macbeth and the Jesuit Priest." In *Essays in Persuasion on Seventeenth-Century Literature*. Chicago: UP, 1981.

Husain, Itrat. *The Dogmatic and Mystical Theology of John Donne*. New York: Macmillan, 1938.

James I (James Stuart). *The Political Works of James I*. Introduction by Charles McIlwain. Cambridge, Mass: Harvard UP, 1918.

Jardine, Lisa. "The Place of Dialectic Teaching in Sixteenth-Century Cambridge." *Studies in the Renaissance*, 21 (1974), 31-62.

Jones, David Martin. "Sir Edward Coke and the Interpretation of Lawful Allegiance in Seventeenth-Century England." *History of Political Thought*, VII (1986), 321-340.

Jones, R. F. "The Humanistic Defense of Learning in the Mid-Seventeenth Century." In *Reason and the Imagination: Studies in the History of Ideas 16001800*. Ed. J. A. Mazzeo. New York: Columbia UP, 1962.

Jonsen, Albert R. and Stephen Toulmin. *The Abuse of Casuistry: A History of Moral Reasoning*. Berkeley: Univ. of California Press, 1988.

Kelly, Kevin. *Conscience: Dictator or Guide? A Study in Seventeenth Century English Protestant Moral Theology*. London: Geoffrey Chapman, 1967.

Kenyon, J. P. *The Stuart Constitution: Documents and Commentary*. Cambridge: UP, 1978.

Kermode, Frank. *Discussions of John Donne*. Boston: D.C. Heath, 1962.

Kerrigan, William. "The Fearful Accommodations of John Donne." *English Literary Renaissance*, 4, No. 3 (1974), 337-363.

Kirk, Kenneth. *Conscience and Its Problems: An Introduction to Casuistry*. London: Longmans, Green and Co., 1927.

___ *Some Principles of Moral Theology and Their Application*. London: Longmans, Green and Co., 1926.

Knafla, Louis. "Conscience in the English Common Law Tradition." *Univ. of Toronto Law Journal*, 1, No. 26 (1976), 1-16.

Knott, John, Jr. *The Sword of the Spirit: Puritan Responses to the Bible*. Chicago: UP, 1980.

Legouis, Pierre. *Donne the Craftsman*. New York: Russell and Russell, 1962.

Leishman, J. B. *The Monarch of Wit*. London: Hutchinson Press, 1962.

Lewalski, Barbara K. *Donne's "Anniversaries" and the Poetry of Praise*. Princeton: UP, 1973.

___ *Protestant Poetics and the Seventeenth-Century Religious Lyric*. Princeton: UP, 1979.

Long, Edward Leroy. *Conscience and Compromise: An Approach to Protestant Casuistry*. Philadelphia: The Westminster Press, 1954.

Macklem, Michael. *The Anatomy of the World: Relations Between Natural and Moral Law From Donne to Pope*. Minneapolis: Univ. Minn. Press, 1958.

Malloch, A. E. "The Definition of Sin in Donne's Biathanatos." *Modern Language Notes*, LXII (1957), 332-335.

___ "John Donne and the Casuists." *Studies in English Literature*, 2, No. 1 (1962) , 57-76.

___ "The Techniques and Function of the Renaissance Paradox." *Studies in Philology*, LIII (1956), 191-203.

Marotti, Arthur F. *John Donne: Coterie Poet*. Madison: Univ. of Wisconsin

Press, 1986.

Martz, Louis. *The Poetry of Meditation*. New Haven: Yale UP, 1954.

___ *The Wit of Love*. Notre Dame: Univ. of Notre Dame Press, 1969.

Marx, Karl. *Early Writings*. Ed. and Trans. T. B. Bottomore. NY: McGraw Hill, 1964.

McAdoo, H.R. *The Structure of Caroline Moral Theology*. London: Longmans, Green and Co., 1949.

___ "Anglican/ Roman Catholic Relations, 1717-1980." In *Rome and the Anglicans: Historical and Doctrinal Aspects of Anglican-Roman Catholic Relations*. Ed. Wolfgang Haase. New York: Walter de Gruyter, 1982.

McCanles, Michael. "Paradox in Donne." *Studies in the Renaissance*, 13 (1966), 266-287.

McGrath, Lynette. "John Donne's Apology For Poetry." *Studies in English Literature*, 20, No. 1 (1980), 73-89.

McGrath, Patrick. *Papists and Puritans Under Elizabeth I*. London: Blandford Press , 1967.

McNeill, John T. and Helena M. Gamer, ed. and trans. *Medieval Handbooks of Penance*. New York: Columbia UP, 1938.

Meuller, Janel, Ed. *Donne's Prebend Sermons*. Cambridge, MA: Harvard UP, 1971.

Meyer, Arnold Oskar. *England and the Catholic Church Under Elizabeth*, trans. J. R. McKee. New York: Routledge and Kegan Paul, 1967.

Miller, Perry. *The New England Mind: The Seventeenth Century*. Cambridge, Mass.: Harvard UP, 1954.

Milton, John. *Complete Poems and Major Prose*. Ed. Merritt Y. Hughes. Indianapolis: Odyssey Press, 1975.

Miner, Earl. *The Metaphysical Mode From Donne to Cowley*. Princeton: UP, 1969.

Molony, Frank. *John Donne: His Flight From Medievalism*. Urbana: Univ. of Illinois Studies in Language and Literature, Vol. 29, 1944.

Moore, Thomas V. "Donne's Use of Uncertainty As A Vital Force In 'Satyre III,'" *Modern Philology*, 67, (1969), 41-49.

Morgan, John. *Godly Learning: Puritan Attitudes towards Reason, Learning and Education, 1560-1640*. Cambridge: UP, 1988.

Mosse, George L. *The Holy Pretence: A Study in Christianity and Reason of State from William Perkins to John Winthrop*. Oxford: B. Blackwell, 1957.

Nelson, Benjamin. "The Early Modern Revolution in Science and Philosophy: Fictionalism, Probabilism, Fideism, and Catholic 'Prophetism,'" *Boston Studies in the Philosophy of Science*, III (1966), 1-40.

___ "Response to Edward Grant." *Daedalus*, 9 (1962), 613-15.

Nicolson, Marjorie Hope. *The Breaking of the Circle*. New York: Columbia Univ. Press, 1960.

Norbrook, David. "The Monarchy of Wit and the Republic of Letters: Donne's Politics." In *Soliciting Interpretation*. Eds. Elizabeth D. Harvey and Katharine Eisaman Maus. Chicago: UP, 1990, 3-36.

O'Connor, D. J. *Aquinas and Natural Law*. London: Macmillan, 1967.

Ong, Walter Jackson. "The Province of Rhetoric and Poetic." *Modern Schoolman*, XIX (1942), 24-27.

___ *Ramus, Method and the Decay of Dialogue*. Cambridge, Mass.: Harvard UP, 1958.

___ "Tudor Writings on Rhetoric." *Studies in the Renaissance*, 15 (1968), 39-

69.

Ornstein, Robert. "Donne, Montaigne, and Natural Law." *Journal of English and Germanic Philology*, LV (1956), 213229.

Osler, Margaret J. "Certainty, Scepticism, and Scientific Optimism: The Roots of Eighteenth Century Attitudes Toward Scientific Knowledge." In *Probability, Time and Space in Eighteenth Century Literature*. Ed. Paula R. Backscheider. New York: Ams Press, 1979.

Parfitt, George. *John Donne: A Literary Life*. London: Macmillan, 1989.

Pascal, Blaise. *Pensées and The Provincial Letters*. Trans. W. F. Trotter and Thomas M'Crie. New York: Random House, 1941.

Patey, Douglas L. *Probability and Literary Form*. Cambridge: UP, 1984.

Patterson, Annabel. "All Donne." In *Soliciting Interpetation: Literary Theory and Seventeenth-Century English Poetry*. Eds. Elizabeth D. Harvey and Katharine Eisaman Maus. Chicago: UP, 1990, 37-67.

____ *Censorship and Interpretation: The Conditions of Writing and Reading in Early Modern England*. Madison: Univ. of Wisconsin Press, 1984, 103.

____ "Misinterpretable Donne: The Testimony of the Letters." *John Donne Journal*, 1, No. 1 (1982), 39-53.

Pebworth, Ted-Larry. "'Let Me Here Use That Freedome': Subversive Representation in John Donne's 'Obsequies to the Lord Harrington." *Journal of English and Germanic Philology*, 91 (1992), 17-42.

Pepperdene, Margaret. *That Subtle Wreath*. Atlanta: Darby Printing, 1973.

Perkins, William. *A Discourse of Conscience Wherein Is Set Downe The nature, properties, and differences thereof: as also the way to get and keepe good conscience*. Ed. Thomas Merrill. Nieuwkoop: B. De Graaf, 1966.

____ *The Whole Treatise of Cases of Conscience*. Ed. Thomas Merrill. Nieuwkoop: B. De Graaf, 1966.

Peterson, Douglas. "John Donne's Holy Sonnets and the Anglican Doctrine of Contrition." *Studies in Philology*, LVI (1959), 504-518.

Pinka, Patricia Garland. *This Dialogue of One: The "Songs and Sonets" of John Donne*. Alabama: Univ. of Alabama Press, 1982.

Popkin, Richard. *The History of Scepticism From Erasmus to Spinoza*. Berkeley: Univ. of California Press, 1979.

____ "The Sceptical Crisis and the Rise of Modern Philosophy: I." *The Review of Metaphysics*, 7, No. 1 (1953), 132-151.

____ "The Sceptical Crisis and the Rise of Modern Philosophy: II." *The Review of Metaphysics*, 7, No. 2 (1953), 307-322.

____ "The Sceptical Crisis and the Rise of Modern Philosophy: III." *The Review of Metaphysics*, 7, No. 3 (1954), 499-510.

Rajan, Tilottama. "'Nothing Sooner Broke': Donne's Songs and Sonets As Self-Consuming Artifact." *English Literary History*, 49 (1982), 805-828.

Raleigh, Sir Walter. *The Sceptic*. Vol. 8 from The Works. 8 vols. Oxford: UP, 1829.

Ramsay, Mary Paton. "Donne's Relation to Philosophy." In *A Garland For John Donne*. Ed. Theodore Spencer. Gloucester, Mass: Peter Smith, 1958.

____ *Les Doctrines Medievales Chez Donne*. Oxford: Clarendon Press, 1917.

Roberts, John R. "John Donne's Poetry: An Assessment of Modern Criticism." *John Donne Journal*, 1, No.1 (1982), 55-68.

____ "Donne's 'Satyre III' Reconsidered." *College Language Association*, XII, No. 2 (1968), 105-115.

Rose, Elliot. *Cases of Conscience: Alternatives Open to Recusants and Puritans*

Under Elizabeth I and James I. Cambridge: UP, 1975.

Rostenberg, Leona. *The Minority Press and the English Crown: A Study in Repression, 1558-1625.* Niewkoop: B. De Graaf, 1971.

Roston, Murray. *The Soul of Wit.* Oxford: Clarendon Press, 1974.

Rowlands, Marie B. "Recusant Women 1560-1640." In *Women in English Society 1500-1800.* Ed. Mary Prior. London: Methuen, 1985, 149-180.

Saint German, Christopher. *Doctor and Student.* Ed. T. F. Plucknett. London: Seldon Society, 1974.

Sanderson, Robert. *Works.* 6 vols. Ed. William Jacobson. Oxford: Oxford UP, 1854.

Schmitt, Charles. *Cicero Scepticus: A Study of the Influence of the "Academica" in the Renaissance.* The Hague: Martinus Nijhoff, 1972.

___ "Giulio Castellani (1528-1586): A Sixteenth Century Opponent of Scepticism." *Journal of the History of Philosophy,* 5, No. 1 (1967), 15-39.

___ "Who Read Gianfrancesco Pico della Mirandola?" *Studies in the Renaissance,* II (1964), 105-132.

Michael C. Schoenfeldt. *Prayer and Power: George Herbert and Renaissance Courtship.* Chicago: UP, 1991.

Scott, James Brown. *The Catholic Conception of International Law: Suárez and Victoria.* Washington, D.C: Georgetown UP, 1934.

Sencourt, Robert. *Outflying Philosophy: A Study of the Religious Element.* New York: Haskell House, 1966.

Sextus Empiricus. *Outlines of Pyrrhonism.* Cambridge, Mass.: Harvard UP, 1976.

Shami, Jeanne M. "Donne's Protestant Casuistry: Cases of Conscience in the Sermons." *Studies in Philology,* LXXX, No. 1 (1983), 53-66.

___ "Donne on Discretion." *English Literary History,* 47 (1980), 49-66.

Shapiro, Barbara. "Latitudinarianism and Science in Seventeenth Century England." In *The Intellectual Revolution of the Seventeenth Century.* Ed. Charles Webster. Boston: Routledge and Kegan Paul, 1974.

___ *Probability and Certainty in Seventeenth Century England.* Princeton: UP, 1983.

Shawcross, John T. *The Complete Poetry of John Donne.* Garden City, New York: Anchor, 1967.

Shebbeare, Charles J. "Probabilism." *Church Quaterly Review,* LXXIV, No. CXLVIII (1912), 327-346.

Sherwood, Terry G. *Fulfilling the Circle: A Study of John Donne's Thought.* Toronto: UP, 1984.

___ "Our Connexion of Causes: John Donne and Reason." Diss. Univ. of Calif., Berkeley 1969.

Shuger, Deborah Kuller. *Habits of Thought in the English Renaissance: Religion, Politics, and the Dominant Culture.* Berkeley: Univ. of California Press, 1990.

Sidgwick, Henry. *Outlines of the History of Ethics.* London: Macmillan, 1931.

Sidney, Sir Philip. *Defense of Poesy.* Ed. Lewis Soens. Lincoln, Nebraska: Univ. of Nebraska Press, 1970.

Siegal, P. N. "Donne's Paradoxes and Problems." *Philological Quaterly,* XXVIII, (1949), 506-519.

Simpson, Evelyn. *A Study of the Prose Works of John Donne.* Oxford: Clarendon Press, 1962.

___ "Donne's Paradoxes and Problems." In *A Garland For John Donne.* Ed.

Theodore Spencer. Gloucester, Mass.: Peter Smith, 1958.

Sinfield, Alan. *Faultlines: Cultural Materialism and the Politics of Dissident Reading*. Berkeley: Univ. of California Press, 1992.

___ *Literature in Protestant England 1560-1600*. London: Croom Helm, 1983.

Slights, Camille Wells. *The Casuistical Tradition in Shakespeare, Donne, Herbert and Milton*. Princeton: UP, 1981.

Sloane, Thomas O. *Donne, Milton, and the End of Humanist Rhetoric*. Berkeley: Univ. of Calif. Press, 1985.

___ "The Persona as Rhetor: An Interpretation of Donne's 'Satyre III.'" *Quarterly Journal of Speech*, LI, No. 1 (1965), 14-27.

___ "The Rhetoric in the Poetry of John Donne." *Studies in English Literature 1500-1900*, 3 (1963), 31-44.

Smith, A. J. "No Man Is a Contradiction." *John Donne Journal*, 1, No.1 (1982), 21-38.

Sommerville, Johann P. "The 'new art of lying': equivocation, mental reservation, and casuistry." In *Conscience and Casuistry in Early Modern Europe*. Ed. Edmund Leites. Cambridge: UP, 1988, 159-184.

___ *Politics and Ideology in England, 1603-1640*. London, 1986.

Sprott, S. E. *The English Debate on Suicide From Donne to Hume*. La Salle, Ill.: Open Court, 1961.

Steadman, John M. *The Hill and the Labyrinth: Discourse and Certitude in Milton and His Near-Contemporaries*. Berkeley: Univ. of Calif. Press, 1984.

Stein, Arnold. *John Donne's Lyrics: The Eloquence of Action*. Minneapolis: Univ. of Minnesota Press, 1962.

Stone, Lawrence. *The Causes of the English Revolution, 1629-1642*. NY: Harper, 1972.

Strier, Richard. "Radical Donne: 'Satyre III.'" *English Literary History*, 60 (1993), 283-322.

Suarez, Francisco. *De Legibus*. In *Selections From Three Works*, II, "The Classics of International Law." Oxford: Clarendon Press, 1944.

___ *Opera Omnia*, 24 vols. Paris, 1859.

Sullivan, Alvin. "Donne's Sophistry and Certain Renaissance Books of Logic and Rhetoric." *Studies in English Literature*, 22, No. 1 (1982), 107-120.

Summers, Claude J. "The Bride of the Apocalypse and the Quest for True Religion: Donne, Herbert, and Spenser." In *Bright Shootes of Everlastingnesse: The Seventeenth-Century Religious Lyric*. Eds. Claude J. Summers and Ted-Larry Pebworth. Columbia, Missouri: Univ. of Missouri Press, 1987, 78-92.

Taylor, Jeremy. *A Dissuasive From Popery To The People of Ireland*. London: William Ball, 1837.

___ *Ductor Dubitantium*. Ed. Alexander Taylor. London: Longman, Brown, Green and Longman, 1855.

Tentler, Thomas N. *Sin and Confession on the Eve of the Reformation*. Princeton: UP, 1977.

Thomas, Keith. "Cases of Conscience in Seventeenth-Century England." In *Public Duty and Private Conscience in Seventeenth-Century England*. Eds. John Morrill, Paul Slack, and Daniel Woolf. Oxford: Clarendon Press, 1993.

Tierney, Brian. *Religion, Law, and the Growth of Constitutional Thought, 1150-1650*. Cambridge: UP, 1982.

Trimpi, Wesley. "The Quality of Fiction: The Rhetorical Transmission of Literary Theory." *Traditio*, 30 (1974), 1-119.

Tuve, Rosemond. *Elizabethan and Metaphysical Imagery*. Chicago: UP, 1972.

Unger, Leonard. *Donne's Poetry and Modern Criticism*. Chicago: Henry Regnery Co., 1950.

Van Leeuwen, Henry. *The Problem of Certainty in English Thought 1630-1690*. The Hague: Martinus Nijhoff, 1963.

Vinogradoff, Paul. "Reason and Conscience in Sixteenth Century Jurisprudence." *Collected Papers*. Vol. 2. Oxford: Clarendon Press, 1928.

Wakefield, Gordon. *Puritan Devotion: Its Place in the Development of Christian Piety*. London: Allenson-Breckinridge, 1957.

Wallerstein, Ruth. *Studies in Seventeenth Century Poetic*. Madison: Univ. of Wisconsin Press, 1961.

Walton, Izaac. *The Life of Donne*. New York: Oxford UP, 1973.

Warnke, Frank J. *John Donne*. Boston: G. K. Hall, 1987.

Webber, Joan. *Contrary Music: The Prose Style of John Donne*. Madison: Univ. of Wisconsin Press, 1963.

Westfall, Richard S. *Science and Religion in Seventeenth-Century England*. Ann Arbor: Univ. of Michigan Press, 1973.

Wiggins, Elizabeth. "Logic in the Poetry of John Donne." *Studies in Philology*, 52 (1945), 41-60.

Wiley, Margaret. *The Subtle Knot: Creative Scepticism in Seventeenth Century England*. Cambridge, Mass.: Harvard UP, 1952.

Willey, Basil. *The Seventeenth Century Background*. New York: Columbia UP, 1942.

Williams, C. "Conscience." *New Catholic Encyclopedia*, Vol. 4. New York: McGraw Hill, 1967.

Williamson, George. *The Donne Tradition*. Cambridge, Mass.: Harvard UP, 1930.

___ "The Libertine Donne." *Philological Quarterly*, 13, No. 3 (1934), 276-291.

Wilson, Scott W. "Process and Product: Reconstructing Donne's Personae." *Studies in English Literature*, 20, No. 1 (1980), 91-103.

Winter, Ernst F. *Erasmus and Luther: Discourse on Free Will*. New York: Frederick Ungar, 1961.

Wood, Thomas. *English Casuistical Divinity During the Seventeenth Century*. London: Billing and Sons, 1952.

Wordsworth, C., ed. *Bishop Sanderson's Lectures on Conscience and Human Law*. Oxford: James Williamson, 1877.

Wright, Louis B. "William Perkins: Elizabethan Apostle of 'Practical Divinity.'" *Huntington Library Quarterly*, 3 (1940), 171-196.

Zagorin, Perez. *Ways of Lying: Dissimulation, Persecution, and Conformity in Early Modern Europe*. Cambridge, MA: Harvard UP, 1990.

Zunder, William. *The Poetry of John Donne: Literature and Culture in the Elizabethan and Jacobean Period*. Sussex: Harvester Press, 1982.

___ "The Poetry of John Donne: Literature, History and Ideology." In *Jacobean Poetry and Prose: Rhetoric, Representation, and the Popular Imagination*. Ed. Clive Bloom. London: Macmillan, 1988, 78-95.

AN INDEX OF NAMES AND PLACES

AN INDEX OF SUBJECTS

90-91, 94, 115 n. 24, 116, 123, 130; of the lawmaker, 5-6, 87, 92-93, 95, 142. *See also* Equity

Interpretation: and authority, 12-13, 31, 33-34, 48-61; debate about, 1, 62-64, 125, 140-143; relativity of, 23, 66-75, 128-134; and Scripture, 71-75, 74 n. 17, 90-97, 107

In utramque partem. See Debate

Jesuits (Society of Jesus), 8, 27, 27 n. 61, 40-41, 42 n. 22, 51, 59, 59-60 n. 57, 63 n. 64, 84 n. 40, 86, 86 n. 42

Justa Defensio, 3

Language, 1-2, 5, 16-17, 66-75, 113 n. 22, 121

Law: against religious assembly, 92-94; conflict among, 84-98; contingency of, 22-23, 22 n. 46, 28, 33, 51-61, 76-83, 87; deficiencies of, 1-2, 5-6, 51-52; intention of, 5-6, 21, 28 n. 62, 87, 90-95; in the *Songs and Sonets* 17-18, 99-138; recusancy, 9, 39, 40, 85, 85 n. 41, 90, 93-94; of religious conformity, 12, 93-94; sumptuary, 23. *See also* Casuistry; Convention; Equity

Mental reservation, 40-41, 41 n. 21, 121 n. 34

Moral theology, 1, 5, 20

Oath of Allegiance, 4, 9, 39, 79, 83-91. See also *Pseudo-Martyr*

Pacis Compositio, 3

Peace of Augsburg, 3

Penitentials. *See* Confessors' Manuals

Perplexity (as category), 25, 28, 28 n. 62, 55, 85-92, 97, 111-112, 111 n. 19, 116-117, 120, 124, 127

Petrarchism, 30, 101, 123

Practical theology. *See* Casuistry

Probabiliorism, 60-61

Probabilism, 14-15, 35, 57-60, 79, 139

Probability, 2, 17, 61, 66-67, 91, 95-96, 141

Protestant casuistry: criteria for judgment, 22, 23-26, 29, 31, 33-34, 46, 48-61, 76, 85, 90-98; Donne's endorsement of, 14-15, 20-26, 50-61, 66-67, 72, 76, 97-98, 139-143; emphasis on process, 20, 25-26, 46-47, 60 n. 60, 91-92, 96, 139-140; and external authority, 24-26, 29, 37-38; importance of debate, 23-25, 29-30, 33, 46-47, 54-61, 70-72, 76, 139; privileging of individual, 23-26, 24 n. 51, 30-31, 36-38, 54-61, 57 n. 50, 60 n. 60, 80-81, 116, 141-142

Reason: and casuistry, 5, 7, 23, 37, 48-61, 74 n. 17, 83-91, 95; deficiencies of, 1-2, 17-18, 113 n. 22, 115 n. 26, 120; Donne on, 61-65, 67-75. *See also* Catholic Casuistry; Protestant Casuistry

Regnans in Excelsis, 38, 39

Rule of faith controversy, 48-50, 48 n. 35

Scepticism, 13, 46-47, 49 n. 37, 62, 65, 69-70, 70 n. 10, 72, 77, 138, 141

Scholastic article, 46-47

Suicide. See *Biathanatos*

Studies in the History
of Christian Thought

EDITED BY HEIKO A. OBERMAN

50. HOENEN, M. J. F. M. *Marsilius of Inghen.* Divine Knowledge in Late Medieval Thought. 1993
51. O'MALLEY, J. W., IZBICKI, T. M. and CHRISTIANSON, G. (eds.) *Humanity and Divinity in Renaissance and Reformation.* Essays in Honor of Charles Trinkaus. 1993
52. REEVE, A. (ed.) and SCREECH, M. A. (introd.) *Erasmus' Annotations on the New Testament.* Galatians to the Apocalypse. 1993
53. STUMP, Ph. H. *The Reforms of the Council of Constance (1414-1418).* 1994
54. GIAKALIS, A. *Images of the Divine.* The Theology of Icons at the Seventh Ecumenical Council. With a Foreword by Henry Chadwick. 1994
55. NELLEN, H. J. M. and RABBIE, E. *Hugo Grotius – Theologian.* Essays in Honour of G. H. M. Posthumus Meyjes. 1994
56. TRIGG, J. D. *Baptism in the Theology of Martin Luther.* 1994
57. JANSE, W. *Albert Hardenberg als Theologe.* Profil eines Bucer-Schülers. 1994
58. ASSELT, W.J. van. *The Covenant Theology of Johannes Cocceius (1603-1669).* An Examination of its Structure. *In preparation*
59. SCHOOR, R.J.M. van de. *The Irenical Theology of Théophile Brachet de La Milletière (1588-1665).* 1995
60. STREHLE, S. *The Catholic Roots of the Protestant Gospel.* Encounter between the Middle Ages and the Reformation. 1995
61. BROWN, M.L. *Donne and the Politics of Conscience in Early Modern England.* 1995
62. SCREECH, M.A. (ed.). *Richard Mocket, Warden of All Souls College, Oxford, Doctrina et Politia Ecclesiae Anglicanae.* An Anglican Summa. Facsimile with Variants of the Text of 1617. Edited with an Introduction. 1995
63. SNOEK, G.J.C. *Medieval Piety from Relics to the Eucharist.* 1995
64. PIXTON, P.B. *The German Episcopacy and the Implementation of the Decrees of the Fourth Lateran Council, 1216-1245.* Watchmen on the Tower. 1995

Prospectus available on request

E. J. BRILL — P.O.B. 9000 — 2300 PA LEIDEN — THE NETHERLANDS